# FROM GRAMMAR TO PARK

# FROM GRAMMAR TO PARK

## 100 YEARS OF A BARNSTAPLE SCHOOL, 1910-2010

Sic nos non nobis

**Trevor Hill**

HALSGROVE

First published in Great Britain in 2010

Copyright © Trevor Hill 2010

British Library Cataloguing-in-Publication Data
A CIP record for this title is available from the British Library

ISBN 978 1 84114 997 4

**HALSGROVE**
Halsgrove House,
Ryelands Industrial Estate,
Bagley Road, Wellington, Somerset TA21 9PZ
Tel: 01823 653777    Fax: 01823 216796
email: sales@halsgrove.com

Part of the Halsgrove group of companies
Information on all Halsgrove titles is available at: www.halsgrove.com

Printed and bound in Great Britain by Cromwell Press Group, Trowbridge

# A Hundred Years

The mornings would come
With yet another fresh start.
The young would rush in
To fill our ageing heart.
A new start,
A first day,
An old teacher
With lots to say.
Row on row,
Line on line,
All in order,
Looking fine!
We taught them well,
We made them strong,
We filled them up
And sent them along.
For a hundred long years
And countless nights,
We've filled up their minds
And charged up their lights
To shine.

*(Alfred Jones, Year 9 Pupil, 2009)*

*"The years teach much which
the days never knew."*

*(Ralph Waldo Emerson)*

# CONTENTS

# FOREWORD

W̲E̲ ̲E̲A̲C̲H̲ regard our own period in history as unique – uniquely different, uniquely challenging, uniquely modern and cutting edge, more enlightened than 'the good old days' and closer to that elusive ideal we all seek to achieve. Or do we simply adopt the prevailing interpretation of continuous threads that run throughout history, each interpreting our role to serve the times in which we live? Certainly in reading this book I come to realise just how easy it is to become caught up in and completely preoccupied by the here and now whilst overlooking an appreciation of all that has been achieved previously.

A hundred years represents some 20,000 school days and thousands of individual life stories. G.K. Chesterton wrote that, *"Education is simply the soul of a society as it passes from one generation to another"*. Since 1910 this school has helped to educate four generations, now moving into its fifth, serving the local community through good and bad times, war and peace. I have a deep respect for our heritage and all that the school has achieved over the last century. It has responded to successive waves of social change that have accelerated in the last 20 years beyond the imagination of previous generations.

Past generations tend to be extremely respectful of their school and the education it offered. I enjoy hosting reunions and watching old-classmates recollect episodes from 'the best days of their lives'. They are usually staggered by how the school has developed and grown. The genesis of this book stems from a reunion organised by Trevor Hill of the 1961-68 cohort from the Boys Grammar School. Clearly they attended an extremely strict and serious school but some of the adventures and pranks they recounted were hilarious. I never imagined then that Trevor would come back to me with a proposal to write a history of the school for the 2010 Centenary. Realising the scale of the project, I urged caution. Thankfully, he proved determined and I am very pleased that he was.

Trevor has managed to capture the atmosphere of this school in a way that will be recognised by all who have learned here, taught here, or worked here. He pays tribute to individuals who dedicated their professional lives to opening pupils' eyes and making a difference. He has brought together a richness and diversity of personal testimonies and archive material that will delight the book's readers and become a valuable record for future historians.

How visionary the school's founders were without even realising it. By building their 1910 school in the fields of Newport they placed the school of 2010 immediately adjacent to the North Devon Link Road which opened 80 years later! Good vehicular access is complemented by a Park and Ride site which adds ample parking and an old rail bridge that now offers a pedestrian short-cut to the Tennis and Leisure Centres. A superb setting overlooking the town is now also wonderfully accessible to the community it serves.

The arrival of the comprehensive era in 1972 began a process of radical change that has continued and intensified. For the first 60 years of life as a grammar school the aims were sharper and narrower, defined in times of greater respect, authority and certainty. The ethos and regime was one of voluntarily opting in, so you therefore became completely subject to the culture and its rules. Dissidents were physically disciplined into line or required to leave! Over the last 40 years we have become progressively more tolerant, more inclusive, more understanding and progressively more accountable to the scrutiny of our constituency.

How will the teenagers of today look back on their school days? They live in a world of instant information and they are the first generation to experience the inversion of the natural order of things, when, as computer experts, it is they who teach their parents and grandparents! Their future will depend on their ability to grasp new concepts, make new choices and go on learning and adapting throughout life. The question *"Did you receive a good education?"* may these days initially be answered by *"It depends what you mean by a good education"*. But I trust the majority would also respond *"Yes"* – and perhaps even *"Yes, thank you"*.

*David Atton at morning assembly in the dining hall, 2009.*

Those boys and girls who registered at the school in 1910 would get a few surprises if they returned today but they would still be able to recognise their school. Will someone be able to write a companion volume in 2110? And how might the world have changed by then? We look to the future with confidence.

*David Atton, Headteacher*
*The Park Community School*
*Spring 2010*

# AUTHOR'S INTRODUCTION

IF MY parents were alive today to see my name on the cover of a book I doubt they would believe it. They owned no books and were in awe of the bookish world I was joining in 1961 when I started at Barnstaple Boys Grammar School. Mum and Dad scrimped and saved to afford the uniform, the dinner money and the bicycle to get me across town from Yeo Vale but they hadn't the foggiest idea about any of the assignments I brought back in my satchel as homework. I was a bit hazy about it all myself for the first year or two.

Nobody would be more dumbstruck to see my name on a history book than my history teachers. History was my second worst subject, after Latin. I assumed that any school which taught Latin must have existed since Roman times. Not until a reunion of my classmates in 2007 did I learn that our old school had been built as recently as 1910 and so had only just celebrated its fiftieth birthday when we started. By the time of our reunion the school's familiar landmarks had been dramatically absorbed into the larger and more sophisticated establishment known as The Park Community School. Yet the odour of changing rooms and science labs was still the same. It was easy to evoke images of the masters and prefects who had ruled the roost in our time and some of them even joined us that day. Memories of pranks we'd played on them came flooding back and I felt an overwhelming fondness for the place. The idea of commemorating the school's hundredth birthday was born and three years later this book is the result.

*Some of the Class of '61 then and at their 2007 reunion. The author is foreground centre, spouting forth as usual.*

I am one among thousands who've passed through the classrooms and corridors at the heart of this story. Some may look back on their schooldays with horror but, as I've sat here scribbling, I've imagined readers who will bring to the book their own affection for the school and their own cherished memories. The chapters are chronological so you may want to jump straight to whichever one deals with your era where you should see familiar names and faces alongside forgotten details. When you dip into other sections you will probably be amazed at how different the school was before your time and/or how much it has changed since you left. I hope the *"Well, I never!"* moments add an extra dimension.

What happened at this single Barnstaple secondary school from 1910-2010 provides insights into the history of English education and into the social history of North Devon. The school has been shaped by Acts of Parliament, by external events, by the whims of fashion and by some strong individuals. It has been dual-sex, single-sex and co-educational. It has charged fees and taken boarders, it has been highly selective, and now it is comprehensive and free to all. Where pupils were once caned into submission, they now get a say in the recruitment of senior staff. Where one building with ten teachers and a telephone once served a mere 105 pupils, today nearly 1500 pupils are served by a veritable village of buildings with 180 staff and 500 computers. But such changes should not obscure some underlying continuities.

Few people in 2010 would disagree with this mission statement from Sir Thomas Acland, the man who laid the foundation stone in 1909: *"This school is intended to awaken thought, to give a broader outlook on life and to prepare young people for their future career, whatever it might be."* Today's students still wear a uniform with a crest and a Latin motto created in 1910 - 'Sic nos non nobis', meaning 'We strive not for ourselves but for others'. Inter-House rivalry is still strong. Time-honoured events like Plays, Sports Days and Swimming Galas remain highlights of the calendar. Despite a myriad of changes to the fabric of the school, parts of it will still be uncannily familiar to pupils from long ago. The exterior front of the original building looks much the same now as it did in 1910 and the old boys' gym still has the very same apparatus as it did when I first stretched my limbs there nearly 50 years ago.

Regardless of particular regimes, the school has always prepared boys and girls to be decent citizens, making it an institution with an important place in the hearts of generations of adults. It was a great privilege for me in the Sixties to be among the elite 20% who had the chance to 'go to the Grammar'. Of course, many people now look back on selective education as 'the bad old days' and I fully understand why. I witnessed at first hand the beginning of the school's mid-life transformation and I view what went before and what has come after with equal dispassion. I'm a great admirer of the more complex and more inclusive establishment which has evolved at Park. It properly reflects the more egalitarian society that Britain has become.

Not all of my teachers were paragons of virtue. Some of them were hopeless and others got away with throwing chalk and board rubbers at us. But I am grateful to several teachers whom I took for granted long ago. I've heard many former pupils talk of being inspired by at least one special teacher. If this book omits to pay tribute to the particular teachers who were special to you then I hope the following example may represent them…

*Mark Roberts.*

My own academic future hinged on being taught Spanish by an energetic young Welshman who also coached rugby. I now know that Mark 'Taffy' Roberts started on the same day as I did in September 1961 and he certainly seemed less prehistoric than many of those who greeted us in their forbidding black gowns. Mark didn't actually teach me until my third year and by then I was already in the 'B' stream, along with all the other dunces at Latin. He believed in the 'direct oral method', which meant that for the first few weeks of Spanish we didn't write anything down. He just entered the classroom and started talking to us in Spanish. *"Buenos días, Señor Roberts"* we learned to say within minutes of starting lesson one. By a combination of patience and acting ability he communicated the meaning of a whole range of verbs, nouns, adjectives and prepositions. We learned to mimic his pronunciation of simple sentences and even to talk to each other in Spanish. By the end of my third year I was on linguistic speed and I came top of the class in Spanish.

There is no tonic quite as powerful as being judged to be good at something and Mark encouraged me to work hard in other subjects too. With renewed confidence, I blossomed. In my fourth year, he sat me down and told me that I might be good enough to study languages at university but that an O' Level in Latin would be one of the entry requirements. He advised me to start Latin again, which filled me with dread, though I trusted his judgement and eventually managed to scrape a pass. By my final year at school a university language course was indeed my best option, just as Mark had predicted. How lucky I am to have crossed paths with this insightful and gifted teacher. Years later I tried to track him down to thank him for launching my career but sadly I learned that he'd died shortly after taking a promotion in Wales. This book is dedicated to all the great teachers whom we may have omitted to thank.

*It wasn't too late to say thanks to Brian Williams, Geoff Smith, David Rowe, Carol Jenkins, Ken Doughty and Fred Lee. 2007 reunion.*

I am neither an educationalist nor a professional historian, so the reader should not expect much in this book by way of pedagogical theory or the detailed referencing of sources. *"Thank God for that"* I hope I hear you say! My main aim has been to document enough of the minutiae of everyday school life to transport readers back through the decades. I hope that even the earliest years, for which there is no living memory, will come vividly into focus in these pages. Sources vary according to the period but Governors' minutes, reports of official inspections, school magazines and Heads' newsletters all provide reliable anchor points. The testimony of former pupils adds colour and amusement from the 1930s to the 1980s and melds with contributions from staff for the most recent five decades. Anecdote and instinct play as much a part as material gleaned from dusty archives.

I have adopted a few conventions to aid brevity and consistency. The abbreviation 'BGS' is used to refer to the Boys, Girls and mixed versions of 'Barnstaple Grammar School'. The abbreviation 'Park' includes the more recent nomenclature of 'The Park Community School'. OBA stands for Old Boys Association and Old Bardians Association (which subsumed the OGA too). Costs are always given in 'new money' to save younger readers puzzling over what a fee of 1/6d might mean, though inflation still makes it difficult to fathom that 7½ pence once bought so much. The main body of the book is written in the third person, which teachers told us would add authority to our writing. I'm not sure that's true but old habits die hard.

Many people have made significant contributions to this book and I cannot here name everyone to whom I owe thanks. Foremost among them, however, is David Atton, the present Head, who has supported this project enthusiastically from the start without ever trying to influence a word of what I wrote. David let me loose on what passes for the school archive - a cupboard full of fairly random stuff. He also pointed many interesting people my way. Tim Wormleighton, Principal Archivist at the North Devon Local Studies Centre directed me to a miscellany of items deposited there by former staff and pupils. Among former teachers, Berwick Coates, Alison Grant and Sue McEldon have offered me much useful advice as well as anecdotes. Publisher Steven Pugsley has a wealth of experience in regional history and his team at Halsgrove has helped a novice to produce a proper book. Andrea Foster at the *North Devon Journal* put me in touch with living witnesses. Her articles led to phone-calls, correspondence and meetings with scores of people, all with stories to tell. My thanks go to everyone who has shared their memories with me - this book is collectively our story. My thanks also go to the copyright holders of photographs and artwork, whether I've been able to trace them or not. In the case of any inadvertent oversight I would be grateful for information which would enable copyright holders to be acknowledged in future editions. Finally, I would like to thank my wife, Sue Hill, a comprehensive school teacher for 37 years. She has endured my unreasonable obsession with this project and every chapter owes a debt to her. Naturally, I take full responsibility for whatever shortcomings may remain.

**Trevor Hill**
**Spring 2010**

# CHAPTER 1

# DAWN OF A NEW ERA

MOST CHILDREN in medieval England didn't go to school. Boys learned farming or other trades from their fathers and girls learned sewing and cooking from their mothers. Occasionally boys from important families learned reading, writing and arithmetic, which gave them authority over others. There may have been universities at Oxford and Cambridge in the thirteenth century but most people in England were illiterate. In fact, education did not significantly empower ordinary people until the dawn of the 20th century. At least it didn't in North Devon.

By the mid sixteenth century a few children from poor families were being taught to read and write by educated priests in Chantry Schools, where they were engaged to chant for lost souls. In the course of the Reformation, one such school was transferred to St Anne's Chapel in Barnstaple, which was built in 1330 and still stands near St Peter's Parish Church. It was purchased by the town in 1549 for use as a 'Grammar School'. The names of all the Masters who taught in that tiny one-room school have been recorded. They were all M.A. educated and almost all had taken holy orders. They focused on teaching Latin and Greek, subjects long regarded as essential to a gentleman's education. Reverend Robert Luck took the job in 1698 and he taught the school's most famous old boy, a local merchant's son called John Gay, who became a poet and playwright. Gay was probably thinking of his schooldays when he penned these words in 'The Birth of a Squire':

> How shall his spirit brook the rigid rules
> And the long tyranny of grammar schools?
> Let younger brother o'er dull authors plod,
> Lashed into Latin by the tingling rod.

*Engraving of the first Barnstaple Grammar School at St Anne's Chapel.*

Classics and caning characterised the entire 360-year history of the first Barnstaple Grammar School. Hugh Sloley, a pupil there from 1852, wrote: *"Imagine small boys spending long hours at Caesar and Ovid before they were nine. Imagine long evenings of prep in a room which has no windows, just a skylight and tallow candles, sitting at a long bench without any back. The inevitable result of bad work was cane, cane, more cane!"* The Headmaster then was a Reverend Johnston and boarders attended the Parish Church where he often preached. The fee-paying pupils were almost entirely the sons of the wealthiest citizens. White's *Devonshire Directory* of 1850 cites one exception: *"The Corporation allow the master the free use of a house, though for this privilege he is required to teach one free scholar, who receives a classical education in common with about 30 other boys."* For the rest of Barnstaple's youth, including everyone of the female sex, there was still no secondary education.

When Victoria became Queen in 1837 some politicians still thought that the education of the poor was unnecessary and even dangerous. One MP contended that *"It was books that produced the French Revolution!"* By this time several elementary schools were already well-established in Barnstaple but real progress was hindered because there was not yet any legal obligation on parents to send their children to school and many families still needed them to work. One solution was to make use of the one day of the week when children's labour was not required, Sunday. By 1851, more than 2 million working class children in Britain were enrolled in Sunday Schools, where basic literacy and numeric skills enhanced their religious instruction.

*Interior of St Anne's classroom with the Master's desk and cane. The room is preserved intact and this photo was taken in 2009.*

The 1870 Elementary Education Act established School Boards and introduced the idea of compulsory universal education. By 1880 attendance was enforced by bye-laws and 90% of eligible children were soon attending, up from just 10% two decades earlier. The 1891 Education Act decreed that elementary education was to be provided free of charge, although fees were not finally abolished until 1918. The school leaving age was raised to 11 in 1893 and to 12 in 1899, making it illegal to employ younger children in factories. By the end of the 19th century some School Boards had begun grouping the oldest and ablest children into higher grade schools and offering a curriculum which in some respects resembled that of fee-paying secondary schools.

A Parliamentary Commission Report of 1869 described the Grammar School at St Anne's Chapel as *"in a languishing state"* and the premises as *"lamentably inferior"*. In an early demonstration of parent power, farmers and tradesmen began sending their sons to the new Devon County School at West Buckland, which offered 100 boarders a more practical and commercial curriculum and no obligatory Latin. Barnstaple Grammar was forced to draw its pupils from further afield and the pupil roll for 1867 shows twelve boarders and only seven day boys from the immediate vicinity. An exchange of letters in the *North Devon Journal* in 1875 suggested that the school seemed *"totally unfit for educational purposes"*. It is hard to imagine how it managed to struggle on until 1910.

*BGS cap badge circa 1900.*

In 1881 Barnstaple's great benefactor, William Frederick Rock, made an attempt to found a new school. Mr Rock had already gifted Rock Park to the town in 1879 *"for the enjoyment of its people."* A Miss Arundell-Yeo then owned a portion of the land in Newport on which Park School now stands and Mr Rock wrote her a solicitor's letter explaining that he wished to establish *"a school, an addition which more than anything else is needed by the town."* The lady declined to sell and nothing more came of it for the rest of the century.

As the twentieth century dawned, the development of a national public system of education in England and Wales was still lagging 50 years behind much of Europe and the USA. In response, the Conservative government of Arthur Balfour presented its 1902 Education Bill. Many politicians feared that the cost of popular education would lose them the support of large landowners and industrialists who were the major taxpayers, but the argument that Britain needed a more educated workforce to maintain its position in world trade eventually prevailed. The Education Act of 1902 laid the framework for County Grammar Schools, the first stage of a national system of secondary education into which higher grade elementary schools and fee-paying secondary schools would be integrated. It abolished the former School Boards and created Local Education Authorities, based on the County Councils, which were to provide grants for school maintenance.

To their eternal credit, Barnstaple's power brokers were swift to respond to the prospect of cash on the table. 'The Joint Committee for Secondary Education for the Borough of Barnstaple' met for the first time on September 29th 1903 and immediately seized the opportunity of laying claims before the County Council for Barnstaple to be provided with a new secondary school. After considering what supplementary money could be contributed from local charities, the committee recommended the County to build a school for 150 boys and 150 girls.

On 8th August 1904 a meeting of all parties to the scheme agreed on all matters and a sub-committee was appointed to find a suitable site. Led by Alderman Reavell, they viewed several possibilities before selecting a site at Newport which included the very land W.F. Rock had sought for the same purpose 23 years previously. Three fields amounted to almost 13 acres and included two houses on the Bishops Tawton Road and a playing-field which had been used for many years by Barnstaple Rugby Club. The first draft plan a year later estimated that £14,000 would be required to purchase the land and build a school upon it. Devon County Council would provide £8,000 and the town would provide the remaining £6,000. The Newport site was duly purchased from Mr Chichester of Hall for the sum of £4,100.

Meanwhile the national Board of Education had published curriculum regulations defining a four year course leading to a School Certificate examination. Subjects included English language and literature, geography, history, a foreign language, mathematics, science, drawing, manual work, physical training, and household crafts for girls. In 1905 the Board added: *"The function of the teacher is to create or foster the aptitude for work and for the intelligent use of leisure. The only uniformity of practice the Board wishes to see is that all teachers should think for themselves and adapt the curriculum to the needs of the children in their charge."* The 1907 Education Act cemented another key brick in the wall - the scholarship and free place system, designed to give promising children from elementary schools the opportunity to go to secondary schools even if their parents could not afford the fees.

*James Hill.*

*Below left: The builders take a break for the first ever school photo.*

The ceremony to lay the foundation stone of the new Barnstaple Grammar School took place on 11th August 1909. Sir Thomas Acland, Chairman of Devon Education Committee, officiated, accompanied by the Mayor of Barnstaple, Mr Hunt, and William Philip Hiern, Chairman of the Building Committee. The first secondary school to be built under the auspices of Devon County Council and Devon's first ever dual-sex Grammar School was finally getting off the ground.

George Pollard and Co. of Taunton had secured the contract to build the school, which was to be completed within one year for a little over £9,418. The photograph of the workmen posing in front of the nearly completed building constitutes the first ever school photo. The Clerk of Works was a local man, James Hill, who had been a pupil at St Anne's Chapel. Four generations of James Hill's descendants would be educated at the new school right through to the 21st century.

The 1910 'Articles of Government' for BGS defined the membership and responsibilities of the Governing Body, which was initially constituted as a sub-committee of the Devon County Council Education Committee. They had to produce an annual budget for submission to the County, which

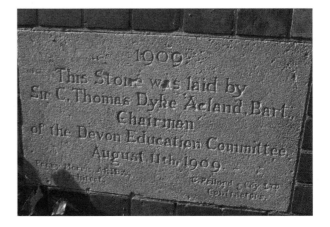

would pay the necessary funds in four instalments each year. The Governors would appoint the staff, prescribe the subjects of instruction, set the fees and the school timetable, and be responsible for the maintenance of plant and apparatus. There would be a Boys Department and a separate Girls Department, each catering for pupils aged 10-18 in single-sex classes. Two Head Teachers would *"control the choice of books, the method of teaching, the arrangement of classes and the whole internal organisation, management and discipline of the school."* The Head Master of the Boys Department would be responsible for matters common to both Departments.

The first Governors' meeting was held on June 22nd 1910. Thirteen Governors were present, all men, and they appointed Mr George Brown as Clerk at an annual salary of £45. They resolved to provide 200 single oak desks in two sizes. At their second meeting on 2nd July, two co-opted women joined eight J.P.s, six Councillors (including The Mayor of Barnstaple), and two Reverends. Mr William Philip Hiern was appointed Chairman, and Alderman Arthur John Reavell became Vice Chairman.

Mr H. G. Abel (M.A., Cambridge) was appointed Headmaster of the Boys Department at a salary of £400 p.a. Miss Annie Jenkin (M.A., London) became Headmistress of the Girls Department at a salary of £250 p.a. Unequal pay for men and women was taken for granted. Governors also appointed two senior masters (at £150), two senior mistresses (at £130), two junior masters (at £120) and two junior mistresses (at £110).

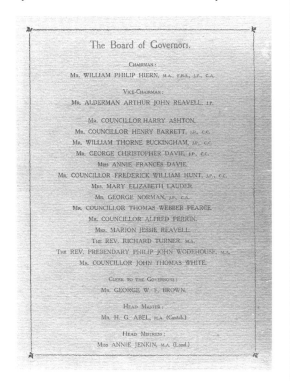

Just ten full-time teachers would cater for boys and girls separately across a wide range of subjects. Barnstaple School of Art was asked to assist with the teaching of drawing and *"manual instruction"* and the County Council also provided the services of a cookery teacher one day per week. Tuition Fees were set at £2.50 per term for pupils under 12 and £3.15 per term for pupils over 12, with a 10% discount for two or more children from the same family. Fees did not include mathematical instruments or books.

The minutes of Governors' meetings in the final few months before pupils arrived convey a sense of frenzied excitement about the job in hand. Sub committees met almost daily to deal with nitty gritty matters. They advertised for a man and wife team to act as caretakers and cleaners at a weekly wage of £1.75; from 44 applicants, Mr and Mrs Sanders were appointed. Governors received tenders for laboratory fittings and accepted a quote for £359.41. They purchased two pianos for £61. They applied to the National Telephone Co. for the school to be connected to the phone system. They ordered items for the cookery and geography rooms, exercise books, tools for the caretakers and blinds for the windows… the list went on and on.

Mr Abel and Miss Jenkin attended their first Governors' meeting on 23rd August. The first prospectus was settled and sent off to the printers. Mr Abel suggested the school motto – Sic Nos Non Nobis. At a sub-committee in late August, Governors chose a brown uniform cap for boys with the Borough Arms and motto in gold, costing 7½ pence from Shellard & Co. Girls' straw hats and hat bands could be obtained from Rowe and Co.

At a meeting on 6th September, just two days before the official opening, it was confirmed which 24 children (12 boys and 12 girls) would be the first to be admitted as Free Scholars. These children from ordinary families were the forerunners of free education for all. They had all attended elementary schools and had all passed an entrance test. Their names reflect the fashion of the times - two girls called Gladys, five Ediths, two Reginalds and one each of Mabel, Florence, Elizabeth, Ethel, Frances, Frederick, George, Stanley, Leslie, Douglas, Maurice, Charles, Alexander, Samuel and Albert.

At 3.30 pm on Thursday 8th September 1910 the Governors, the Mayor and Corporation of Barnstaple, several members of Devon County Council and 600 invited members of the public gathered in the late summer sunshine and looked up at the finished

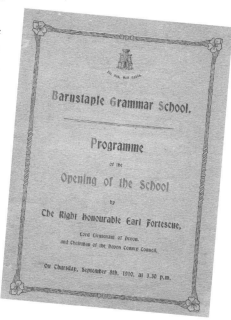

school building with its Borough Arms carved in stone at one end and the Fortescue crest at the other. They witnessed William Hiern hand a silver key to Lord Fortescue, the Lord Lieutenant of Devon, who unlocked the door to the new Barnstaple Grammar School. They processed to the Hall where it became clear from speeches that the school owed *"its inspiration and its existence"* to Mr Hiern.

## William Philip Hiern, Founding Father

William Philip Hiern J.P. B.A. M.A. C.A. and F.R.S. was the key founder of the 1910 School. He was the prime mover in getting Devon County Council to build their first school in Barnstaple, he negotiated the purchase of the site, and he became the inaugural Chairman of Governors.

The *Journal* described him as *"Barnstaple's most distinguished citizen"* and *"a great Devonian"*. He was a Fellow of the Royal Society and an internationally known botanist and mathematician. His published works included catalogues of the flora of Africa and India as well as *The Flora and Botany of Devon*. He probably planted the trees from five continents which still adorn the school's south driveway. He was a Magistrate, a County Councillor and President of the North Devon Liberal Association. He lived in Barnstaple Castle, had the title 'Lord of the Manor of Stoke Rivers' and was a distant relative of John Gay.

Mr Hiern was still an active Governor when he died, aged 86, in November 1925. Headmaster Abel said then: *"Mr Hiern threw wholehearted devotedness into his public service and I was inspired by his example."* Miss Jenkin added: *"At the time the school was built there was considerable opposition to the idea of there being a girls' school. It was through Mr Hiern's determination that girls should have the same chances as boys that the scheme was carried through."* Mr Hiern left a Trust Fund, whose interest was to be used to assist a deserving girl to continue her studies at the school or to further her training on leaving.

The *North Devon Journal* described the facilities of the new school in great detail. It said that the Architect, Percy Morris, had *"made the first public secondary school in Devon a model of what such a school should be."* Intended to accommodate boys in the east half and girls in the west half, the school was designed to convert to a mixed school if later required without any structural alterations. There was no mention of the wall down the middle of the playground to keep the sexes apart!

Boys and girls each had four classrooms on the ground floor and two classrooms on the first floor. There was a woodwork room and a cookery room. Two laboratories and a lecture hall were to be shared, along with a *"lofty and handsome"* 84 feet long assembly hall in the centre of the building, divided by a folding partition with boys on one side and girls on the other. The two Head Teachers had offices in the basement and there were two staff-rooms, two stationery stores and two sets of toilets with seven basins in each. The floors were polished block-wood and the classroom walls were painted green, cream and white, with red dados to add warmth to the north-facing rooms. The school was lit throughout by electricity, supplied by Barnstaple Municipal Electric Light. Heating was by hot water radiators stoked by basement boilers. Ventilation was by hopper screens attached to the windows. Outside, there were bicycle sheds and a tarmac playground with *"space beyond for a gymnasium and swimming bath"*. Tennis courts were being laid out and a *"beautiful carriage road"* had been constructed to the main Bishops Tawton Road entrance. There was a separate pedestrian entrance from Ladies Mile – for young ladies only, naturally.

The fact that half of the intake would be girls was a major breakthrough at a time when the education of women, who still didn't have the vote, was still not considered a high priority by many in society. The inclusion of pupils who had been selected on merit from ordinary local families and whose places were offered free was a development that would be built on as the century progressed. The use of the pre-existing name, 'Barnstaple Grammar School', belied the changes which were taking place. Yes, the first headmaster was a Classics M.A. and, yes, judged by today's standards, it was still elitist. But there was no mistaking that a new era had begun, the logical conclusion of which would be the Comprehensive School we have today. The founding fathers had done their work well.

*South front, 1912.*

# CHAPTER 2

# FORWARD INTO BATTLE, 1910~1918

TEN FULL-TIME teachers were lined up and raring to grapple with the first cohort of agile young minds. But the new school's first decade would be marred by an altogether more serious battle, a devastating war that would turn boys into soldiers. In September 1910 that was still hidden in the future.

The official opening ceremony may have implied that the school was ready to welcome pupils. It wasn't. Over the next twelve frantic days the Governors' penchant for sub-committees reached new heights. Anticipating a low initial intake, an advertising sub-committee devised ads to recruit pupils through local newspapers. The sub-committee for furnishings resolved that the Clerk should get a barrel of disinfectant! The Headmaster of the St Anne's Chapel school was now out of a job and offered to sell some blackboards, though the minutes don't say whether the Governors bought them. They did purchase a 'magic lantern' and promptly set up a sub-committee to administer it. A boarding sub-committee approved Miss Ackland's house in Landkey Road for the boarding of three pupils. It met the requirements of providing a bath and a suitable place for homework with good artificial light. Since the sexes were to be segregated at school by means of partitions and walls, it followed that *"no boy and girl from the school should board in the same house unless they be brother and sister."*

Supporting Mr Abel on the boys' side were William Turner B.A., Edward Robinson B.Sc., Joseph Charnley M.A. and Frederick Teece. Miss Jenkin's team consisted of Louisa Smith B.A., Olive Crowcroft B.Sc, Nellie Honey B.A., and Lucy Cronin B.A. The boys also had two part-time instructors, Sergeant Major Hudson for 'drill' and Mr W. Evans for 'manual training' (woodwork). The girls had a part-time drill instructress, Miss Grayson, and a part-time cookery instructress, Miss Stevenson. A single part-time Art Master, Mr W. Bryant, was shared by both sides. All of the female teachers were unmarried.

The first customers, 53 boys and 52 girls, arrived for lessons on Tuesday 20th September. Miss Smith offered these jottings 25 years later: *"That first morning the whole building was very new and clean, the floors unstained and destined by their accusing whiteness to call down vengeance on any luckless ink-spiller's head. The ringing of the first bell, the girls filing in for the first morning prayers...the school as a living organism had come into being."*

That Thursday's *Journal* made it sound like a holiday camp: *"Tomorrow they will watch a performance of* As You Like It *at the Theatre Royal. The first school game will be football, and school runs will also be arranged. Hockey will be introduced next term and the tennis courts should be finished for next summer."* What a pity it had to be spoiled by lessons! All pupils did Latin, French, English, Maths, Singing and Physical Drill. Boys also did Greek, Chemistry, Physics, Nature Study, and Woodwork, while girls also did General Science, Botany, Drawing and Domestic Subjects.

*Girls' playground drill, showing the dividing wall.*

The rationale for splitting the sexes and keeping them separate may have been due in part to a sense that sexual contact among young adolescents was to be discouraged. But the main consideration was simply that boys and girls studied different subjects. They had different expectations placed upon them and they had very different career prospects. Boys at the Grammar School were being prepared for serious jobs in industry and the professions. Many parents still regarded the education of girls as less important, as a sort

*Group of boys and staff, 1910-11. Mr Abel is seated centre. John Henry Howard Hill is standing sixth from the left.*

of finishing exercise along the way to marriage and motherhood. Mixed sex classes would simply have been impractical.

The School Archive contains the original School Register in two large volumes and the first entries in each give a flavour of the diverse clientele who arrived that first week and what subsequently happened to them. The first name in the Boys Register is George Frederick Arundell from Crediton, who was born in 1895 and admitted as a fee-paying day-boy in Form V, having previously attended the North Devon County School. His father was described as a *"gentleman farmer"*. George's school record shows that he was absent through ill health during the Easter term of 1911 and that he left the school without any public examination certificates in December 1912 to take up farming. Samuel Trick was a 13 year-old free-place scholar from Bickington Council School whose father was a carpenter. Samuel and his friends will figure later in this chapter. John Henry Howard Hill, the 16 year-old son of Clerk of Works James Hill, joined as a fee-payer for his final year of schooling before leaving to become a clerk in a surveyor's office.

The first name in the Girls Register is Gladys Thorne from Combe Martin Council School, who was born in 1898. Her father was a saddler and she was admitted as a free-place scholar with an exemption from school fees for the duration of her school life, which stretched until July 1915. Her record shows that she gained Cambridge passes in Conversational French and went on to Bristol to train as a teaching assistant, returning to BGS for her teaching practice. Florence Maude Tucker from Tawstock and Edith Anne Robins from Pilton were other free-place scholars who went on to teach and they appear in the earliest surviving class photo. Completing a quartet of scholarship girls to become teachers was Frances Ethel Mearles from Bradiford, one of seven children whose father was a gardener. Ten times a week, including going home for a midday meal, Frances walked from Bradiford to BGS and back again, a weekly total of 30 miles. Her daughter adds: *"Mum used to say she didn't learn to walk until she was three years old but she made up for it later!"* Then there was Ethel Kathleen Hill, the first scholarship pupil from Instow, who left BGS in 1916 to become the first Old Girl to win a university place. She later graduated with a B.A. from Reading.

Miss Smith recalled the first term on the girls' side: *"Games were started at once and vigorously, though outside matches were few. Hockey had to be played at the far end of the boys' field while the girls' field was in construction. At the start there were only two Houses, Alcestis and Penelope. The end of the first term was celebrated by a party at which juniors and seniors combined to play progressive games."*

The first term ended with a dispute over cleaning after Mr Sanders the caretaker had asked for further help. A Governors' sub-committee was established to look into the matter. Mrs Lauder was co-opted - it would need a woman to advise on cleaning matters, obviously - and they concluded that £1.75 per week

*Girls' drill class in the assembly hall.*

*Girls' form class, 1910-11. Florence Tucker is seated front left and Edith Robins is standing second from left.*

was sufficient to cover the cost of cleaning the school. The Governors set out a full and detailed list of duties they expected to be covered: *"The Macadam playgrounds should be swept every day, and all form rooms should be swept with sawdust, sprinkled with disinfectant and the desks all wiped over with a damp cloth every afternoon after school."* Windows were to be cleaned once a month and toilets were to be thoroughly cleaned and scoured daily. The cookery room, laboratories and cloakrooms should be cleaned once a week and the assembly hall once a month. Finally, the whole school needed to be *"cleaned thoroughly from top to bottom and scrubbed"* three times a year during vacations. Mr and Mrs Sanders were told that if they refused to comply with these conditions they would be given notice. On 1st November they resigned. A week later, a Mr William Trapnell was appointed caretaker on the same terms and was given the option of renting a house on site.

*The girls' end of the assembly hall, 1911.*

For the Easter Term of 1911 pupil numbers increased to 61 boys and 65 girls. 27 of the girls were 'pupil teachers' preparing to become Elementary School Teachers, who attended the Grammar School part time for academic tuition, alternating with teaching practise elsewhere. Numbers continued to build. Governors resolved to levy a *"voluntary fee"* of 7½ pence per pupil per term for participating in games. Among their outgoings were horse boots and a horse-drawn roller for levelling the cricket and hockey pitches. The grounds committee decided to plant trees and shrubs so they hired a groundsman at 15 pence per day. One of his first jobs was to erect a flagpole.

In competitive sport the boys had an inauspicious start, with two humiliating defeats at cricket. On June 10th 1911 West Buckland School visited and played against *"the first representative eleven of Barnstaple Grammar School"*. West Buckland won comfortably. In the return match at West Buckland a month later, the home team declared at 381 for 9 wickets, which remained the highest score ever recorded against a BGS side. The BGS reply was a meagre 21 in the first innings and a disgraceful 6 all out (including 2 extras) in the second innings, which remains the lowest total ever. No victory was recorded against West Buckland until the 1913 season, when BGS found a couple of useful bowlers.

The Governing Body contained some pretty canny business brains. They negotiated the rateable value of the building down from £320 to £160. They put the supply of coal and coke out to competitive tender and got it for 97p and 90p per ton respectively. They arranged a dancing class for girls at a cost of 55p per term, of which 50p would go to the dance teacher, leaving a small profit. They turned down a request from the Education Committee to admit a boy from Ilfracombe as a free student on the grounds that they had already met the required quota. He was later admitted on a County Day Scholarship, which meant income. They turned down a request by the only non-graduate teacher, Fred Teece, to attend a course in Cambridge in his own time during the summer vacation. Presumably he'd asked for reimbursement of the course fee. At other times the Governors showed they had a collective heart. Samuel Trick was offered an annual bicycle allowance of £2 so that he could cycle in from Fremington.

The second academic year began with 89 boys and 89 girls, plus 16 pupil teachers. The number of free scholarship pupils also rose to an aggregate of 42. John Lewis Smallcorn from Instow became one of them. John left school in December 1915 and worked as a railway clerk at Waterloo Station before becoming Mayor of the London Borough of Carshalton. A chance communication with John Smallcorn's son revealed this unlikely career path and leaves one wondering what other things the early alumni went on to. Apparently John always treasured his old school books and magazines until they went up in smoke one day when a bonfire spread to his garden shed.

In his first annual report as Head in October 1911, Mr Abel wrote: *"The work and calibre of the school are improving. There is one distinctly promising Form consisting of 18 boys, of whom 11 are scholarship boys. Every effort must be made to keep them for their own and the school's sake"* So already the scholarship pupils were proving to be the brightest buttons in the box. Mr Abel also reported *"a grave misuse of a free place"*- a boy withdrawn without notice by his father to work at an office in town when he would have better profited by continuing his education. The simple fact was that beyond the legal leaving age a boy at work was earning whereas a boy at school, even if he received a scholarship, was still a drain on an average family's resources. Mr Abel had another concern: *"The general physique of the boys is not as good as I should like. Of fifteen boys who have sandwiches or pasties at school, twelve are under weight by an average of half a stone."* The dinner hour was lengthened to give every boy a chance of getting home for a meal.

*John Lewis Smallcorn.*

*Mr Robinson's science class.*

*Miss Crowcroft's science class.*

500 copies of a new School Prospectus were printed as a marketing aid in 1912. It contained some of the earliest photographs of boys and girls at work and a few new insights into school life.

## From Barnstaple Grammar School Prospectus, 1912

Girls must be provided with a white sailor hat, a school hat band, and a drill costume. No jewellery may be worn except what is absolutely necessary. Boys must wear the school cap or a straw hat with the school ribbon.

It is essential that homework should have first claim on a pupil's attention in the evening.

There is provision for boarders at £10.50 per term at a house in Newport with an experienced matron.

Religious instruction is given in accordance with the principles of the Christian faith but no particular denomination's formulary may be taught.

The holidays for the academic year 1912-1913 will be December 21st to January 13th; April 5th to April 28th; July 31st to September 15th. There is a whole day holiday in the middle of each term. A further 'Merit' half-holiday in the middle of each half-term is conditional on each Form's good behaviour and satisfactory work.

*Barnstaple Grammar School for Girls.*

*Needlework class.*

Budgets for the year to 31st March 1913 showed estimated costs for each half of the School (boys and girls) to be approximately £1,600. After allowing for income from fees and so on, each needed a balance of around £900 from the County. The joint bill for teachers' salaries was £1,790. The next highest costs were for Cleaning/Caretaker and Fuel/Light, which each came to £115 per annum. The most bizarre entry in the budget was £5 for *"manure"*.

Miss Smith's 1935 jottings noted that: *"For the first two years, joint concerts were held in conjunction with the Boys School but, as our numbers increased, the Girls School became sufficient to itself for such occasions and soon exchanged an inadequate school platform for the stage of a real theatre in town."* A few photographs have survived of tableaux from those early girls' dramatic performances before they tackled Shakespeare.

In September 1912 the first girls' fifth form was created. 42 years later ten of them held a reunion and Mrs Winifred Farley (née Burgess) wrote up her memories for the girls' magazine. *"In those days, we had no prefect system. We wore straw boaters and black stockings."* Nostalgia was very strong among the reunion ladies: *"Through all of our varied life experiences, the atmosphere and background of our School and its associations has gone with us, held in our memory with gratitude and pride."*

*Mr Evans' woodwork class.*

December 1912 brought the publication of Volume I, Number I of the *Barnstaple Grammar School Magazine*, a title which showed male arrogance given that it only covered the boys' side of the school. From its second edition in April 1913, the magazine was renamed *Rock Magazine* and it continued without interruption until 1964. Some of the traditions of the first edition endured throughout, like listing the arrival and departure of pupils under the Latin headings 'Salvete' and 'Valete'.

*Girls' drama tableau circa 1913.*

The first magazine's Editorial Foreword made it clear that it was written *"through boys, for boys and by boys"*. There was a report on a school visit to the Barnstaple Gas Works and news of a pupil who fell off his pony while riding to school! In sport, the first cross country run was described as a 'Paper Chase' with two 'hares' scattering a trail of paper litter for the 'hounds' to follow. The route skirted Codden Hill, followed the Venn stream towards Landkey, and then headed home to complete a distance of 7½ miles. There was a boxing class on Friday evenings from 6.30 to 8 o'clock. In the first mention of boys' Houses, an evening football match between Fortescue and Kingsley became one-sided when a number of Kingsley boys didn't turn up. Among miscellaneous items of note, Form II had a flower garden from which boys were able to send flowers to the North Devon Infirmary. And a school hymn emphasised the work ethic with this as its final verse:

> There's no place for the slacker who shrinks at play or work;
> Sufficient this, our lesson, that nobody must shirk.
> With brain, with hand and muscle for His true service lent,
> God calls us to be doing and use what he has sent.

Girls did not start their magazine until 1923 and so insights into their preoccupations are somewhat diminished for several of the intervening years. Fortunately for the historian, BGGS had a four-day inspection by the Board of Education in December 1912. Overall, the inspectors said the school was a valuable addition to the very limited provision for the public secondary education of girls in Devon. *"With careful guidance it should have a prosperous future."* Their Report included the following specific findings and recommendations:

Rock Magazine *cover design, 1913-1934.*

- The school had 5 boarders and 78 day scholars. 6 pupils were under 11 and the most senior Form (VB) had 15 girls with an average age of 15½.
- 68% of the girls came from Barnstaple and 30% were from elsewhere in Devon. 39% came from the homes of Traders and Contractors, 15% from Professional classes, 11% from Artisans, 10% from Clerks & Agents, 8% from Farmers, 7% from Public Service workers and 3% from Labourers. 59% of the girls had entered from public elementary schools.
- On the teaching of English: *"Shakespeare work seemed to be too advanced for Form IVB. The reading of good fiction out of school hours might be more directly encouraged."*
- On Housecraft: *"In needlework, the girls have made shoe-bags and blouses by hand. They badly need a sewing machine and cutting out tables. Cookery is rather better provided for."*
- On Religious instruction: *"The life of Christ should find a place in the early stages and more attention might be paid to learning by heart at all stages".*
- On transport: *"Girls from Ilfracombe should be allowed to return home by the 3.48 train instead of being kept at school until 4pm, as the next train (the 6.12) arrives at Ilfracombe at 6.51. The girls have to be up again to catch the 7.20 morning train, which makes their day exceedingly long."*
- On general welfare issues: *"The approach to the School (via Ladies Mile) is lonely and unprotected and a lamp should be provided at the entrance for the winter months... The amount of homework tends to be heavy and needs to be carefully watched lest it becomes excessive... Many pupils have a long school day with no adequate mid-day meal. It is strongly urged that arrangements are made to provide a daily hot dinner at moderate cost."*

*Ladies Mile entrance (2009).*

Governors duly considered providing a school dinner service by creating a separate building with a kitchen, dining room and scullery. The purchase of a Singer Sewing Machine for £3.25 had to wait a further two years.

By 1913 scholarship pupils were coming from all over North Devon, including Ilfracombe, South Molton and Bideford. An examination was held in June and the 12 year-olds with the highest marks were recommended for free places. The exam lasted six hours and included mental arithmetic, English composition, dictation, history and geography. In October 1913 there were 102 boys and 91 girls at the school. Seven boys sat Cambridge Exams and four of them ranked among the top ten results in all England, a remarkable achievement. Mr Abel made a plea to Governors on behalf of a 15 year-old boy who was in great need of assistance: *"His father is dead and the widow is barely supporting them. The boy has ability and a hard struggle is being made to keep the boy at school."*

The *Rock Magazines* for 1913 included an article on moth collecting and a report on a visit to the Raleigh Cabinet Works of Shapland & Petter. 'Form Notes' consisted largely of trivia and jokes, the best of which was: *"What's the difference between caustic soda and the man who built the Ark? Answer: one is Noah and the other is NaOH!"* The football first XI suffered some heavy defeats – 0-10 against the Devon County School, 2-4 against Ilfracombe YMCA, 0-4 against Barnstaple Banks and 2-5 against BGS Old Boys. They were playing against adults in the latter matches. A School Concert in April included a selection of songs, a Latin play, a gym display and a scene from Molière's *Le Bourgeois Gentilhomme*. The biggest school event of 1913 was the first ever Boys' Sports Day, held on June 11th. Events included throwing the cricket ball, high jump, 100 yards, 220 yards, 880 yards, one mile, sack race, egg and spoon race, and 3-legged race. The House Cup went to Fortescue but Raleigh won the Tug of War.

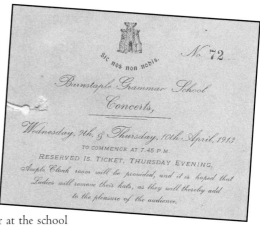

On June 6th 1913 the German Reichstag passed a bill authorising the German army to be increased to 863,000 soldiers forthwith and up to 5 million in extremis. British newspapers largely ignored this and focused instead in the ensuing months on conflicts in the Balkans, Ireland and India as well as on protests by suffragettes at home. The July 1913 meeting of the BGS Governors gave one small indication that Britain might be responding to the German military build-up when it recorded that Sergeant Major Hudson had given up his position as drill instructor at the school because *"his other work at the Territorial Army was becoming more pressing"*. The Head stressed the importance of 'Drill': *"The physique of boys is immensely improved if physical exercises are regular and daily"*. A Mr Ashford was quickly appointed to fill the staffing gap. One wonders if they had any inkling that they would soon be preparing schoolboys to be soldiers.

The Governors were confident enough about the future in April 1914 to accept a tender to paint the whole of the outside of the school at a cost of £74. They also accepted a tender of £266 to build a dining hall and kitchen, proving the value of school inspections. That April's *Rock* made no mention of international tensions. There were feature articles on photography and walking in the Quantocks. There was a snippet of gossip that *"a certain master has a favourite trick of squashing boys against the wall while they are coming upstairs"*, and news that the Landkey contingent was blown off their bicycles eleven times one morning as they came to school. Seeds had been planted in the school garden and boys were hoping for a good crop of turnips, carrots, radishes, potatoes, cauliflower, lettuce and flowers.

How calm was the lull before the storm.

---

&#10022;

---

On June 28th 1914 Archduke Franz Ferdinand, heir to the Austro-Hungarian throne, was assassinated during a tour of Sarajevo and there were strong suspicions that Serbians were behind it. An international domino effect was set in motion and by early August Germany had declared war on Russia and France. Prime Minister Asquith announced that Britain would protect the French coast and stand by a treaty guaranteeing Belgian neutrality. On 4th August Germany ignored the implied threat and invaded Belgium, so Britain entered the war.

*Alan Savory.*

Within a month the first wave of more than 1,500 men from North Devon volunteered to join the Forces. There was a general expectation that 'the hun' would be defeated by Christmas, so many fit men did not want to miss out on the action. Barnstaple Grammar School was not immune. French teacher Joseph Charnley was the first to answer the call but William Trapnell the Caretaker was close behind him. The *Rock Magazine* for December had a hand-drawn Roll of Honour listing the 26 former pupils who had already joined up to serve the King. They included two brothers, Joseph and Alan Savory, both Privates with the 6th Devon Territorials. The Savory boys had competed at Sports Day a few months previously, when Joseph broke the high jump record with a leap of 4 feet 11 inches.

There were other early repercussions of the war. A Belgian refugee and his family evacuated to Barnstaple and Reverend Avery agreed to pay for their two sons to attend BGS. Emile and Antoine Verset duly arrived and their classmates began a collection for the Belgian Refugee Fund. A Mr Watts wrote to say that he couldn't send his youngest son to school because he was needed in the family business, owing to the fact that two older sons were away on active service. The builders of the new dining hall asked for more money to cover the increased cost of timber and ironwork *"caused through the war"* and an increase in the price of coal was also minuted.

The magazine reported that *"in the workshop some of us have been busy making crutches for the wounded"* and *"Mr Crowe now runs an Ambulance Class on Friday evenings at 6.30."* Mr Abel started up a rifle range. Striving to do better and encouraging a sound esprit de corps became a constant theme in all aspects of school life. Fifteen pupils from various forms joined staff on an Exmoor hike. They caught an early morning train to Lynton and walked 20 miles via Countisbury Hill and Brendon to Simonsbath before returning home by 'char-a-banc'.

In other respects normal business continued. The dining-room sub-committee advertised for a lady cook and Mrs French was appointed at a weekly wage of 50 pence, which was only payable during term time and included washing up. It was decided that control of the dining hall would come under Miss Jenkin. This is the first sign that the Head Mistress had jurisdiction over anything to do with boys, even if it was only determining what they ate. She was authorised to take over land to grow vegetables for the kitchen. School dinners became extremely popular and the dining hall was said to be a noisy place.

By 1915 most normal economic development in Barnstaple was affected by the War. There were sporadic strikes for higher pay as the cost of living increased. Local engineering works were turned over to the making of munitions. Large numbers of horses were requisitioned and shipped to France, where they were used as officers' mounts and for pulling gun-carriages. In September there was a 40% increase in income tax and a 50% increase in Customs duty on various goods, all to fund an escalating war. British troops were engaged in a massive offensive in the trenches of the Western Front.

With so many men at war, women were taking over traditionally male jobs at home. Assistant Master Mr Crowe was called up for military service and the Governors approved his temporary replacement by a female, noting that his job would be kept open pending his return. The balance of genders within the school was shifting, reflecting what was happening in society at large. While the number of older boys was dwindling because of the war, the number of girls was on the increase. There were 146 girls by September 1915 and two new mistresses were requested. Louisa Smith wrote that *"the sewing class made garments for the Belgian refugees and a little Belgian girl was for a time among the junior pupils. With a food shortage threatening, the school flower garden was commandeered for rabbit hutches and a run of fowls and ducks."*

BGS girls were also providing much-needed entertainment. In March 1915 their production of *Twelfth Night* was performed at Barnstaple Theatre Royal to raise money for the Belgian Relief Fund. Girls played all the parts, including the distinctly un-ladylike roles of Sir Toby Belch and Sir Andrew Aguecheek. One glorious photograph shows a suitably bearded May Ingerson as Sir Toby engaging with Edith Robins as Olivia. The photo has survived thanks to Edith's descendants who also preserved a testimonial letter from Miss Jenkin.

There was now no attempt to disguise the fact that senior boys were being prepared for possible military service. They had training in Morse and Semaphore codes. Under the supervision of Mr Cameron, an ex Army man, there were army-style drill exercises every Tuesday afternoon during the autumn term of 1915. What must younger pupils have thought when the shouts of *"Left, right, left right, left right"* filtered through from the playground to mingle with the recitation of Latin verbs? The *Rock* reported that *"some people were found to have two left feet"* during two route marches through Bishops Tawton.

In July 1916 the *Rock* published extracts from a letter the Head had received from former pupil F. Bond, who wrote from the trenches: *"We are on the alert*

*Miss Jenkin's Testimonial Letter for Edith Robins.*

Thoughts were of staff
and former pupils who
were now at war.
Drawing by Art Teacher
Allan Smith.

*during the night. On the order 'Stand to Arms' each man jumps to his post with his rifle. Sentries keep watch on the enemy trenches by peering through periscopes. During the day we clean our rifles for inspection, light camp fires to fry bacon and make tea, and hope to get a few hours sleep between further turns on sentry duty."* The letter inspired Art teacher Allan Smith to sketch an accompanying picture of a sentry asleep. One wonders what the boys in Form VI must have thought as they tried to focus on their exams or their cricket that summer. Some of them would soon be enlisted.

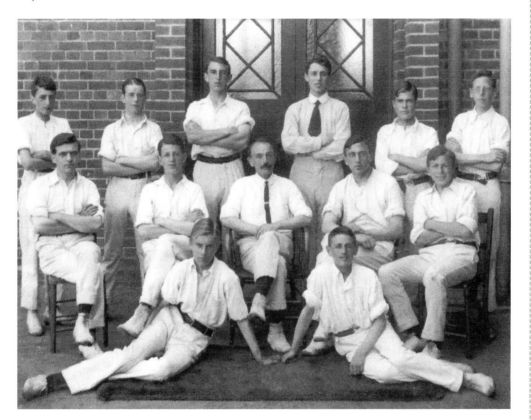

*The cricket team for July
1916 is the first team
photo for which all
names have survived.
Back row from left:
Squire, Collings,
Brokenshire, Cowie, Slee,
Rowden; Middle row:
Richards, White
(Captain), Mr H. G.
Abel (Headmaster),
Jones, Oatway; Front
row: Abbott and
Bennett.*

A flood of vivid letters from serving soldiers occupied twelve full pages of the *Rock's* December edition. Some are so evocative that they demand inclusion here.

Lieutenant Hudson (formerly Sergeant Major Hudson, the School Drill Master) wrote from Mesopotamia, where he had gained another bar to a DCM won in the Boer War. *"One doesn't expect to find things very comfortable when on active service but this beats everything I have been through. It's such an awful country, flat as a pancake. The soil consists of mud and clay that sticks like glue. We are beset by flies and insects of all kinds by the millions, together with excessive heat registering 105° and upwards. In order to get a night's rest you have to smother yourself with kerosene oil and get under a mosquito net. The boys from the school who have served with the Battalion have turned out earnest and good soldiers."*

Hudson's staffroom colleague, R. M. Crowe, seemed to be more comfortably off, writing from India as an officer in command of a recruiting unit. *"I do not think I shall ever do anything for myself again. My bearer (a sort of butler-valet) does everything — he dresses me and, at first, insisted on drying me down after my bath. I have been subjected to a process which I hardly believed to be possible, viz. shaved before I woke up in the morning. One of the first chaps I saw on the platform at Muttra, when we arrived, was A. B. Savory, looking very fit and very big."*

J. H. Brindley wrote from France. *"Earlier in the year, the country was really pretty — bluebells and anemones in the woods, poppies in the old cornfields between the lines, and green growth everywhere. But the intense bombardments mean death to everything. I remember one little village in a beautiful wood which sloped down to the river, a chateau and church nestling in the middle and all the houses intact. We gradually watched until it was nothing but a low heap of brick dust with a forest of bare poles around it."*

*Stanley Buckingham.*

A. Smith was also in France. *"You should see the dug-outs in the trenches we captured from the Huns. They are about 30 feet deep and are divided into different rooms fitted out with beds. I have been put in as a runner. My duties are to go about with our officer and take any message he may wish to send. Our steel helmets are very useful as protection against small pieces of shrapnel. I have been hit several times on the helmet without being hurt."*

Stanley Buckingham expressed surprise that France was *"such a farming country"*, but he didn't have long to dwell on the fact. *"I have moved up rapidly from my first day of landing to within the sound of the guns, which were simply roaring a few days ago. A few big ones woke me up this morning."*

Samuel Trick wrote from Grantham, where he had been trained to drive mule wagons. *"We have been raided by Zepps on one or two occasions but, luckily, no damage has been done to the camp. I was made Lance Corporal on July 14th and am now on the Machine Gun Transport, awaiting a draft for the front. One cure for timidity is to make a man ride a mule at full gallop with arms folded and no stirrups. The life here is rather rough but I'm quite happy… Chugg and Sparks left here a week ago and are now on their way to Mesopotamia to join an armoured car battery. I am sure they will render a good account of themselves behind a machine gun."*

Trick and Buckingham had both been free-place scholars in the 1910 intake, as had Frederick Slee and Reginald Chugg, who were also now at war. They had only left school in July, when Buckingham and Slee shared the 6th Form Prize. War had already diminished the Boys' Sixth Form but even the Fifth Form was suffering a drop in numbers now and was down to nine for the final term of 1916. One of the younger leavers became a Boy Artificer at Plymouth. None of this affected sales of the magazine. On the contrary, it was reported that interest in the *Rock* was growing among 'old boys'. They were charged 5 pence for three editions, unless they were *"serving with the Colours"*, when it was free of charge. The December 1916 edition congratulated an un-named member of BGGS for coming first in the whole of England in the Cambridge Junior Examination, a rare example of girls' news getting into the boys' magazine.

*Samuel Trick.*

In January 1917 Mr Abel reported on the school's first fatality: *"Stanley Gordon Buckingham, lately a student at the school, has been killed in action in France on 29th December."* He was 19 years old. Six months earlier he had been a prefect and *"the most brilliant boy scholar at the Grammar School"*. Condolences were sent to his family at Bittadon Barton. The April magazine had a 3-page obituary and a photograph of Buckingham in uniform. He was described as *"the most popular fellow in the school"*. This edition also had 15 pages of letters from old boys, including several who were writing for the first time from postings overseas or training camps in the UK. In March, Mr Charnley's replacement, Mr Critchley, was himself called to military service.

In July, there was a *Rock* obituary to another of the twelve scholarship boys from 1910, Samuel Trick. He had left school in July 1915 and spent one term at Battersea Teacher Training College before joining the Army. Towards the end of 1917 a third old boy, Arthur Squire, was killed in action at the Battle of Cambrai. He had been a fee-paying boarder from Lynton.

Another old boy, John Harley Brindley from Rumsam, was awarded the Military Cross. He became a Lieutenant in the Royal Field Artillery, serving in France and then Italy. Military records show that he won his M.C. for: *"Conspicuous gallantry and devotion to duty. Under an intense hostile bombardment of his battery he displayed the greatest promptness and magnificent disregard for danger in attending to the wounded and, working energetically to extinguish a fire which had broken out, he saved the ammunition which was starting to explode. His gallant action undoubtedly saved great loss of life and material."* In 1938 John Brindley became the first 'old boy' to serve as a BGS Governor.

There were further financial stringencies in the latter part of 1917. Head Teachers were asked to exercise *"the strictest economy"* in the use of stationery. Governors were informed that, owing to increases in wages and materials, it would now cost 32½ pence per page to print their minutes and so the minutes immediately become shorter and more succinct. Even the thriving *Rock* magazine was obliged to reduce the number of letters it published from soldiers.

In October Henry Abel gave notice that he intended to take up a Headship in London in December. On his last day at BGS he was presented with a library writing table and was thanked profusely for setting such a high standard as the inaugural Head of the School. The *Rock* described him as *"an English gentleman and a Christian."*

## Henry George Abel M.A.
## Headmaster, 1910-1917

Henry Abel was only 35 when he became Head at BGS. He was a Cambridge Classics graduate who also taught English and Scripture. Little else would be known of him as a man if Mr Teece had not written a splendidly detailed tribute to him for the March 1945 edition of the *Rock* magazine, which reported Mr Abel's death in retirement...

*"From the outset he flung all his energies into making BGS a really notable school. He had a way with him and in an incredibly short time he won the love and trust of the boys and bound the staff together in a bond of Brotherhood. Everyone's trouble was his trouble. Everyone's well-being was his concern. If you were despondent, he encouraged you. If you were ill, he visited you. If you had done well, he rejoiced with you.*

*He was a keen coach at cricket, he played football with the boys and he enjoyed a game of tennis with his staff. He was a pianist and he composed some of the hymn tunes we used at school. He loved a joke and was the life and soul of a party. He knew about art and we soon began to see reproductions of fine pictures on the walls of our classrooms. Most outstanding in him were his moral outlook and his belief that boys needed the guidance of God in their daily affairs. Old boys have told me that Mr Abel's Scripture lessons were wonderful.*

*He never forgot BGS. On his frequent visits to North Devon he would ask after various boys. He remembered their names and their cheerful rogueries. He always brought along a favourite tobacco for Mr Worth, the caretaker, and he visited the widowed mothers of boys lost in the war.*

*It was good to have known Henry George Abel. His was a very rare and choice spirit. We ought to thank God that he was given to us for a time to be an example and an inspiration to serve our fellow men."*

Four men applied for the vacancy of Headmaster and Mr Harold Sydney-Jones, formerly of Manchester Grammar School, was appointed at an annual salary of £400. An application was received from the Devon War Agricultural Committee for the housing of 30-40 boys at the school, who were to be sent to Barnstaple to assist agriculturists in the district. The boys were offered half of the central hall as sleeping accommodation and also use of the dining hall.

January 1918 marked the start of the government's policy of *"two meatless days a week"* to deal with the grave food shortage. It was decided to plant potatoes in the two long strips of land at the boys' entrance. A round of house visits by members of the Governors' boarding sub-committee led to the unexplained withdrawal of Mrs Turner's property as a boarding house for boys. Instead, twelve boys would be boarded at a hostel in Pilton Street run by Miss Godden. The boarding fees were 90 pence per 7 days and 82½ pence per 5 days – plus laundry in each case.

The April 1918 edition of the *Rock* carried two more obituaries for former pupils. Reginald Bale, 19, was killed in northern France. Mr Abel wrote a personal tribute to Leslie Fear, a boy he'd seen develop to manhood and then answer the call of duty. There was also a tribute to George Northey, a 1910 starter who went missing in action but who was later reported to be a prisoner of war.

For light relief, the magazine had a feature on current school nicknames. These included Sago (for a boy whose surname was Rice), Wiry, Hair-oil, Hippo, J-HON (for someone who had once mis-spelled his own first name), Inky, Cow (for a big, shy boy), Granfer, Oxo, Dreamy, Spider, Big Ben, Friar Tuck, Mustard, Pimple, Bunter, Froggy, Kaiser, Studious Bill, Zulu and Dormouse. The compiler of the above list added: *"When I think of Smeth, Podgy, Policeman, Pip, Sparkle, Golliwog, Beaky, Buck, Giant, Tiny, Worm, Lawrie, Izzy and dozens of others doing their duty overseas, I am proud to have lived and worked with them."* One was left to imagine 'Pimple' and 'Podgy' striking fear into the hearts of the Hun!

Among other developments in 1918, the Governors started a Cadet Corps. The introduction of the BGS Old Boys Association was announced, with an annual subscription of 12½ pence to include the cost of sending the magazines. A tuck shop was opened in the Form IV room, where bottles of lime juice and soda could be purchased for 2½ pence.

Seventeen girls took up free places in another expanded intake on their side in September. Additional desks and chairs were being ordered on a regular basis, along

*Hockey Team, 1918.*

with extra plates and cutlery. The girls' cloakroom was converted to an extra classroom and the cloakroom moved to a play shed outside. Miss Jenkin's office became another classroom and her office moved to a curtained off area of the stage. The overall teaching staff now consisted of 6 men and 12 women.

At 11 am on the eleventh day of the eleventh month, after more than four years of war, the guns fell silent on the battlefields of Europe. Germany had accepted defeat. Armistice Day became a red letter day for William Richards, one of the 1910 BGS boys. William had left school in 1917 to serve as a medical orderly in Italy and France, putting on hold an offer of a place at Cambridge to study medicine. On 11th November 1918, he arrived at Barnstaple Junction Station for his first period of leave and was met by his

*Soccer Team 1918-1919. William Richards is standing second left, Mr Critchley is seated left and the teacher standing is Mr Teece.*

family who told him the war was over. William had wondered why church bells had been ringing in all the villages along the route from Exeter. He was demobbed within a few weeks and returned to school for two terms to get back into the routine of study before going up to Cambridge. As an ex soldier, William refused to wear his school cap, although he did wear the rest of his school uniform for those two extra terms. At Sports Day he won the Mile (in 5 minutes and 8 seconds) and the 440 yards (in 57 seconds), both of which were still school records in 1934. He eventually became a doctor in Ealing.

Alan Ballantyne Savory also returned to school for a term after four years of military service. News came that Charles Alfred Perrin had died of his wounds and was buried in Flanders, aged 19. The list of the School's fatalities finally rose to seven when it became known that Emile Verset, one of the first two Belgian evacuees, was killed in action while acting as a motorcycle dispatch rider in the final days of the conflict. Messrs Critchley, Evans and Turner returned to their teaching duties and the ladies who had covered for them moved on elsewhere. Mr Crowe's military duties kept him away until September 1919.

The Governors resolved to provide a Roll of Honour for those who had served in the War. It contains 119 names and it is still displayed at Park School to this day. There is no surviving Girls' Honour Board though there were probably unsung heroines among Old Girls serving as nurses and munitions workers.

Peace seemed to bring an immediate appetite for change at BGS. Drake House was created, adding to the original three boys' houses of Fortescue, Raleigh and Kingsley. One of the new Head's first initiatives was to introduce rugby, the national game of his native Wales, and for the first few years after the war boys played soccer and rugby in alternate terms. A Musical Society was established with the formation of a violin

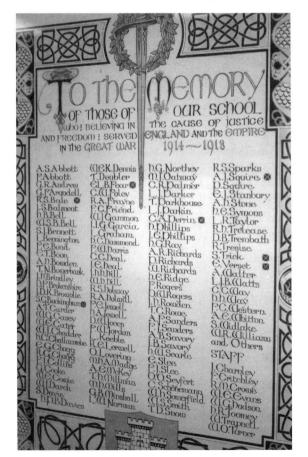

class, which it was hoped would later develop into a full orchestra, though an attempt to organise a boys' choir was quickly abandoned. Three days before Christmas 1918, Mr Sydney-Jones, hosted 35 old boys for an evening Whist Drive with refreshments and a short musical programme. It was the first official meeting of the Old Boys Association.

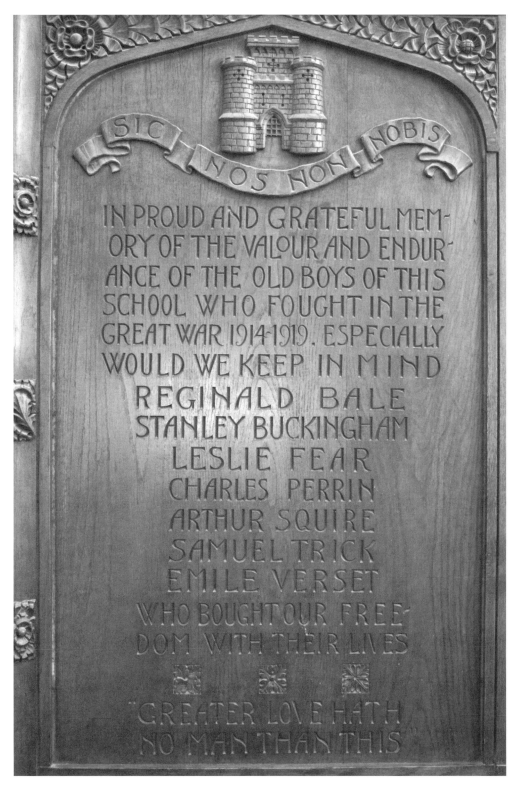

The OBA commissioned a wooden memorial board with the names of the fallen and began raising funds to build a Memorial Cricket Pavilion in honour of the seven keen sportsmen who had given their lives. A funding target of £400 was set, to be achieved by jumble sales and fund-raising concerts. The pavilion was formally opened in May 1922. Not long after that, the Barnstaple War Memorial was unveiled in Rock Park. It carries the names of all 227 local men who paid the ultimate sacrifice. In what came to be called 'The Great War' nine million Britons had been mobilised and three quarters of a million of them died.

# CHAPTER 3
# TWINKLING TWENTIES, 1919-1929

WHEN MR SYDNEY-JONES took over as Headmaster in 1918 he inherited a school that was a twinkling star in the Devon education firmament. The new Head soon gained a reputation as "*a typical boys' master*". It was said that "*a merry twinkle came into his eye whenever he related pranks and episodes from his classes.*" The combined school had 450 pupils in 1919 and by 1922 the number had increased a little more. Throughout the remainder of the Twinkling Twenties, however, pupil numbers fell again owing to the decline in birth rate during the war years. From 1921 the school leaving age was raised to 14 but BGS pupils were already staying on later than that as a rule, despite the fact that tuition fees were reported to be higher than at any other secondary school in Devon. 18 boys and 18 girls were granted new free places from September 1919. Nine of the boys and five of the girls came from Ashleigh Road School in Barnstaple.

*The Radley family in 1920. All five children went to BGS – from left, Olive, Morrish, George, William and Mabel.*

The first bus service from Ilfracombe to Barnstaple via Braunton began in 1919, bringing some new customers within reach but a new secondary school in Ilfracombe also brought new competition. George Radley was determined that his three sons and two daughters would attend Barnstaple Grammar so he leased his remote farm in the wilds of Exmoor and rented a house in Goodleigh. For several years the children travelled to and from school by pony and trap. George Radley Junior began as an eight year-old in a new Preparatory Class catering for a mixed group of boys and girls under eleven. Although some 'Prep' pupils subsequently went elsewhere, George progressed to the Grammar School proper and stayed there until 1925.

With the war stringencies behind them, the Governors turned their attention to improving staff pay. The caretaker got a rise to £2 per week. Teachers were overdue a salary increase and a document submitted to the County gives further evidence of the inequalities of pay between men and women. Mr Critchley (with 8 years of teaching experience) and Mr Scott (3 years) were both on a salary of £230 whereas the two most senior female teachers, Miss Smith (17 years) and Miss Cronin (14 years), were both graduates yet were only earning £210. It's doubtful that the unfairness was resolved because in 1921, when Burnham salary scales for secondary teachers provided national parity on pay for the first time, Devon County Council opposed it.

*Miss Annie Jenkin (centre) and staff, 1919.*

Boarding accommodation exercised the Governing Body a lot in 1919. Fourteen girls were already boarding at Miss Nicholls' house in Park Lane and a further six were at Mrs Webber's in South Street, but Governors were also keen to purchase Pill House as a hostel. Mrs James' house in Newport was declared unsuitable for boarding sixteen boys and Governors even considered an ex-Army hut on the premises as bedroom accommodation. Two wooden huts were erected but they became 'temporary' classrooms - so temporary that they were still in use after World War 2! It was decided to have a whole school library instead of separate Form libraries. A boiler was installed for teaching laundry work to girls.

There were some off-beat sporting notes in the *Rock* magazines for 1919. The tennis club had had a successful season but, *"hard hitting has resulted in the breakage of a few windows."* The Editor speculated about what the *Rock's* report on Sports Day 1969 might contain and suggested there might be a 500 mile race won by *"a 500 horsepower Pentaplane covering the distance in 1.969 centiseconds."* This was quite imaginative considering North Devon still had fewer motor cars than horse-drawn vehicles. On 15th November the first inter-school rugby match ended with Blundell's Reserves beating BGS 33-0. The *Rock* report said there was a need for tackling lower and that, *"knocks on and forward passes were frequent as our boys got used to the new game."*

In the autumn term, the boys' Concert was revived, the first since 1914, and the programme included Sheridan's *The Rivals* with boys playing the female roles. The girls' Prize-giving Ceremony was held in Barnstaple's Albert Hall in December. After two successful whist drives and 'smoking concerts' the first annual dinner of the OBA was held at the Imperial Hotel.

In 1920, the *Rock* welcomed Mr Markham as Drill Instructor and Games Master, saying: *"He has played for Neath, the stronghold of the rugby code, so he must be hot stuff."* Two advertisements appeared in the April edition. One was for a pair of football boots - *"only used for three seasons and well-repaired several times"*. The other was for *"100 neatly-typed lines guaranteed to be accepted by any prefect - large variety in stock."* A Debating Society motion that *"Birds' egg collecting is a cruel sport and should be abolished"* was defeated by 14:12. A motion that *"Capital punishment should be abolished"* was

*First ever representative rugby team, 1919. Back row from left: Rogers, Webber, Jennings, Mopper, Hill, Croot, Baker; Middle row: Baker, Whitlock, Mr T. Jones, L.C. Jones (Captain), Mr Crowe, Friend, Dunn; Front row: H.S. Jones, Casey, Crang.*

*Mr Sydney-Jones (sitting centre) and staff, circa 1920.*

defeated by a much larger majority. One new event at Sports Day was the Steeplechase Handicap, a ¾ mile circuit of the school grounds including fields, hedges and a scramble across the railway cutting. In an impromptu tug of war *"the sudden and unexpected collapse of the Old Boy's team revealed the presence of two masters at the end of the rope!"*

Governors purchased another army hut for use as a caretaker's house. They also bought a gramophone and records for the teaching of voice production and French across both schools. But their main initiative was to create Riversvale hostel for 25 girls on a site they had purchased in Litchdon Street. Boarders would be charged £60 per annum including laundry but had to provide their own cutlery and bedding. The sewing class was soon making pillow-cases. Mrs Passmore was appointed as matron at an annual salary of £80.

*Form 2 boys, 1921.*

It is clear from two photographs from 1921 that neither boys nor girls yet had a strictly-defined uniform dress-code and so, although each pupil was well turned out, there was considerable variation in their appearance. Maintenance Grants of around £10 per term were being awarded in 1921 to needy scholarship pupils, who could also be awarded rail and ferry tickets or other travel costs, a book allowance of £3 and

a bicycle allowance of £2. Girls now had their own Chemistry and Botany laboratories and no longer needed to share labs with boys. Improved gymnastic facilities included ropes between the hall pillars.

The appointment to the staff of 'Soldiers Three', as Mr Sydney-Jones called Messrs Hughes, Shercliff and Allen who were all recently demobbed and all keen rugby men, led to a vast improvement in standards of rugby at all levels and it was therefore decided to abandon soccer. The prowess of all fifteen first-team players was individually and colourfully described in the *Rock*. Watts was *"a fast wing who frequently demoralises his opponents by the unbridled ferocity of his countenance"*. Hopper was *"a vigorous, hard-working forward who worries his opponents as much with his hair as with his hands"*. Baker was *"a sturdy forward, who should not tackle masters so roughly"*. The first ever school medical examination found all the boys to be in robust health in a school *"pervaded by an atmosphere of cheerfulness"*.

In 1921 Cecil Spiegelhalter was welcomed as a Science teacher. He also took over the duties of cricket master and arranged an ambitious programme of 18 matches. His hand-written account of cricket at the school would one day become a treasure of the archive, recording as it does the highest ever batting partnership of 157 in 1924 and the highest ever single-innings score by a BGS pupil of 156 runs by Aubrey Hill in 1926 against Hele's School. At Sports Day, someone threw the cricket ball 87½ yards and the Long Jump was won with a record leap of 18 feet 4¾ inches. The first ever School Exchange involved two boys going to France in the summer under a scheme organised by the French Academy of Education.

The Girls' School Prize-giving ceremony at the Albert Hall in December 1921 was reported in the newspaper. Miss Jenkin told a large gathering of parents and relatives that 18 of the 19 senior girls had obtained school certificates. The County Medical Officer had concluded that *"it would be hard to find a healthier, happier lot of girls"*. Their seventh annual Shakespearian production, *Romeo and Juliet*, had played to full and appreciative houses and the Choir had won a North Devon competition. Two representative teams each for hockey and netball had played against Edgehill, West Bank, Ilfracombe Secondary School, Barnstaple Ladies and Westward Ho! Ladies. Miss Jenkin appealed for a shield or cup to be donated as a prize for a new inter-form competition for 'Neatness and Order'.

In a telling creative essay for the *Rock* in April 1922, K. M. of Form IVa suggested an architectural improvement: *"Each classroom should have a desk for the Master with a wall around it and doors that lock when the Master enters and only open when the bell sounds, in order that the Master cannot come down and bang you about."* The library had grown and was now big enough to have a card index system. After ten years at BGS, School Captain S. H. Croot departed for Cambridge to study medicine.

The OBA-funded Memorial Cricket Pavilion was formally opened on May 13th at the first match of the season between the Old Boys XI and the School XI. The Rock carried critiques of school cricketers. F. B. Marshall's bowling was described as *"remarkable for its breadth"* – which presumably meant he bowled wide! The other main sporting news of the year was about a spectator, the Headmaster

*Cricketers at the new Memorial Pavilion in 1922. Standing from left: Croot, Huxtable, Williams, Marshall, R. Yeo, T. Yeo, Vickery, Taylor, Mr Bill Hughes, Jones, Mr Cecil Spiegelhalter, Mr Allin, Mr Curtice; Sitting: Incledon (Captain), Gammon, Watts.*

Boys and Masters,
June 1923.

Girls and
Mistresses, June
1923.

GOSPEL
Monday
17 JULY 1922
2.15 to 3.45

UNIVERSITY OF CAMBRIDGE

SENIOR LOCAL EXAMINATION

The Gospel according to St Mark

(One hour and a half)

All the answers to this paper are to be sent up in one bundle.
Part II (English) and Part II (Greek) are alternatives. No candidate
may attempt both. Higher credit is given for Part II (Greek) than
for Part II (English).

PART I.

1. "The Gospel of St Mark is essentially a picture drawn
from life." Illustrate this statement.

2. Narrate and explain the parable of the Mustard Seed.

3. What is meant by "the tradition of the elders"? Shew
from this Gospel our Lord's attitude towards it.

4. Comment on **four** of the following passages giving the
context in each case:

(a) The sabbath was made for man, and not man for the
sabbath.

(b) Is not this the carpenter?

(c) They kept the saying, questioning among themselves
what the rising again from the dead should mean.

(d) How hardly shall they that have riches enter into
the kingdom of God!

(e) And not even so did their witness agree together.

PART II (ENGLISH).

Candidates who take Part II (Greek) must not attempt the two
questions next following.

5. Give an account of the appearances of the Risen Lord
recorded in this Gospel.

6. Write notes of explanation on **five** of the following extracts, giving the context in each case: When Abiathar was
high priest—as sheep not having a shepherd—a Greek, a Syro-
phoenician—a ransom for many—as angels in heaven—the father
of Alexander and Rufus.                    [Turn over

no less, who was knocked down by a rugby player crashing into touch during a match against Barum in early December. Mr Sydney-Jones broke his leg and was absent from school for the remainder of the term.

The Governors asked the County for £8,057 to run the school for the year to March 1923. The County in turn required fees to be increased to £3.50 per term. The earliest long-format photographs in the school archive are dated June 1923. They show boys and girls more uniformly attired than two years previously.

A handful of 1920s reports on individual pupils are held by the North Devon Record Office. Olive Cole, who was 14 in 1922, received a separate report every term for class work and additional reports for examinations. There was a percentage mark for each subject along with the subject teacher's comments, plus separate notes on attendance, punctuality, conduct, number of detentions and progress. Boys received just one report per year showing their position in class for each subject but no percentage marks. The examples filed were all signed by the Headmaster, who added comments like, *"An ugly incident occurred during an examination"* and *"Wake up!"* Unsatisfactory reports were sent home by post. The numbers of pupils per class varied between 19 and 32.

The *Rock* recorded that poor weather in 1923 turned playing fields into a quagmire. House matches were eventually abandoned after several postponements. The Debating Society reversed their 1920 verdict on capital punishment and voted to abolish it by 50:21. The December edition had a section devoted to the Old Boys Association and the Editor wrote: *"Old Boys are doing well in many varied spheres, reflecting credit on their school.*

*From Turkey, Australia, South America, Canada, the High Seas and all parts of Britain we receive letters from Old Boys who cherish the memory of their school and make its ideals a guide to their conduct and life."*

We have reached the point where living memory comes into play for the first time. In 1924, Victor 'Cracky' Uren was 9 years old and he joined the mixed BGS Prep. class, in a 'temporary' hut beyond the playground. His teacher was Miss Erna Cowie, whose sister taught at the Girls Grammar. Victor later graduated to the Boys Grammar and he is believed to be the oldest living Old Bardian, male or female, at the time this book goes to press.

Victor is 96 in 2010 and he is still quite physically active, attributing his health and longevity to the rigorous exercises and games he did at school. He recalls that P.E. Master Dixie Dobell was one of the few teachers willing to talk about his wartime experiences: *"He had fought in the Battle of Jutland and had tales of bodies flying through the air".* Victor skipped a year because he was bright but missed doing the maths module on fractions and says he has preferred decimals ever since. He remembers each day starting with a hymn at 9 o'clock. He says there were still no rigid rules about school uniform: *"You could wear what you liked as long as it was decent and not flamboyant."* Victor's most abiding memory of school is peering out of the first floor laboratory window, from where it was possible to see over the dividing wall into the girls' playground. *"We used to speculate about what colour knickers each girl was wearing and then wait for them to do cartwheels or handstands to see who was right!"* Victor went on to pass his Higher Certificate and played at wing forward for the rugby 1st XV. He later became an architect.

*Victor Uren, the oldest known 'Old Boy' in 2009.*

*Dick Youings, Peter Hill and Victor Uren, 1927.*

An article about Victor Uren in the *North Devon Journal* in 2009 prompted two of his contemporaries to come forward. Peter Hill and Bill Stone joined as Prep Boys in 1925 and 1926 respectively and both went on to play first XV rugby. Peter Hill has vivid memories of his schooldays: *"I can remember one morning when the Assembly Hall had to be cleared because Jack Wood had dropped some stink bombs. The Headmaster was 'Grampy' Jones. Grampy was a short man and a big lad called Mothy, who went to be caned, picked Grampy up and sat him on his office table!"* There was also a short-sighted teacher who didn't last long: *"We moved his desk back by a yard and he kept bumping into it!"* Peter made a chair in woodwork which he still has to this day. He can remember swimming in the River Taw at Newbridge on group outings with history master Bill Hughes.

Bill Stone grew up in a house bordering on the school but his father never let him take a short cut over the back fence. He has retained a remarkable piece of ephemera - a complete handwritten list from the 1920s showing all the boys names against their cloakroom peg numbers. Bill became a civil engineer. Peter Hill went into the family jewellery business and was a founder member of Barnstaple Swimming Club at Rock Park Baths. If there are any surviving BGS girls from the 1920s, they have sadly not volunteered details of their cart-wheeling days!

In 1924 storms brought down a lot of the elm trees around the school, leaving the field *"like a lumber forest".* Drake House had

*Boys' cloakroom list from the 1920s.*

extraordinary success over the winter and held every House Cup, Shield and Championship except cricket. Miss Jenkin filed an analysis of what had become of the girls who left school in 1924. Five of them, all free-place pupils, went on to universities. Twelve, all free-place pupils, went into Teacher Training Colleges. eight, including 6 free-place pupils, taught in Prep School or Elementary School, requiring no further qualifications. Six were employed in office work, 3 worked in shops, 2 worked in nursing and 2 worked for the Post Office. Ten, including 9 fee-payers, left North Devon. Twenty-six, including 16 fee-payers, simply *"stayed at home"*.

By 1925, the *Rock* had slimmed down to twenty very dull pages of sports results. This coincided with a five-year gap in the archived Governors' minutes until they mysteriously re-appear for 1930. A researcher looking for documentary evidence of school life might have despaired were it not for the imminent arrival of a breath of fresh air. The *Alpenant*, the magazine of the Girls Grammar School, took its name from the first syllables of the three girls' Houses - Alcestis, Penelope and Antigone. The 1926 edition is the first to be archived and there was one edition per year until 1964. The magazine cover would change colour according to which of the three Houses was achieving the most. The 1926 edition was green because Penelope was top House but the editor hoped that Alcestis or Antigone would soon make it red or purple respectively.

A report on girls' sport revealed that prizes of tennis racquets and cutlery sets were given to winners and runners up. There were also inter-House and Form prizes for many other activities, including cooking, needlework, music, science, neatness, and drill. That wasn't all: *"It has been decided to award a deportment stripe to those girls who walk well, hold themselves well, and have a good general appearance."* One sixth form girl described *"the classic atmosphere of our Form room"* enhanced by pictures from Miss Jenkin and a statue of Cupid and Psyche: *"by subscribing a small sum yearly, we hope to form a collection of these delightful statues and thus adorn our room as befits an Abode of Wisdom."* There were hostel notes from Riversvale where *"serenity still rules despite many youthful and innocent pranks. We still joyfully submit to the tyrannical rule of Miss Cronin and Miss Crowcroft."* Among hostel events were a trip to Clovelly, a tennis tournament and a Christmas social.

*Hockey Match against Barum Ladies, 1926.*

Perhaps the *Rock* editor of 1926 sensed the competition from the *Alpenant* when he wrote: *"the magazine is degenerating and there are not nearly enough humorous or interesting articles."* In the short term, they relied on news of some rather geeky interests, like a feature article on 'wireless' as a hobby, news of several lectures with lantern-slides from railway companies, and a camera club to *"utilise the dark room which has lain fallow"*. An 11-member 'orchestra' augmented by boys on toy instruments played Haydn's 'Toy Symphony' at Speech Day. A School Swimming Gala was held for the first time but the absence of facilities in Barnstaple meant a journey to Ilfracombe, with an unexpected setback: *"One of the charabancs conveying the party broke down and we had to curtail the programme of events."* The Old Boys Association now had an impressive 392 members.

The 1927 *Alpenant* was more than covering its costs, thanks in part to commercial advertising by school uniform suppliers, something which the *Rock* had not yet tried. The magazine carried a review from the *North Devon Herald* of the girls' production of *A Winter's Tale*, *"which played to large and appreciative audiences for three nights in the Theatre Royal, Barnstaple"*. All the costumes were home made and, in a rare collaboration, the boys' orchestra provided the music. This production continued an annual tradition of girls' Shakespearian productions unbroken since 1915. The magazine even had a Shakespeare-inspired poem by M. Clarke of Form IVb...

### A Speech Before Examinations

Once more into the room, dear friends, once more,
Or stay outside to your eternal shame.
In school there's nothing so becomes a girl
As modest stillness and humility,
But when examination time draws nigh
Stiffen your back-bones, summon up your brains;
Disguise your ignorance with wise aspect.
Now set your teeth and set as if with joy;
Hold hard your breath and walk in jauntily,
With fearless gaze. On, on, you noblest schoolmates,
Whose blood is fet from all the choicest minds,
Be copy now to girls of duller wit,
And teach them how to answer in exams,
For there is none of you so seeming dull
That hath not knowledge stored inside that head.
I see you stand impatient to commence;
The bell has rung, the game's afoot, and all
With dauntless mien must answer to the call.

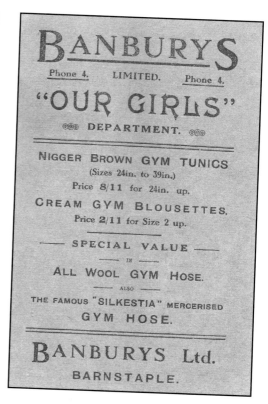

1927 brought the first Inter-School Athletic Sports, marking a new phase in the rivalry between BGS, Crediton Grammar and West Buckland. The latter came en masse in a special train and were dominant, although Harry Bradley, who would one day become a BGS teacher, won the Long Jump with a leap of 19 feet. Bradley completed a clean sweep of victories in the school's own Sports, winning at 100 yards, 220 yards, Long Jump, High Jump and the Mile, and earning the Open Cup for Drake for the second year in succession.

In February 1927, 83 boys were away with influenza when Inspectors called to see how things were going. This is thought to be the first ever external inspection of the Boys Grammar School. Its main findings were as follows:

- Of the 231 boys, 23 were under 11 and 22 were over 16. The average stay at the school was just 3 years and 4 months. 66% of boys came from Barnstaple and the rest were from elsewhere in Devon.

- Fees were now £10.50 per annum. The number of free places was a stipulated 40% of the previous year's admissions. 30 boys were taking up the option of a midday meal for 4p at the school refectory.

*Advert from 1927 Alpenant.*

*Harry Bradley winning the Mile, 1927.*

- There were nine full-time and two part-time teachers plus the Head, who taught Maths and Physics. Inspectors found the teaching timetables very heavy: *"This is particularly noticeable in the case of the Head, whose teaching duties must render other aspects of his work difficult if not impossible."* More self-study classes for Sixth Formers were suggested.

- Latin was taught to everyone from Form II and French was then taken by the more able linguists in Form III. But Inspectors remarked that *"the teaching of French over a three year course is quite inadequate and the pupils' pronunciation is poor. The teaching of both subjects is weak and much of the Latin teaching is dull, with insufficient oral work and translation."*

- In R.E. there were two lessons a week on Old and New Testament teaching: *"The Master gets boys to read passages aloud and then he comments and asks questions about them."*

- English lessons were lively and varied, ranging from a debate to learning poetry, as well as grammatical and literary study. Geography and History displayed a good standard of work overall. The two Science laboratories were well maintained and the standard of teaching was satisfactory.

- Inspectors saved their highest praise for Art Master Allan Smith: *"It would be difficult to believe that the quality of work shown had been done without any proper facilities or a proper room to work in. Every effort should be made to give this Master a better chance."*

The Girls Grammar School was subjected to a similar inspection in October 1928. The overall conclusion of the report was that: *"This is a very good school, with an atmosphere of cheerful work. The girls are receiving an excellent training."* Detailed findings included the following:

- There were 258 girls enrolled, including 28 boarders and 16 girls under the age of 11. 58% of pupils came from Barnstaple and the remainder from elsewhere in Devon. In 1927 60 girls had left the school after an average of 3 years and 5 months at the school.

- The Head and her 12 staff were said to be a well-qualified and harmonious team. Exam results were *"creditable, with no real weakness in any subject"*. The inspectors had lots of detailed praise, speaking of this *"scholarly and level-headed mistress"* and that *"vigorous and interesting teacher"*. They found that: *"The sixth form show unusual ability in thinking out and discussing topics suggested by their reading."*

- Huts provided a Sixth Form room, two classrooms, and a sewing room.

- About 40 girls were taking a hot dinner at 20p for five days. Others brought packed lunches to eat in a supervised room.

- Housecraft included needlework, housewifery, laundry-work and cookery, but the latter three were taken only by girls who had dropped Latin.

The programme for the boys' Speech Day in 1928 had an irksome printer's error. The girls' Sports Day in July was rained off and postponed to the first week of October. Fun events included a *"flower pot race"*, a skipping race, an obstacle race, a potato race, a three-legged race, a sack race, a wheelbarrow race, a *"bunny jump"*, an egg and spoon race and *"hobble and poodle"*.

Antigone was now top House, having won the cricket, netball and choir shields. It was keen to keep its position, which would mean everyone pulling their weight and losing fewer points through detentions: *"If we are to gain Junior and Senior Shields next term we shall need much more enthusiasm and esprit de corps from everyone."* Where the Boys School kept order with the stick, the Girls School kept order with a whole bunch of carrots!

In 1929 the entire Boys School went on a full day excursion to the Great Western Railway Works at Swindon, involving a 3½ hour train journey each way. They saw the whole process of making trains from white hot iron being cast in the foundry to new locomotives being assembled, painted and tested. The school was ahead of its time in giving pupils the opportunity for such experiences.

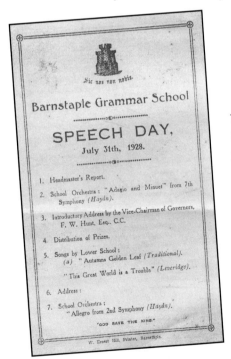

# CHAPTER 4

# THREADBARE THIRTIES, 1930-1939

IN AUGUST 1930 crowds thronged Ladies Mile to celebrate the opening of the Rock Park extension, which would soon include a new outdoor public swimming baths, a children's boating lake and two tennis courts, all beautifully landscaped with paths, lawns, and flower beds. A sundial was gifted by Barnstaple Girls Grammar School to be situated near the tennis courts. It was a year for gifts. At the girls' Prizegiving, *"buttonholes and nosegays"* were presented to the Governors. Pupils of both schools were using a new wireless donated by the Old Bardians Association. And an armchair was presented to Mr Worth who retired after 19 years as the school caretaker.

A Latin teacher called Mr Lamb moved on to pastures new and the *Rock* commented: *"Perhaps the greatest thing Mr Lamb has done here is to make Latin a subject that boys do not dislike."* There was more sarcastic wit when another *Rock* contributor wrote: *"In November we were given a talk by an eminent temperance lecturer on 'the effects of alcohol on the human brain'. Since the pupils do not drink, this must have been intended for the staff, wherein he had a perfect illustration for his lecture!"* Humour was returning to the boys' magazine and the prefects came in for some stick.

### Prefects' Song – by A. Thorn

When a boy is not engaged in his employment,
Of maturing his extremely little brain,
His capacity for innocent enjoyment
Is one that 'Impos' never could restrain.

When the enterprising boy is not a learning,
Or the student isn't occupied with Maths,
He spends his time in all the school rules spurning,
And rides his bike along forbidden paths.

And since we have all these poor boys to mother,
Of happy leisure hours we have none.
Taking one consideration with another,
A prefect's lot is not a happy one.

The pupil intake went up in 1931 and 1932, owing to the increase in the birth rate in 1920 and 1921. With more boys to police, prefects were given distinctive maroon caps with a wide orange band, a silver and red crest and a tassle. It was suggested that the prefects were such an ugly-looking lot that *"they needed to be disguised with gaudy caps!"*

In July 1931, Mr Sydney-Jones retired after 13½ years as Headmaster. The *Rock* described it as *"the end of an epoch"* and devoted three pages to their outgoing leader, whom they knew as 'H.S.' or 'Grampy'. The pupils presented him with a clock and the OBA gave him an armchair at a special evening in his honour.

*Prefect's cap.*

# Harold Sydney-Jones, M.A.
## Headmaster, 1918-1931

Mr Sydney-Jones was a Welshman who had previously taught at Manchester Grammar School. As well as his leadership duties he taught a full timetable of Maths and Physics and founded the chess club and the Old Bardians Association. Academic standards were high during his tenure and BGS had its full share of County and State Scholarships at a time when both were scarce and competition was fierce.

When H.S. died in November 1946, maths and music teacher H. J. Martin, wrote this in tribute: *"His textbook* A Modern Arithmetic *revolutionised the teaching of the subject as did his text-book on the calculus which was the first to provide a rational introduction. His best work was done with sixth formers who had a mathematics bent, but he could fascinate ten year olds too with stimulating problems. He had a very warm corner in his heart for some of those who were officially regarded as incorrigible scamps."*

Mr Sydney-Jones was replaced in September 1931 by Wilfrid Canham B.A. M.A., a Cambridge man. In November the County asked Governors to reduce admin expenditure by 15%. D.C.C. made it clear that the Governors could not sue parents for non payment of fees without specific authority. The matter arose because eleven late payers had not responded to reminders. In spite of the cash flow problem Governors agreed to contribute to the medical expenses of a boy who had been injured at rugby.

The very next year there seemed to be money in the kitty again judging by the sudden splurge of spending. Governors purchased 17 new desks, 50 chairs, and four hearth rugs for the staff rooms and new blinds for the girls' hall. They converted light switches, painted doors and lavatories, creosoted huts and fences, and re-surfaced the entrance path. They even contracted out the winding of school clocks. There was discussion about providing a common room for students, who were willing to pay towards it.

In 1932 the opening of the Rock Park Swimming Baths resulted in swimming being included in the school curriculum for the first time and the *Rock* magazine soon gave a long list of boys who had swum their

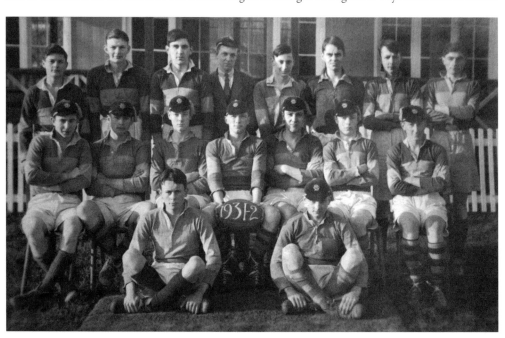

*Rugby Team, 1931-32. Captain Guy Casey was later Mayor of Barnstaple.*

first length. Gannaway set a new high jump record at 5'4". In the annual gymnastics competition there was a new trophy, the Hill Cup, presented by Reverend Hill and awarded to the best under-14 gymnast.

Four oral informants, all pupils at BGS in the 1930s, were in their 80s when they shared their memories with the author. They all have multiple family connections to the School...

Jack Prowse remembers a contingent from Appledore who travelled daily to Instow by ferry and then on to Barnstaple by train. He reckons that standards of discipline dropped during the 1930s: *"Ties became optional, teachers didn't always wear gowns and the Head didn't use the cane much."* Among the landmark pranks Jack recalls was an occasion when somebody removed the school bell and hung it on the weather vane on the roof. Once a group of pupils broke into the school office and found the exam papers. He says that Mr Evans (woodwork) worked part-time in both Barnstaple and Ilfracombe Grammar Schools and lived in one of the two designated teachers' houses with two Lynton pupils. 'Dixie' Dobell used to complain about the girl's P.E. mistress, whose voice boomed through from the other side of the partition in the main hall as if she were drilling his class as well as her own. Jack's favourite teacher was H. J. 'Jerry' Martin (Maths and Music) *"who could really impart his subjects and who transformed my school life"*. Mr Martin was organist at Holy Trinity Church, so Jack joined the choir there and later became choirmaster. Jack's wife Lillian and their two sons, Richard and Malcolm, also attended BGS and all three went on to play significant parts in North Devon politics.

Sylvia Dulham entered Miss Cowie's Prep Class in 1934 before joining the main school two years later. Not all Prep children stayed on. *"Miss Cowie wore a wig and a velvet headband and she was adored by all who knew her, despite having no teaching qualifications."* Sylvia recalls that finishing times for boys and girls at the big school were staggered by 15 minutes to reduce the risk of girls meeting older boys after school. But Sylvia's friend Dora Richards lived in Newport, so the pair of them often loitered there to flirt with the prefects. Talking to boys was against the rules but Sylvia never got caught and she remembers her first kiss with an impish smile. There was a School Dance every summer for Fifth and Sixth Formers and the boys' band played the music. She took her School Certificate exams before she was 15, passing in Art, English, Geography, Cookery and Sewing. She left to train as a shorthand typist but later married a BGS boy and then became a BGS governor when their two children joined the school.

Hazel Webster and her sister Joy only got to see boys by standing on the benches along the dividing wall in the playground. Girls in their day wore a Panama hat in summer and a brown-brimmed hat with badge in winter. The uniform was completed by a brown gym slip, white blouse, brown knickers, brown shoes, and a school tie in brown and gold. Hazel has no recollection of a culture of pranks at the Girls School but she did confess with a giggle to tipping salt and pepper into someone else's pastie mixture during a cookery lesson. Hazel later became School Secretary and the second wife of science teacher Harry Bradley.

Eddie Spiegelhalter was ill with pneumonia and TB as a young child and was taught at home before joining the BGS Prep School, so his entire schooling was at the Newport site. Brother Frank was two years older and used to come over to the Prep School to tie Eddie's shoelaces. Eddie found the big school *"formal, routine and very disciplined. You had to wear a cap in town."* His father, Cecil, was a popular teacher, famous for saying, *"Och, what have you done?"* whenever someone dropped a test-tube or similar and this led to his nickname, 'Okker'. Cecil was a pipe smoker and had a gutta-percha lining to his jacket pocket, which boys would sometimes fill with cold water via a Bunsen burner tube. Eddie recalls that art teacher Allan 'Snooker' Smith had been shot through the cheek during the war. He had a mantra for teaching perspective drawing, delivered in a Northern accent: *"If one line goes oop to the right, the other goes oop to the left"*. Herr Seckler, who taught German, lived near Codden Hill and pupils used to visit him to sample his farmhouse cider.

*Mr Canham's first school photo - he is central with arms folded. To his left are Messrs Hughes, Martin, Seckler and Dobell. To Mr Canham's right are Messrs Critchley, Teece, Evans, Spiegelhalter and Smith.*

Eddie Spiegelhalter's name appears in the 1933 *Rock* magazine for winning the Form II prize. Others mentioned in dispatches that year included G. Dalling, who set a new long jump record with 21'3" and E. J. Slee, who won the Grade III Elocution Competition. Mr Hughes the history teacher became engaged to Marjorie Oliver, a Governor's daughter. 80 boys learned to swim in one term leaving *"only a very few boys who still cannot swim"*, though there was a suspicion that the numbers included some pupils whose feet touched the bottom and who were allowed to perform at the shallow end on gala day! Drake House was in the doldrums, unable to raise a team to take part in the senior rugby matches, and a year later it was dissolved and its members divided equally among the three original Houses.

In 1933 the County insisted that any Secondary School wishing to circulate Governors' minutes should get them stencilled to save on printing costs so the financial year for 1933-34 is the last to have detailed archived accounts. They show salaries for teachers. Headmaster Cranham on £547 p.a. received less than the longer-serving Girls' Head, Miss Jenkin, who got £556. Mr F. Critchley was next highest at £430 and the lowest paid female teacher was earning £180 p.a. The accounts already had an entry for 'supply teaching'. The minutes included decisions about additional allowances paid to individual free-place scholars. Hilda Turpitt received £1.50 for books, £2 for a bicycle and £5 for maintenance. Kenneth Irwin received his rail fares and a free midday meal. On other expenditure, one month's gas and coke cost £68.50, while electric light cost £14.45. It cost £1 for a chimney sweep to clean the school chimneys. The window cleaning bill was 42p per term and telephone costs were £8 per term. £82.25 went on University of Cambridge Examination fees and £5.40 to Nicklins for piano tuning.

Two new events appeared at the girls' Sports Day in 1934 – a slow bicycle race and an Old Girls Race. A report on the Old Girls Association said numbers had steadily increased and a distinctive blazer was now available for members. There was a long list of marriages, a few births, and a few notes on old girls who had gone into teaching and nursing.

In 1934 boys were invited to submit designs for a new cover for the *Rock* magazine and the December issue featured the winning design by Victor Uren, now in his tenth year at the school. Inside there was news that swimmers were being entered for Royal Lifesaving Society certificates. The most news-

*Kathryn Yeo's 1934 examination report.*

*Girls' Sports Day 1934, showing huts flanking the path to Ladies Mile.*

---

**Easter 1934**

**RESULT OF TERMINAL EXAMINATION.**

Position in Form 3    No. of Pupils in Form 37    Average Age of Pupils 12·10 full

| SUBJECT. | Maximum Marks Obtainable in each subject. | Marks gained by Pupil. | SPECIAL REMARKS. |
|---|---|---|---|
| Arithmetic | 100 | 70 | 2nd. |
| Algebra | 100 | 72 | 2nd |
| Geometry | 100 | 63 | 1st |
| Trigonometry | | | |
| Scripture | 100 | 69 | |
| English Grammar and Essay | 100 | 63 | |
| English Literature | 100 | 60 | |
| History | 100 | 73 | 2nd |
| Geography | 100 | 70 | 1st bracketed |
| French | 100 | 71 | |
| Latin | | | |
| Chemistry or Biology | 100 | 61 | |
| Physics or Physiology | | | |
| Botany | | | |
| Needlework | 100 | 45 | |
| Cookery | — | — | |
| Art | 100 | 31 | |
| Drill | | | |
| TOTALS | 1200 | 748 | 62·3% |

Conduct   Good.
Progress   Good.

Annie Jenkin

worthy school event of 1934 attracted remarkably little comment in either side's magazine. Miss Annie Jenkin retired after 24 years of devoted service to the School, having been Headmistress since opening day. There were no lengthy tributes or reports of emotional farewells, which must have been how she wanted it. Miss Jenkin was succeeded by Miss Elsie May Atkins M.A., who taught History and Latin.

*Victor Uren's new* Rock *cover design which endured until 1952.*

## Miss Annie. Jenkin, B.A. M.A.
## Headmistress, 1910-1934.

Miss Jenkin was born in 1872 and educated at High Schools in Sheffield and Bath before graduating from the University of London with a B.A. in Classics and M.A.s in Classics and French. In her Cambridge Teaching Diploma she gained a distinction in the practical part of the exam. She had taught in Wales and had been Senior Mistress at Grimsby Municipal College for 3 years before joining BGS, where she taught Latin, Scripture and some Maths.

Miss Jenkin lived alone in a house on Taw Vale and rode to school on a bicycle with a large basket on the front. She steered BGGS from 52 girls in 1910 to become one of the leading girls' schools in the West Country with 270 girls in 1934. The short announcement of her retirement in the *Alpenant* revealed nothing about her beyond *"her untiring energy and devotion to an exacting standard of duty"*. Rather little personal trace remains of her 24 years of service, which leaves one to infer colossal humility. Her legacy was in the daily impact she had on the lives of her girls, which was considerable. Former pupil, Marjorie Blackmore recalls helping Miss Jenkin with her office flower arrangement and says, *"She was very gentle and kind and a good listener."*

The *Rock* Editorial for April 1935 was written by School Captain F. Colwill, who clearly had a sense of history. It began: *"We are approaching the 25th birthday of our school. Boys who came here in the early days are now men and some of them have sons with us. It must be a great comfort to a son to be told he is just like his father in his confusion of the Latin cases, his naïve excuses for missing homework, and his incorrigibility as a gym-shoe loser. As the years roll on, BGS strikes her roots deeper into the heart of the community and some day, not far ahead, there will hardly be one noteworthy citizen of Barnstaple who will not be an Old Bardian."* He clearly hadn't allowed for incomers.

*Boys' orchestra from 1930s with Mr H. J. Martin who ran it.*

Boys and girls, parents, former pupils and a joint choir gathered at St Peter's Parish Church in October 1935 to celebrate the School's Silver Jubilee. Just a few weeks later the same company assembled there again at a memorial service for their Headmaster, Wilfrid Cranham. Mr Canham's health had begun to deteriorate during 1934 and he died of cancer in late November. Mr Fred Critchley stood in for two terms as Acting Head until Rodney Marshall Pasley B.A. M.A. was appointed to start after Easter.

# Wilfrid David Canham, B.A. and M.A.
## Headmaster, 1931-1935.

Mr Canham was born in 1896 and attended the City of Norwich School. In the Great War he served in France, Salonica and Palestine, earning the Military Cross, before going on to graduate at Magdalen College, Cambridge. He was then Senior English Master at Warwick School from 1925-1931. At BGS he taught English, History and Divinity and was said to be good at soccer, athletics, cricket and hockey. He was a Christian Scientist. Pupils recall that he wore spats and was big on etiquette. Mr Martin wrote that *"his rule was smooth and efficient."* The *Rock* described, *"a loyal colleague and a sincere friend whose personality was rich and colourful."*

The *Rock* for December 1935 mentioned a major change ahead when it reported that a scheme by Old Bardians to fund the installation of showers had been put on hold following the announcement by the County of their intention to build a new Grammar School for boys on the Newport site. The plan was that the existing school building would then be taken over by the Girls Grammar.

*1935 Girls and Staff. The teachers in the third row (working from the left) are: Miss Cowie (Prep School), Miss Johns (Sport), Miss Kerrison (French), the other Miss Cowie, Miss Gaze (Science), Miss Crowroft (Biology), un-identified, Miss Atkins (Head), Miss Cronin (Music), Miss Percy (Maths), Miss Harris (English). The remainder are un-identified.*

The 1936 *Alpenant* congratulated former pupil and teacher Mrs Manaton on becoming Mayoress of Barnstaple, A wide variety of creative writing include this splendid rhyming couplet: *"Nobody thinks of a poor school desk - It's much too old to be picturesque."*

The boys' steeplechase was lengthened in 1936; juniors were now running the original course of 3½ miles while seniors tackled a more manly 6½ miles. A BGS swimming team competed against Bideford Grammar School and Shebbear at Westward Ho! and they won every event bar one. The eight prefects were all appointed ex officio from other positions of responsibility - the School Captain, Captains of all three Houses, the Captain of Rugby, the Librarian, the Magazine Editor and the President of the Rock Debating Society. Play reading and a mock Town Council Election were among the activities of the Debating Society.

The *Alpenant* for 1937 had a bumper 52 pages, giving a real flavour of the rich cultural life of the Girls Grammar School. There had been a conference about the political situation in Europe, with girls presenting papers on Bolshevism, the rise of Fascism in Italy, and life in Germany under the Nazis. Other reports covered a recital of *"pianoforte music"*, two touring plays, botanical field work and a school tour of the town's municipal offices. There were 15 pages of poetry and prose with a few puzzles and riddles thrown in for good measure. Form notes confirmed the enormous competitive spirit among the girls, who even vied with each other to have the best bowl of bulbs and the best Christmas play. Form IIIB had received a lot of detentions but two girls had won deportment stripes. Form IVA was very proud of its hyacinths and scillas but disappointed by poor neatness marks. 'Form IV Remove' was scythed down from 36 girls to 15 by a flu epidemic but came first in neatness despite having a bowl of dead hyacinths. Penelope House now had its own Latin motto – *"Nos pudet ultimas venisse"* (*"It shames us to come last"*).

Girls' uniform socks changed from black to brown and there was discussion of the former practice of disguising a hole in a black sock by writing in ink on the leg beneath. Sports Day now included a *"chariot race"* - which involved four girls running in formation at high speed. Two dinner ladies, Mrs Pile and Mary, were retiring as cook and server respectively after 23 years at the school. The 29 girls of Riversvale Hostel started their own Hostel Houses - Windsor, Sandringham and Balmoral: *"It has proved useful in giving the girls something to work for, since they lose marks for disregarding certain rules, but gain marks for general good behaviour."* There was a House rota for making tea on Sundays. Old Girl Beth Wood wrote about her voyage to Australia, where she was now an interpreter for a German businessman. The *Alpenant* ended with nine full pages of adverts, including one for uniform blazers.

The *Rock* must have had an eye on its feminine rival because 1937 brought its first advertisements. Among them were ads for four Barnstaple outfitters and one for County Garage (*"distributors for Alvis, Armstrong Siddeley, Standard and Jowett cars"*). Advertising rates were 12½p for a quarter page and £2 for the full rear or inside cover. At Speech Day Mr Pasley reported terrific exam results - over 90% success in School Certificate exams, which was 25% above the national average. The 'Barumites in London' were thanked for donating prizes. Prefects were entertained to tea and table tennis by the Head and his wife.

Board of Education Inspectors visited the Boys School for three days in November 1937. Their overall conclusion that, *"the school continues to make good progress since the last inspection in 1927 and appears to be in a healthy state"* was rather undermined by many detailed points of criticism. There was a sense that the whole school had perhaps become a bit threadbare.

Inspectors stressed that *"the need for fresh accommodation for both schools has become urgent"* and they hoped there would not be further delays in providing new buildings agreed by the County. The report mentioned *"the superior attractions of the new buildings at the Grammar School in Bideford"* as a factor in the further decline in the number of boys attending BGS and said: *"The present numbers are not economic, since there are not enough pupils to provide a complete two-Form organisation in each year."* Staffing levels were compromised, the range of subjects on offer was limited and there were only 19 students in the Sixth Form. Inspectors felt that BBGS needed to expand from 220 pupils to about 350 - 7 years of 50 pupils in each would be ideal - and that meant new accommodation to ease the *"serious congestion"*. There was no purpose-built gymnasium, no art room, no proper library and inadequate laboratories. The school was particularly badly off for changing and washing facilities for Games and P.E.

There were critical observations on individual subject teaching too. Only one boy in three years had failed the School Certificate exams in English but *"many boys are poor at reading aloud and their written work is best described as stolid"*. Progress of pupils beginning Latin was hindered by ignorance of the elements of English grammar. In Geography the teaching was rather old fashioned. The master in charge of French had a slight German accent, though he was *"zealous and painstaking"*. The timetable provided for little Physics in years 1 and 2. Boys under 13 got Music lessons but then there was nothing until the Sixth Form. All in all, it was a case of 'must try harder'. The report shows the real value of external inspections. This was substantially the same school that had been praised a decade earlier, but the world had moved on and the school had become insular and unaware that it now lagged behind improved standards elsewhere. On a positive note, only 11% of leavers in July were under 16, making the average school life at BGS longer than the average for Devon.

In view of the negative comment about Physics provision, the career of Ken Grinstead seems all the more remarkable. Ken began as a pupil at this time and then went on to a 30 year career at Porton Down as a bio-physicist and then 20 years at Aldermaston as archivist for weapons research. Ken provides one or two additional notes covering the latter years of the decade. He describes Mr Pasley as *"a very fair-minded man who taught Economics and Public Affairs to the Sixth Form"*. He also remembers a Latin teacher, Bill Day, who joined in 1937 and rode a motorbike and sidecar to school. Mr Day had a crash and was off for a while but was heartily cheered by all the boys on his return. Some things hadn't changed since the early days: *"If you were upstairs in room 5A, you could open the window and whistle at the girls!"*

Marjorie Blackmore tells a stirring tale of her romance with one of the boys. Marjorie was a pupil from 1933-38, a pretty girl who was only 11 when she won a deportment stripe in a competition that involved parading around a room. Her mum sewed the stripe onto her gymslip but she was later stripped of it by Miss Johns *"for receiving notes from boys"*. Marjorie was chosen to ring the school bell and this brought her to the attention of a boy five years her senior called Claude Dix because *"the boys would jump up to look over the wall."* Claude was a Prefect, Head of Fortescue and the 1st XV rugby captain. How she and Claude developed their relationship in a divided school is a matter that Marjorie is coy about but she says that Claude made the running and figured out ways to meet secretly outside of school. He used to help her with her Maths

*Marjorie Blackmore.*

*Claude Dix, far right, winning a sprint race in 1933.*

*Claude and Marjorie Dix on their wedding day.*

homework, so she got great marks for Maths in the non–exam terms and then came almost bottom of the class in the exams.

Marjorie left school at 16 to work in the office at Shapland and Petter. She and Claude got married in 1942. Years later Claude Dix became Head at Pilton Primary School where Marjorie's schooling had started. She remembers cycling to BGS past girls at Pilton glove factory who jeered *"Grammar School gutter scraper!"* It was a common taunt back then from those who were less educationally fortunate. But Marjorie used her talents well. In 2005 she was awarded an MBE for her charity work.

The 1938 Spens Report on Secondary Education recommended that there should be three types of secondary school: grammar schools for the academically able, technical schools for those who had a practical bent and new 'modern' secondary schools for everyone else. Spens also recommended that the school leaving age should be raised to 16 but it wasn't actually raised to 15 until 1946 and didn't reach 16 until 1973.

The terminology of qualifications in this period can be confusing. Pupils who passed the 'Ordinary School Certificate' in 8 subjects were said to have 'gained matriculation', which meant they could continue to the 'Higher Certificate'. They had to pass five of the Ordinary Certificate exams (including Maths and English) with credit in one sitting, and then get three further credits, which could be taken separately. The phrase 'County Major Scholarships', which dominated huge wooden boards in Reception, were effectively bursaries enabling pupils who had done best at the Higher Certificate to go to university. They were not awarded lightly.

The *Rock Magazines* for 1938 contained news that the school's electricity supply was changed from DC to AC and that the telephone was now linked to the automatic exchange system. The death was announced of Mr Reavell, Chairman of Governors, who had been a Governor since the school opened in 1910. Raleigh held a House Tea to celebrate their numerous successes in sport. The swimming sports saw the addition of a one length *"divesting garments"* race. A pre-Christmas event in the School Hall featured *"the Sixth Form nigger minstrels"*.

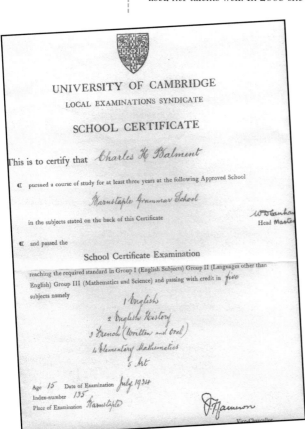

The Barnstaple Boys Grammar School Prospectus for 1938-39 contained a mission statement that few people would argue with even today: *"The aims of the School are to maintain a high standard of sound learning, to develop character, to instil a spirit of citizenship and a high standard of manners, and to provide for a healthy physical development."* Boys from the '50s and early '60s would be surprised to see far fewer school rules than in their day. There seemed to be just three rules: boys must not be absent except in case of illness; a boy returning to school after illness must bring a note stating the reason for that absence; books, caps, overcoats and sports kit must be plainly marked with the owner's name. Tuition fees were £3.50 per term including stationery but not mathematical instruments or textbooks, which could be hired from the school for 30p per term. There was a subscription of 14p per term for the supply of cricket bats, footballs and the school magazine.

In February 1939 it was the turn of the Girls Grammar School to have a Board of Education Inspection. In many ways, the detail of their report was quite damning, suggesting that the school had not moved with the times. In the previous three years only nine girls in total had gone on to university. Inspectors regretted that too few girls were staying on after 16. On the other hand, teachers were perhaps staying too long: *"Nine of the thirteen staff have been in the school for at least 12 years. Their long stay in one school has necessarily limited their outlook and they should realise that changes in some directions are necessary."*

As with the report on the Boys School a year earlier, the 'threadbare' theme continued in the subject notes. The work in Science was seriously handicapped by the lack of proper facilities and too little Physics and Chemistry was being taught in the lower school to make these subjects viable in the Sixth Form. Art, P.E. and Games were all struggling with inadequate resources. Inspectors recommended a second hockey pitch with better drainage than the first, <u>hard</u> tennis courts with 'run back' space, and a proper netball court to replace the uneven asphalt playground. Inspectors felt that too few girls were deriving any benefit from Latin and that the numbers should be reduced. The number of examination subjects was considered too great for some girls and Inspectors hinted at streaming the two parallel classes in each year. The Senior Mistress was the only one qualified to teach Geography, Music and Needlework, which limited the timetabling in these subjects. All forms had a meagre 35 minute lesson a week in Music, though the School Choir was described as *"delightful"*. There was no advanced Maths being taught in the Sixth Form and a revision of the syllabus should take account of modern methods and textbooks.

As if to answer the two adverse inspection reports, the Easter term of 1939 saw the beginning of work on the new boys' school site. The opening date was expected to be September 1940.

September 1939 brought to an end Barnstaple Grammar School's reign as the only fully-fledged secondary school in Barnstaple. Ashleigh Road School, which had taken boys and girls up to the age of 14 since 1920, now gave rise to two 'Senior Schools'. The Barnstaple Boys Senior School opened at the former Miller Institute in Derby Road, which the Borough Council had bought and modified. It was renamed the Boys Secondary Modern in 1945. Ashleigh Road School became the corresponding Senior Girls School in 1939 and was then renamed the Girls Secondary Modern in 1945.

These major capital investments in education gave no clue that Britain was on the threshold of becoming embroiled in another costly war. Both BGS magazines played down the tension for much of 1939. The *Alpenant* Editorial said: *"Despite a fearsome number of international crises, life at school has pursued its regular course."* The *Rock* had a hilarious account of a school trip to Paris: *"Mr Dobel got himself lost one day but everyone assumed he was at the Folies Bergères…Mr Wilmot's brother-in-law gave us an interesting tour of the ancient districts of Paris. But we were delighted to be allowed to explore more modern things by ourselves!"*

On September 3rd 1939 Prime Minister Neville Chamberlain announced that war had been declared on Germany. The following day Winston Churchill joined the War Cabinet as First Lord of the Admiralty.

The *Rock* for December said: *"With the present buildings already overcrowded, we were called upon at the beginning of term to accommodate 34 evacuees."* At Speech day, Mr Pasley assured parents that ample precautions had been taken to safeguard pupils in the event of an air-raid. So that pupils could reach home before the blackout, afternoon school would finish at 3.30. There was a long list of Old Boys known to be serving with the armed forces — 15 in the Royal Navy, 28 in the RAF, and 70 in the Army.

One Old Boy who was training to be an airman circled low over the school on a training flight, but it was the Christmas holiday so nobody waved back to him.

*Aerial view from the 1930s. The field to the right was about to become a building site.*

## CHAPTER 5

# FIGHTING FORTIES, 1940-1949

THE STORY of the 1940s at Barnstaple Grammar School was by no means just about World War Two but the decade began with it already in progress. One of the earliest and most dramatic effects of war on school life was the arrival of evacuees fleeing the risk of German bombing raids on Britain's cities. The first wave of sixty evacuees was welcomed in September 1939. Large contingents of children came with their own teachers and had separate lessons, hopping between vacant labs and classrooms as BGS pupils went for games or P.E. There were 160 boys from Handsworth School in Birmingham, plus girls from Haberdashers Aske in London, and others from Croydon and Plaistow. Years later 'Jerry' Martin wrote: *"Mr Pasley toiled night after night in his study at school, often until the early hours, improvising arrangements for the maximum comfort of all. Handsworth owe him much. His own boys do not know how much he sacrificed himself to ensure that the war should not touch their schooling."*

The *Alpenant* for June 1940 said that the first nine months of war had not stopped normal school activities, although at Riversvale Hostel the lack of 160 yards of blackout material had played havoc with their usual parties! Some evacuees had apparently already returned home and the remainder now seemed to be an integral part of the school.

Ruth Tenchio was 12 years old in June 1940 when she arrived as one of 30 girls evacuated from Coloma Convent in Croydon. They were accompanied by a nun and two teachers. One morning Ruth's mother said goodbye to her, not knowing where she was going. During the train journey to Devon the girls were called individually to their teachers' carriage and told they were heading for Barnstaple. They were met at the Junction Station by a group of scouts with handcarts for their luggage. *"One of them was Jackie Barrow, a Grammar School boy who called me a 'blonde bombshell'. They took us to our billets. I was put with an elderly lady who had a large house with a maid. Coming from a humble family, it was luxury. For the first week or two we had lessons in a dilapidated building in South Street and then we were split up and integrated into classes with the local girls. There were more than 30 girls in each class but we had a good education."*

Not all evacuees came as part of school groups. Eric Smith's family home was destroyed during the bombing of Plymouth and Eric was buried alive in the rubble. His family moved first to Exeter and then, after further bombing there, to Barnstaple. Reta Calton's mother brought her to Barnstaple at the outbreak of the war and she stayed at BGS for six years. She says: *"The staff seemed very old and rather severe. If we forgot to bring our gas mask to school, we approached them with fear."* Elizabeth Baxter came from Guernsey. She remembers that each class had a patch of garden outside the classroom window. Terry Hatton recalls: *"Some of the evacuees brought impetigo with them. One of them also brought in a banana skin and auctioned it*

*Evacuee Ruth Tenchio (left) with her mother and sister. This rust-marked photo went with her father to Italy and Egypt.*

*off for a penny or two!"* A group of Jewish refugees from Czechoslovakia came just to watch a school rugby match. One evacuee, Ian Gillies, went on to achieve broadcasting success, winning BBC Radio's 'Brain of Britain' contest and then becoming chairman of the programme in the 1970s.

The *Rock Magazine* was unable to include letters from serving soldiers as it had done throughout World War One, saying: *"We are requested by the Ministry of Information to abstain from publishing many things we know would interest you. Our members in the various forces are playing their parts in this stand against bullies and tyrants but we are not able to quote from their letters."* What they could say was that eight members of the 1939 OBA committee were now serving with the armed forces and that some Old Boys had already been declared 'missing in action'.

Staff and pupils of both sexes undertook salvage activities over the summer holiday of 1940. Hand carts were used to collect metals for sorting in the playground. There were 12 tons of iron, 2½ tons of mixed paper, 7 hundredweights of brass, 4 hundredweights of lead, and 3 hundredweights of aluminium. They took frequent rests for lemonade. In the woodwork room, boys made leg-rests, back-rests and bed tables for the hospital. Girls knitted balaclavas and scarves for troops overseas. Squads of boys picked potatoes on Saturdays at a farm near Braunton. The Girls School adopted a Royal Navy warship and part of their English homework was to write letters to the crew. Occasionally pupils became the beneficiaries of kindness, as when a consignment of dried milk and cocoa turned up as a present from the people of Canada or when bananas reached school from U.S. soldiers.

Evacuees *Reta Calton (left) and Irene Green in Rock Park.*

School windows were protected with muslin to prevent splintering. The *Rock* said, *"Boys cannot see the approach of masters, who in turn cannot see unruly boys!"* 1941 brought the addition of brick blast walls. Two fire pickets, consisting of masters and senior boys equipped with stirrup pumps, fire ladders and other apparatus, were on standby in case of an 'Alert' during school hours. Bill Forward remembers *"staying overnight with a master, ready to put out fires after an air raid. We also dug trenches and practised evacuating into them. I remember one morning the Head gathered us all together in the quadrangle of the new school and told us that a German plane had crashed near Pilton."* Chivenor was strafed and bombers often flew over North Devon en route to South Wales.

Sylvia Dulham often slept on a camp-bed in the staffroom with other Fifth Form volunteers for fire-watching after dark. They were armed with buckets of sand. When the sirens went off at night at Riversvale, the girls would roll up their mattresses and go down to the basement until the all clear was given. Pat Sanders recalls: *"We carried our gas masks to school and back each day. If there was an air-raid siren during school hours, we all marched to Lovers' Lane in Rock Park to lie down on the grass bank, hidden by the trees."*

The *Alpenant* for 1941 reported that pupils had been fundraising for Red Cross ambulances, for the Spitfire Fund and for a 'Wireless for the Troops Fund'. BGS girls helped at the Communal Feeding Centre in Barnstaple Pannier Market, where they peeled potatoes, washed dishes and served stew and jam pudding to refugees. Another group helped out in the hospital kitchens during the summer holidays. A mixed group of boys and girls from BGS planted 250,000 onions at a farm in Tawstock.

The *Rock* for 1942 reported that the war in the Far East was affecting the supply of rubber. Plimsolls had become almost irreplaceable and so it was decided to cancel all athletic sports and cross country running to reduce the wear and tear on rubber shoes. Sports Day only resumed when the war ended. Cricket fared rather better as games against the Selhurst evacuees and the Royal Army Pay Corps helped to swell the fixture list.

In July 1942 most of the boys from Handsworth Grammar School returned to Birmingham and at that point around 300 of the 376 boys at the school were from Devon. 26 boys were now in the Air Training Corps, founded by French master Arthur Newsham. They received training in *"navigation, aircraft identification, foot-drill and Morse"*. There were sixteen boys in the sea cadets and nine in the army cadets. Robert Cann became an Army Cadet at Barnstaple Drill Hall and writes: *"My homework was very quickly done as I was often on night duty with the Home Guard."*

Tony Fletcher was from Croyde, where the U.S. Army carried out landing exercises on the beach. *"The walk through Rock Park to the school in the mornings was littered with evidence of frolics between soldiers and local girls!"* Ray Liverton recalls that, *"One day someone brought in an American bullet found on Saunton beach. They put it in a workshop vice and hit it with a hammer. The shell exploded and the ball inside zinged around the room and ended up lodged inside a light bulb, which had a clean entry hole in it but did not shatter!"* Ruth Tenchio remembers an American Colonel coming to address the school and she reckons that *"Miss Atkins was all over him".*

Beryl Parsley recalls June 6th 1944 when news of the D-Day landings was broadcast on the school wireless: *"A large radiogram stood in the corner of the hall and at lunchtime girls gradually filtered in to listen to the historic news of the invasion. Our French and needlework mistress, Madame Alice Jamart, was from Belgium and she sat beside the radiogram, head bowed, listening. The tears were just dripping into her lap as she anticipated being reunited with her Belgian mother."*

It is quite remarkable that in the midst of a desperate war, the government should have time for other matters but the Butler Education Act was passed in August 1944, claiming that *"Secondary Education would no longer be the privilege of the few but the right of all"*. Devon still had thousands of post-11 pupils in all–age elementary schools and this would now change. The Act would lead to fees in Grammar Schools being abolished, making them freely accessible to the most able 25% of the population who were to be selected at the Eleven Plus examination. Secondary Technical Schools would cater for those with a technical or scientific aptitude and new Modern Secondary Schools would ensure provision for everyone else. The Act also introduced a comprehensive School Health Service providing school meals, free milk, medical and dental treatment, and various support services including transport. Universal free school milk was introduced in August 1946 and the school leaving age was raised to 15 in April 1947. Higher Education too would soon begin opening up to more pupils from ordinary families.

In celebration of the Victory in Europe, both Schools had a holiday on May 8th and 9th 1945. Ruth Tenchio stayed on until October 1945 to do her Ordinary Certificate exams and was the last of the Coloma Convent girls to leave Barnstaple. Years later she came back to live in the town and married a local man. Another evacuee, Jeanette Farthing from Haberdashers' Askes, returned to teach: *"I taught Domestic Science in the very room where I had my own first lessons in cookery twelve years earlier."*

A million British servicemen were demobilised between August and December 1945. At the annual dinner of the Old Bardians Association in December, 82 members were present and they included… *"Men who were at Dunkirk, men who landed on the Normandy beaches on D-Day, men who had helped to plan the D-Day operations, lads who had worked in the military hospitals, and some who had endured the dull misery of P.O.W. camps in Europe and Siam. The Navy men included those who had manned the landing craft on D-Day, others who had carried on the dangerous work of mine-sweeping, and one or two who had convoyed merchant ships on the perilous route to Archangel. One had been torpedoed by enemy submarines and had spent days in an open boat in the stormy Atlantic. There were airmen with distinctions for dog-fighting at 20,000 feet. One of those present had been reported 'missing, probably killed'. Several had helped to chase Rommel from El Alamein to Tunis. Then there were those whose lot it had been to work in the mines. It was a company of whom any school might well be proud."*

An Album of Remembrance was presented to the school together with an oak stand. The album contained the war records and photographs of everyone on the Roll of Honour, researched by Mr Teece and beautifully illuminated by Old Boy Cecil Dunn. The heroic stories neatly summarised in this great book would inspire future generations of boys as they passed though the school Reception where it was always on display. Cecil Dunn visited from Canada in 2000 to see the finished album for which he had done the calligraphy one page at a time by post in 1945.

On Wednesday May 29th 1946 a Dedication Service was held in memory of the 43 Old Boys who lost their lives during the War. Some of their stories are chilling. A Roll of Honour Board made by Shapland and Petter was inscribed with

*Calligrapher Cecil Dunn in 2000.*

*Book of Remembrance.*

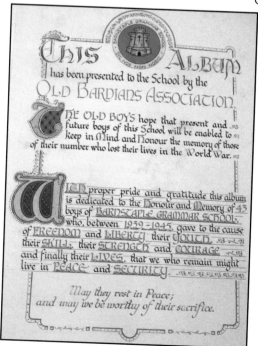

the names of all 43 men who had lost their lives and this is still displayed in 2010 on the staircase leading to the Head's office.

After the war there were desperate shortages of food and heating fuel. In 1946, bread was rationed for the first time. In 1948 there was a serious dock strike and the fresh meat ration was cut further. Clothes rationing continued until 1949, tea until 1952, eggs, sugar and cream until 1953. Rationing only finally ended when restrictions on butter, margarine, cooking fat and meat were all lifted in 1954. No doubt the BGS cooks still managed to keep their 'troops' happy.

———— ❖ ————

Throughout the war years, normal school life continued as best it could. The *Rock* Editorial for December 1940 heralded the most significant development so far in the development of the school site, the completion of the new Boys School: *"At last we have abandoned our former cramped quarters for spacious new buildings. The change has been made very difficult by the war and the consequent lack of equipment."* The summer holidays were extended by a fortnight while volunteers transported books and equipment to the new building (known today as North Building). The boys' morning assembly was held in the gymnasium until the Hall was completed. The combined Speech Day and official Opening Ceremony of the new building was held on Wednesday April 2nd 1941.

*Athletics in front of the new Boys Grammar School building, 1940.*

**Captain L. Roy Bradford**
At school 1926-33. Aged 27. S.A.S. Dropped by parachute in France shortly after D-Day. Disrupted German lines by demolition. Killed in an ambush, 1944.

**Sergeant Christopher Irwin**
At school 1931-36. Aged 21. R.A.F. Navigator with Wellington Bomber Squadron. Did not return from a raid over Germany, 1942.

**Lieutenant Norris Heppenstall**
At school 1929-35. Aged 27. Fleet Air Arm Fighter Pilot. Took part in attack on the Tirpitz. Shot down during attack on Okinawa, Japan, 1945.

**Private Edward Bowden**
At school 1931-36. Aged 23. Royal Signals Wireless Operator. Taken P.O.W. in Malaya. Died of cholera working on the Siam Railway, 1943.

The finished building had ten classrooms on the east side with a Staffroom between numbers 5 and 6. On the west side were rooms for Woodwork, Art, prefects, a reception area and office, a lecture room with tiered desks for Geography and Biology, and separate laboratories for Chemistry and Physics. The north side had cloakrooms and toilets. The south side had the gymnasium and changing rooms. Two grass quadrangles contained tennis courts with unglazed corridors on all sides. At the heart of it all was the Hall, which had a kitchen at one end.

The *Alpenant* declared: *"We are now the sole occupiers of the old building, complete with art room, library, extended cookery room, and new lavatories – all welcome changes after our cramped quarters."* The Girls Grammar School soon began to thrive, with considerably more girls than boys passing the new 11+ exam. There was already an intake of three full classes of 25 girls in 1943, a feat the boys' school never managed in any of its 24 years as a separate school.

Once the new building was occupied the dual-sex Grammar School, which in most respects had been two schools joined at the hip for 30 years by a shared building, became virtually autonomous single sex schools for the next 24 years. It would be 1964 before they came together again for mixed classes in a single unified school. At the outset the dividing line between them was known simply as 'The Gap' - a gap between two huts near the south-west corner of the boys building, through which boys and girls could catch a glimpse of each other. According to Joyce Anderson, *"You could get a detention for peering across at boys through 'the gap'. The penalty for actually crossing the line could have been expulsion!"* Before long, the boundary sprouted a fence and a hedge.

The separation of the sexes applied to all age groups. Pat Sanders attended a dual-sex Sixth Form Conference at Ilfracombe but *"the BGS boys and girls were segregated on separate decks of a double-decker bus for the journey."* Moira Mayne says that the strict rule forbidding girls to wear make-up and jewellery *"was relaxed only for the School Social, a once-in-a-blue-moon evening of fraternising with boys at a supervised dance."* School Socials for Fourth Formers and upwards continued throughout the war years, raising funds for the North Devon Infirmary. Eric Smith found them *"embarrassing for those of us who couldn't dance. I don't think we were that much interested in girls in those days."*

There are renegades in every situation and Reg Gale was one of them. He was twice caught on the girls' side and got caned for it. He says: *"Because it was against the rules it made meeting girls more exciting. Usually we did our courting out of school hours but some of it was done in school uniform."* Joyce Anderson was one of five girls who

*Punished for fraternising with boys - from left Margaret Voden, Barbara Lewis, June Brend, Joyce Anderson, Pamela Knowles.*

got into trouble for just talking to a group of boys out of school hours. They were all in uniform when their 'licentious behaviour' was spotted by Miss Harris and Miss Percy at the bottom of Boutport Street. Next day, the five girls' names were read out in assembly and they were each awarded five after-school detentions for *"fraternising with boys in school uniform"*. Even on Saturdays, girls who were boarding at Riversvale Hostel were not allowed to talk to boys if they went into town. According to Moira Mayne: *"sometimes we met up with boys secretly at places like Tawstock woods. Matron would scrutinise the incoming mail looking for 'billets doux' from boys."*

When Mr Frizzell arrived to teach French, the unaccustomed male presence led one girl to ask him, *'Have you come to mend the windows?'* Miss Atkins and most of the Mistresses were ultra-strict 'Old Maids' and there were at least three pairings who lived together. Miss Atkins lived with her secretary Miss Peacock; Miss Kerrison (French) lived with Miss Johns (PE); and Miss Harris (English) lived with Miss Percy (Maths). Did the girls suspect lesbian relationships? Jean Hill gives the standard response: *"We wouldn't have known what that meant."* Margaret Bonvoisin agrees: *"We were completely ignorant of anything relating to sex. One of my friends at sixteen thought she was pregnant because a boy kissed her and believed that the baby came out of her navel. We didn't know she was wrong. In a human biology lesson, the teacher showed us a very old specimen of a dissected frog in a jar of liquid and pointed vaguely at the reproductive organs. Our mothers never spoke of such things."* Anne Mabbott recalls: *"Miss Boyle pulled down the blinds at the start of the sex education lesson and began by asking, 'Have any of you been on farms?'"*

It's a wonder that the population of Barnstaple ever grew! Fortunately the story of Margaret and Harold Thompson is one that played out time and time again. Harold was Head Boy and captain of the rugby and cricket teams but, even for an alpha male, meeting girls at BGS wasn't easy. Margaret spent the same teenage years on the other side of the great divide. They didn't meet until long after they left school but their subsequent marriage lasted 51 years.

A rich vein of living informants has provided stories for the 1940s and these will now be included under headings for the two separate schools.

# BOYS GRAMMAR SCHOOL

Ray Liverton started in 1940 and so was part of the first intake to the new Boys' School. He remembers a prank played on geography teacher 'Waggles' Teece, whose nickname came from his large waggly moustache: *"Waggles' classroom, which was also our form room, had a large glass case containing samples of rocks for teaching geology. One day, some sixth formers got the key to the case and put in a wad of cotton wool with a label that read 'Waggles' winter woollies'! This went unnoticed for a few weeks, though everyone giggled about it every time Waggles went near the case. The lads got hold of the key again and this time put in a set of false teeth labelled 'False teeth from prehistoric man'. Waggles finally twigged and all of our class was given the cane even though we weren't the perpetrators!"*

Tony Fletcher had an hour's bus trip each way from Croyde but managed to get some homework done on the journey. *"The buses towed gas-producing trailers which burned wood chips because diesel was in short supply. Everyone had to get out and help push up the steeper hills."* Despite the rationing, Tony loved school dinners. *"Friday was always meat and salad followed by prunes and custard to keep us regular".* He remembers one master with particular affection: *"Bill Hughes had shrapnel in his leg and he would regale us with his experiences in the World War 1 trenches. But he had to tone it down a bit after one pupil fainted at some particularly gruesome bit of battlefield description."*

*Boys School Staff, 1942-3: Standing from left: 1 un-named, Watt (Chemistry), Newsham (French), Cheetham (Physics), Williams (English & History), 2 un-named; Sitting: Dobell (P.E.), Spiegelhalter (Chemistry), Smith (Art), Evans (Woodwork), Critchley (English & Deputy Head), Pasley (Head), Hughes (History & Latin), Teece (Geography), Martin (Maths & Music), 1 un-named, Shercliff (Maths & Physics), Wilmot (French).*

In April 1943 Mr R. M. S. Pasley resigned after seven years as Headmaster to take up the Headship of the Central Grammar School in Birmingham.

## Rodney Marshall Sabine Pasley, B.A. M.A.
## Headmaster, 1936-1943

Mr Pasley was born in 1899. He attended Sherborne School and read Modern History at University College, Oxford. He taught in London before joining BGS, where he managed the school during four difficult war years. His main teaching subjects were History, English and Divinity. Pupils and colleagues regarded him with high esteem and sincere affection.

'Jerry' Martin wrote: *"There was something in Mr Pasley that persistently reminded me of H. G. Abel, unlike him though he was in stature. He planned for and oversaw the changeover to the new school building and a certain tenacity of purpose veiled by a very charming personality succeeded in securing many facilities and amenities that schoolmasters know to be vital but that architects are likely to overlook and public authorities are often short-sightedly unwilling to pay for."*

Some time after he left, Mr Pasley inherited the title of Baronet.

Frederick Teece had served for all of the 33 years (99 terms) since the school first opened and he was now retiring. In addition to teaching Geography, he also taught singing, English, nature study, and History and had responsibilities for school finances, the library, and the magazine. He was the convener of the OBA from its beginning in 1918. When his untimely death from a stroke was announced in 1947, Mr Critchley wrote: *"He **was** the Old Boys' Association and letters used to pour into him from Old Boys all over the world. We shall remember his devoted service and kindly personality."*

Another 1943 retiree was Cecil Spiegelhalter. He had joined as a Chemistry teacher though his 22 years included stints of German, Physics, Maths, Latin and History. He was a talented musician, Treasurer of the OBA, an energetic librarian and the convener of the stamp club. He was umpire for more than 200 school cricket matches. After leaving the staff he occasionally returned to give guest lectures on local history and to take part in Brains Trusts for the Rock Society. He died in 1964, aged 81.

At Speech Day in 1944 Headmaster Haywood reported that Biology had been introduced and was being taken by the first three forms. There were now 38 boys in the Sixth Form. With over 200 'entries' in the boxing competition two new weights were created below Flyweight – Paper Weight and Midget Weight. Drake House was reintroduced in September under House Master Arthur Newsham. In 1945, two new masters arrived who would be well remembered by boys over the next 20 years - Mr C. S. 'Charlie' Taylor (Latin) and a former pupil Mr H. E. 'Brigadier' Bradley (Chemistry).

The new Head, E. T. L. R. Haywood, soon earned a reputation as a very strict disciplinarian. Nobody seemed to know what the initial 'E' stood for but his other names were Thomas Lancelot Reed and his initials earned him the nickname 'Etler', which allegedly bore a somewhat fitting resemblance to the name of a certain German dictator! Doug Reid remembers that there were no school photos in Mr Haywood's time as Headmaster – *"that would have smacked of fun!"* Indeed there is no surviving photograph of 'Etler' himself. It has been alleged that he was ferocious with the cane and that a court injunction once decreed he could only cane a boy if another teacher was present and then only if he didn't raise the cane above shoulder height.

Eric Smith says, *"Monitors and Prefects could administer corporal punishment with a slipper. I came close to it a couple of times for smoking behind the cricket*

*Boxing Finalists, 1946. Eric Smith and Gordon Ridd are standing rear left and second left respectively. A young Reg Gale is front centre with Des Perryman to his right.*

*pavilion!"* Eric may have got away with such things because he was as a star boxer whom Mr Dobell used to take to box against other schools.

Reg Gale was another boy with prowess in boxing. Everyone was obliged to enter the annual boxing tournament and Reg reached the finals three years in a row. But Reg's main interest lay elsewhere: *"The teacher who transformed my life was 'Snooker' Smith. I must have had a talent for art but he nurtured it. He encouraged me to attend his weekly evening drawing class at the Art School in Barnstaple."* Mr Smith never had an exam failure and some pupils were convinced he touched up their work before it was submitted! Reg Gale passed his School Certificate in 9 subjects, getting an A for Art, and went on to become the youngest qualified architect in Britain. He has since built thousands of homes and commercial properties in North Devon.

*Reg Gale in 2009 with some of his own watercolour paintings.*

Doug Reid has amusing anecdotes about several teachers: *"'Snooker' Smith's nickname may have come from his habit of playing pocket billiards! If you did anything wrong in Bill Hughes' class, he just used to let his monocle drop, which was quite dramatic."* According to Doug physical violence was rife in the 1940s. 'Doggo' Critchley's quirk was to get two boys out the front to beat each other with a plimsoll at the start of each lesson. *"We didn't mind – it took up time in the lesson! Brig' Bradley used a cat-o-three-tails* (three Bunsen burner tubes tied together)*. Dai Williams was a dead-eye with a piece of chalk and he also used to rub the nape of your neck with his knuckles, which really hurt. 'Dixie' Dobell used to get boys running around the gym, whacking them on the bottom as they passed with a baton of wood like a mock sword blade, chanting Chinese numbers each time he scored a hit: Yung! Che! Ta! Pei!"* It seems that Mr Dobel taught swimming in similar style: *"He used a webbing belt on the end of a pole, leading boys into the deep end and then upending the pole with the words 'Swim, you bugger, swim!'"*

Brian Williams has his own 'Dixie' Dobel story: *"He once invited me to punch him with my right hand in a boxing lesson so that he could demonstrate how to counter punch. I hadn't listened properly and I used my left hand which actually landed on his nose. He chased me all around the gym and I hid in the toilets. At the end of the lesson, all was forgiven. Dixie said it had taught him to be prepared for the unexpected."* Ray Liverton says that 'Dixie' Dobel had served for many years in the Navy and taught them how to dance the Sailor's Hornpipe for a public display. He adds: *"I once saw him climb up a rope in the gym and come down it head first with his hands outstretched, just holding on by his feet. He would have been well over 60 at that time."*

*Mr 'Dixie' Dobel (right) supervising 1940s Swimming Sports at Rock Park baths with (from left) Messrs Newsham, Mabbott, and Critchley*

In 1946, Mr Dobel retired after 25 years at the School. The *Rock* said: *"an abounding sense of humour and a copious fund of anecdotes (true and fanciful) went to make up the Mr Dobel who has gained such a hold on our affections. He will leave a gap in school and staff-room which can never really be filled."* Mr Dobel's death was announced in November 1952. His obituary said that he had taught 1,000 boys to swim!

*Watercolour of the school by Art teacher Allan Smith, presented to 'Dixie' Dobel on his retirement in 1946.*

A young lad called David Vine started his BGS career in 1946. 62 years later, having become arguably the most famous old boy in the school's history, David spoke fondly of his old teachers. He remembered Bill Hughes, the *"one-legged teacher of cricket"* and the *"painful and legendary canings"* dished out by Mr Haywood. Then there was George Stapleton, a Chemistry teacher who committed suicide by drinking poison in the staff toilet and whose death was announced in assembly. Asked to recall a mischievous school-related moment, David confessed to getting revenge for a long-held grudge against his old Physics master, 'Diddler' Cheetham. Shortly after he left school, David reported for the *Journal* on a tennis tournament at Ashleigh Road Tennis Club and his article put the home team's defeat entirely down to the club's star players - Mr and Mrs R. Cheetham!

## David Vine
## Star Pupil, 1946-52

David Vine was born in Newton Abbott but came to BGS from Barnstaple Bluecoat School. David became a Monitor and played at number 8 for the 1st XV. After taking A' Levels in Pure and Applied Maths, Chemistry, Physics and Technical Drawing, *"I bought a trench-coat and a trilby hat and went down to the offices of the* North Devon Journal Herald. *They thought my A' Level subjects an odd choice for a would-be journalist, but they gave me a job covering weddings, funerals and Parish Council meetings."*

From the *Journal*, David moved first to the *Western Morning News* in Plymouth and then joined Westward TV as a Sports Producer on a programme called Sportscene. One day, when the presenter was sick, David stood in for him and that transformed his career. He moved to the BBC in 1966 and went on to present *Ski Sunday, Grandstand, A Question Of Sport*, the World Snooker Championships, the Horse of the Year Show

and Wimbledon. He also fronted coverage of Miss World and the Eurovision Song Contest. Covering the weightlifting at the Sydney Olympics in 2000 was his 14th Games (winter and summer) and he decided to call it a day. David Vine died in January 2009, aged 73.

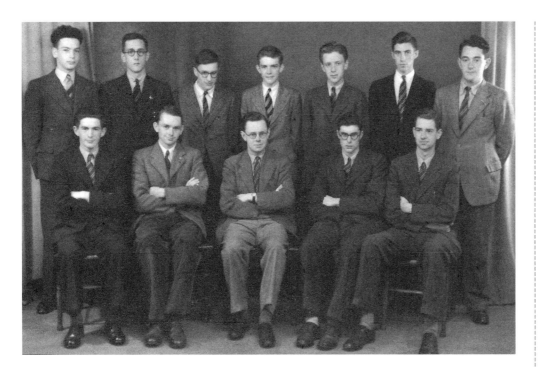

Prefects and monitors, 1946. Back row from left: A.T. Darch, G.H. Martin, L.J. Hart, P.J. West, W.B. Parkhouse, F.D. Brayley, D. Morell; Front row from left: C. Folland, W.E. Simpkins, T.R.H. Godden (School Captain), P.J. Tucker, J.W. Reed.

A surviving photograph treasured by Geoffrey Martin shows the seven prefects and five monitors from 1946. Between them they held all the positions of student responsibility as well as *"playground duty, keeping order in assembly and clearing the school at the end of each day."*

At the start of the 1946-47 academic year 210 boys on average were taking school dinners each day, the maximum that could be accommodated. There were only 328 boys in total, however, and the Head contended that the number was low because three times more girls than boys in North Devon passed the 11+ Test, which was now the only method of entry. A year later, at Speech Day in 1947, the Head again lamented the paucity of new entrants, which were down by a further 30. The intake was so small that it constituted a single Form class, which would upset the balance of the school for at least five years as that cohort moved through the school. If this trend continued, Mr Haywood said, the school would be unable to maintain its present standards of efficiency and cuts would have to be made.

A book in the school library gave Ray Liverton and Lesley Moody the idea of making crystal radio sets. They bought crystals and copper wire and constructed them inside matchboxes, selling them to other boys for 12½p. Later in life, Ray became a Consultant Electrical Engineer. He recalls that one night after dark there was an explosion in the school chemistry lab, causing windows to be smashed. It turned out that some bright spark had put a clip on a rubber pipe leading from a gas retort and the build up of pressure caused it to blow with spectacular consequences. We shall never know whether the perpetrator went on to a career as a demolition man.

'Bill' Hughes left in 1947 after 25 years of teaching History at BGS. Mr Critchley wrote: *"He was a brilliant teacher with a real insight into the nature of boys. He knew they might cheat, bluff and even be impertinent at times, yet he had been a boy himself and, while ruling them with a kindly rod, he had a true and undisguised affection for them. That affection was reciprocated in full measure."* Brian Williams wrote in his diary: *"Bill Hughes left today. I feel really sad because he's been a friend as well as a master to me."*

Brian Williams is a testament to the power of hard work and application, admitting: *"I was put into the "B" stream in my first year and came 31st in the class out of 34 boys".* By his Lower Sixth year in 1947, Brian was a monitor, a librarian and Captain of Fortescue House. As stand-off half and captain of the 1st rugby XV, the 1947 *Rock* said, *"he has been playing better than ever".* By 1948, he had added more honours - as prefect, member of the magazine committee and Captain of Cricket. At Sports Day he won the 440 yards, 220 yards and Long Jump. Future 'teacher material' one might have said, and that is precisely what

1948 Cricket First XI, captained by Brian Williams (front centre).

*David Fry in his new uniform, 1947.*

*What became of these high-flying boys from 1946-50?*

happened. After a period of National Service, a B.A. degree at Manchester University and a spell of teaching in Kent, Mr B. Williams joined the staff of the Boys Grammar School in 1958.

David Fry kept a diary in 1948 during his second term at BGS, recording the sort of quirky stuff a boy would put in a diary: *"6th February: Boxing. I fought a boy called Terry Hope but it gave me a splitting headache so I went to bed early when I got home... 23rd February: The Headmaster let us go on the rugby pitch for a snowball fight with the prefects and monitors... 2nd March: Had my third Imposition from Mr Bradley for being out of bounds."* Chemistry teacher Harry Bradley was the brother of David's uncle by marriage. Being family didn't alter school rules.

A Handicraft Club started on Wednesday evenings in 1948 with Mr Thoday; it covered a wide range of crafts from copper beating to making picture frames. A Natural History Society which had begun in 1945 as a bird-watching club now broadened its reach to include butterflies and moths and was still going strong in 1959 with a botanical garden behind the gym. The Boys School Hall finally had a decent stage, which would facilitate the production of plays.

In 1948-9 more scope was given to the House system so that, in Mr Haywood's words, *"the spirit of service may develop. This spirit is not what it should be."* House badges were instigated to encourage keenness and interest in the Houses and there were prizes for *"boys displaying the best attitude toward school life"*, won by D. Short and D. Fry. Mr Haywood regretted that more boys did not support out-of-school activities. Numbers were also down again for a third consecutive year. The Boys Grammar School was clearly in the doldrums. How different the situation was from the thriving Girls Grammar on the other side of 'The Gap'.

# GIRLS GRAMMAR SCHOOL

Pat Sanders must surely hold the record for the longest time spent as a pupil at either school – eleven years from 1938 to 1949. She began in the Prep class and then joined the Girls Grammar, where she repeated her second year because she was struggling and later spent a third year in the Sixth Form to get a third exam pass.

*Gymslip Girls. Rear from left: Barbara Fillery, unidentified girl and Pat Sanders; Front: Lorna Trussler and Anne Sleigh.*

*Form 2A Girls, 1945.*
*Back Row from left:*
*Phyllis Barrow, Alice*
*Mitchell, Mary Short,*
*Diana London, Beryl*
*Parsley, Sally Bushen,*
*Priscilla Harding,*
*Valeries Gould. Middle*
*Row: Ruth Morrish,*
*Christina Wyborn,*
*Gwen Holcombe, Jean*
*Millar, Penelope Scoins,*
*Margaret Gubb, Nora*
*Greenslade, Suzanna*
*Cole, Margaret Brough,*
*Patsy Chugg. Front*
*Row: Rosemary Everett,*
*Elizabeth Lake, Vanessa*
*Agutter, Miss Evelyn*
*Davis (Maths), Mme*
*Alice Jamart, Miss Jean*
*Watson (Maths), Sally*
*Blair, Sheila Yeo, Vida*
*Wonnacott*

As the entry base broadened more and more children were becoming the first in their family to go to the Grammar School. Beryl Parsley's mum was concerned that they wouldn't be able to afford the uniform and books and so her Auntie Gwen bought her a satchel and a bicycle. She says that Miss Christianson taught pupils 'from the wrong side of the tracks' how to speak properly. They actually used to practise saying 'How now brown cow' in front of a mirror. Beryl says: *"My own sister called me a 'Grammar School Gutter Snipe'!"*

Reta Calton says that most misdemeanours were trivial but that even chewing blades of grass was deemed 'unladylike' and keeping the beret on the head could be nigh on impossible. On uniform, Margaret Bonvoisin remembers: *"We had to wear white silk gloves to school because it was lady-like. The two Miss Cowies would stop you on Taw Vale in mid summer and say, 'Where's your gloves?' They were both Plymouth Brethren."* Pat Sanders says, *"The worst crimes were passing notes to boys through the hedge and not wearing your beret in town."* Beryl Parsley adds: *"You could get a detention for not wearing your hat. Also, they measured the length of the hem of your gymslip or dress and it had to come above your knee when you were kneeling down. I was always conscious that I might reveal my stocking tops and suspenders when I was cycling."*

After eight behaviour detentions (as opposed to homework detentions) pupils were banished from their House for a term. Jean Hill only had two detentions during her whole school career and one of them was for boys throwing her hat around! Margaret Bonvoisin was demoted from the top stream at the end of her first year, *"owing to a regrettable tendency towards lively behaviour"*. Their French teacher confided that lupin flowers or their seed-pods brought on her migraines. *"Needless to say we brought in armfuls of the things and hid them in the cupboard below her desk with magical results... 'Girls, I can feel a migraine coming on! Just get on with your work – I must go and lie down!' We never did own up to that one. Then there was an art teacher who left to join a silent order of Carmelite nuns – were we too noisy for her?"* Anne Mabbott recalls other pranksters: *"During needlework classes, when Mrs Manaton was distracted with embroidery, one or two daring girls would raise the sash windows, climb out and then walk back in through the classroom door without being noticed!"*

In 1944 one of the original 1910 teachers retired. Miss Lucy Cronin had taught a variety of subjects in her 34 years. When she died in 1949 she merited a couple of well-honed sentences in the *Alpenant*: *"Hers was a character made unforgettable by qualities of wit and humour, an honesty and integrity of purpose, and an eager intellect that explored so many fields from classical studies to geography, from mathematics to the gentler arts of music and needlework. Her unfailing wisdom, kindness and courage will always be a source of inspiration to those who were privileged to know her."*

Miss Frances Lock taught Maths at BGGS from the mid 1940s to the mid 1960s and she recounts an April Fool's trick from 1946. *"Dinner money was 4s 2d per week in old money and every Monday I grumbled because most girls turned up with 5 shillings and I had no change. April 1st fell on a Monday that year and every single member of the Fourth Form turned up with the right money - 50 pennies! Poor Miss Peacock had to carry all that to the bank on her bike."*

Current Head David Atton hears anecdotes from former pupils returning to Park School for reunions: *"Elderly ladies have told me of being punished for speaking to their boyfriends, or for sending little notes in split tennis balls over the dividing wall. Two ladies reminisced how, on a hot day, the window had to be closed during their English exam as a steam train on the nearby railway line set fire to the embankment and filled the school with smoke."*

Moira Mayne was a pupil from Woolacombe between 1939 and 1947 and for most of that time she boarded at Riversvale Hostel on Litchdon Street, which the Governors had purchased in 1920. Her notes give a good insight into hostel life.

*Dilapidated former hostel in 2009.*

## Riversvale Hostel for Girls

Riversvale had been a grand Victorian house and in the 1940s it still had a tennis court and a croquet lawn which the girls could use. A former billiard room was converted into a dormitory for 12 girls. The Hostel was run by Matron (Miss Louise Hall or 'Lou'), who was strict but fair, a combination of Housekeeper and Personal Tutor. She was very particular about table manners. *"If anyone spilled anything at table, they would have to serve a penance by peeling potatoes or helping the cook."* Matron organised cleaning rotas for the girls. Everyone had a job to do each evening and an extra job on Saturdays, such as polishing brass.

There were around 33 girls there at any one time, a mixture of all ages from 10-17, all from Devon but from remote places like Brendon. Boarders stayed for a whole term and were allowed one home visit each side of half-term holidays. Each girl was allowed sixpence per week pocket money to cover things like toothpaste.

During the week, the girls would all gather at 8:30 to go to school together in a crocodile and those who weren't staying on after school would also return 'in croc'. There would be High Tea, followed by a compulsory homework period when older girls would help younger ones. *"Then, in our free time, we played Halma, cards and Monopoly before gathering downstairs for a collective hymn and prayer. Bedtime was 8pm and lights had to be out by 8:30. There was supposed to be no talking after that but we used to whisper to each other."*

A rota allowed everyone a chance to play the piano. Matron had a steam radio and on Thursday evenings girls would gather to listen to Bing Crosby. Another treat was when 'Lou' got out her ice-cream-making machine. At the end of each term girls would save up goodies from home and have a midnight feast. There was a good spirit. Girls were quite competitive but they would stick up for each other.

Saturday was the only day of the week when girls could choose how to dress. On Sundays they had a special bottle-green hostel uniform for attending Trinity Church ('in croc' of course), but this was abandoned during clothes rationing. Each summer there would be a day trip to Saunton and during the war they witnessed a boy from the Duke of York's Royal Military School come to grief with a live hand-grenade. *"Matron stepped in to offer first aid and apply a tourniqué. The boy lost an arm and had to go to the North Devon Infirmary, which was opposite the hostel, so the girls set up a rota to visit him."*

The 1947 *Alpenant* recorded a harsh winter. The River Taw froze over and the school was closed for two days because the buses didn't run. Indoor activities flourished, chess and letter-writing were both encouraged and choirs warmed themselves with hearty singing. The usually dignified staff cut loose and performed their own play at the School Christmas Party *"prancing around on the stage in motley hue."* Miss Brokenshire was a harassed businessman, while the meticulous accents of Mrs Plaister and Miss Harris, who played two grubby maids, were transformed into *"Cor it don't 'arf niff!"* and *"Blimey it fair stinks!"*

Science teacher Miss Olive Crowcroft had been part of the school since it began and was now retiring after 37 years. It was part of the character of BGGS that they didn't trumpet the success and long service of their staff in laudatory tributes, as the boys' side did. It was sufficient to note that, *"every girl who has passed through this school has felt Miss Crowcroft's kindly interest in her and the school will miss her greatly."*

For Beryl Parsley, some of the best memories were of musical moments: *"At the end of each term we assembled in the hall to sing 'Forty Years On', the school song. At Speech Days, Miss Atkins used to introduce an elderly tenor friend with the* words, 'And now Mr Sidney Harper will delight us with a few of his songs.' He would proceed to sing rather badly while we girls stuffed handkerchiefs into our mouths to stop us laughing."

The *Alpenant* for 1948 had lino-cut illustrations and photographs of sports. There were prizes awarded for the best contributions to the magazine, which was now being sent to Old Girls all over the world. There were 14 prefects and a Sixth Form Society, which discussed topics such as Justice, Journalism and Agriculture. The Editorial said that the Girls Grammar had once again outgrown the accommodation available, the numbers having reached 450. The new canteen hut allowed the conversion of the old dining room into two extra classrooms. But everyone looked forward to a time when there would be no hut dwellers and when the lessons on the lower floor would cease to have a background of P.E. and music.

Miss Ellenora Darch was appointed to teach Biology in the Girls School in 1948. She thought the classrooms in huts with their coke-burning stoves left a lot to be desired. She remembers that Miss Atkins' secretary, Miss Peacock, *"was always efficient and patient, even when I addressed her at first as Miss Partridge!"*

In 1949 pupil numbers were such that the annual Prize-Giving had to be split into two separate events because there wasn't room to accommodate everyone. The new canteen was crowded at each of two sittings. An embryonic orchestra had been formed and held practises in the lunch hours.

From 29th November to 2nd December 1949 the Girls Grammar School was visited by Ministry of Education Inspectors. They concluded that, *"Despite the somewhat cramping conditions of the school buildings, creditable progress is being made in the classroom. There are touches of distinction in the aesthetic subjects and in certain aspects of PE. There is not much inspiration in the general work, yet much of the teaching is sincere and thorough. The school is still without certain vital needs - a gymnasium and a library large enough to be the school's intellectual centre."*

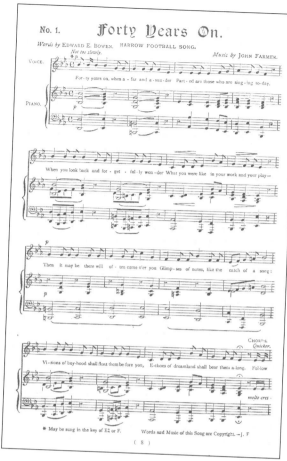

School Song adopted and adapted by the BGS Girls.

Girls' Staff, 1948. Standing from left: Miss Rossiter, Mrs Plaister (née Percy) (Maths), Miss Johns (PE), 3 unidentified, Miss Kerisson (French), Miss Cowie (Prep), Miss Hemmings (Chemistry), 3 unidentified, Miss Peacock (Secretary; Sitting from left: Miss Brokenshire, 2 unidentified, Miss Christiana (English), Miss Atkins, Miss Cowie (Geography), Mrs Manaton, Miss Lock (Maths), Miss Davis, Miss Boyle (Biology). The unidentified teachers may include Miss Cronin (Music), Miss Larman (Latin), Miss Graham (Art), and Miss Litton (Domestic Science).

Since the last inspection in 1939 the number of girls in the school had practically doubled to 480. Fewer girls now left before 16 and most were taking the School Certificate Examination. 15 Sixth Form girls hoped to go to university and a further ten intended to take up other further training. 16 members of staff had been appointed within the last four years but around a third of them were not qualified to teach the upper forms.

Inspectors said the school would benefit from a grand piano for the hall, housecraft reference books and physics apparatus for Sixth Form work. There was the first ever mention of a need for a laboratory assistant. The school now had three hard tennis courts and two extra hockey pitches but the Hall was still doubling as a gymnasium. A serious shortcoming which had not been mentioned before was that there were no changing rooms or showers — *"what change of clothing the girls attempt has to be done in the cloakrooms"*.

The 1950 *Alpenant* drew the curtain on another decade, declaring: *"We are now a three stream school throughout and we have reached the limit of expansion within the present accommodation."*

# CHAPTER 6

# FIZZING FIFTIES, 1950-1959

T HE FIFTIES was not an eventful decade in terms of significant change – there was frankly more fizzle than fizz – but former staff and pupils have brought plenty of sparkle to this account. The Girls Grammar consolidated its successes of the 1940s and the Boys Grammar eventually emerged from the doldrums in terms of numbers and results. Since they continued to function as separate institutions they continue to be treated here under separate headings. But one major national development would affect them both equally and there was one respect in which they were still joined at the hip.

It would not have been obvious from the previous chapter, nor was it to pupils of the time, that throughout the 1940s the separate Boys and Girls Grammar Schools shared a common Governing Body. Governors' minutes for the '40s and '50s were confidential and are now missing from the public archive. But another document which was confidential in its day, the 1953 H. M. Inspectors' Report on the Boys Grammar School, reveals the extraordinary fact that: *"The Governing Body is now responsible not only for the two Grammar Schools but also for the two Modern Secondary Schools in Barnstaple. All four Heads normally attend the meetings. This is not conducive to developing the four schools as distinct communities, nor does it encourage Heads to bring up difficulties such as may concern members of staff."* On the ground this arrangement continued to be invisible.

Nationally, the General Certificate of Education (GCE) was introduced to replace the old 'School Certificate' from 1952. It was designed for the most able 25% of pupils in England and Wales. GCE exams would normally be taken at 16 (Ordinary or 'O' Level) and 18 (Advanced or 'A' Level), but it was mainly grammar schools and independent schools who introduced them. 'Parity of esteem' between Grammar and Modern schools, as envisaged by the 1944 Education Act, never really came to pass. The Certificate of Secondary Education (CSE) was not introduced for Modern Schools until 1965. Competition for places at Grammar Schools increased because they offered the best chance of progressing to university and a well-paid job. But there were equalizing influences on the far horizon. In 1951 Withywood Community School in Bristol became the first purpose-built Comprehensive in the South West.

———— ❖ ————

## GIRLS GRAMMAR SCHOOL

The catchment area of BGGS for those who passed the 11+ was a 20-mile radius from Barnstaple, taking in Torrington, South Molton, Combe Martin, and Bideford. Many girls travelled to school by train or bus. Those who came from places like Hartland, where there was no convenient daily transport, boarded at Riversvale.

Classes were bulging. A girls' school report from 1950 shows 35 pupils in Form IVx. Prize-giving was split across two days for lack of a large enough hall to accommodate juniors and seniors together. Subject prizes included Spoken French, Cookery, Speech, Original Composition and Scripture. Science was now split into the separate disciplines of Physics, Chemistry and Biology and the old first floor lecture room was converted into a Biology laboratory with modern equipment. The *Alpenant* magazine reported at length on school visits to the County Show at Chivenor and the Torridge Vale Dairies in Torrington, as well as Youth Hostel trips to Brendon and Clovelly.

Anne Mabbott was in the first group to sit GCE A' Levels in 1952 and she remembers that *"Felicity Chugg then had to sit in a room all on her own to do the Oxford Entrance Exam."* The *Alpenant* stressed that Sixth Form work would not be confined to grooming university students but would give a variety of courses with different standards within each subject. German, Anatomy & Physiology and Current Affairs were soon on offer.

The 1952 *Alpenant* announced that the school had a French Assistant for the first time, Mademoiselle Charpantier. A party of girls was entertained aboard SS *Ulysses* at Avonmouth. Its skipper Captain Foulkes was married to a BGS old girl and his previous ship had been 'sponsored' by BGGS since 1947. The House Captain of Antigone deplored the high level of detentions, especially in the Junior School, saying: *"The first and second forms should divert their energies to netball, hockey, tennis, theorems and irregular French verbs."* The Captain of Penelope went further: *"Penelope House has excelled in nothing this year except an astounding capacity for mediocrity."* The Old Girls Association pages were full, as they always would be from now on, with news of marriages, births and career successes. The magazine conveys a real sense of pride among girls for their school.

There was praise in the 1953 magazine for the open-air production of *A Midsummer Night's Dream* by the Boys Secondary Modern School. Was fraternising being actively encouraged with those 'rough young men' from Derby? It seems to have been the thin end of the wedge, judging by Celia Mullins' article for the 1954 *Alpenant* about two ground-breaking Sixth Form Socials with the boys of Shebbear College: *"One*

*dark December evening, a bus-full of light-hearted members of the Sixth Form, clad in their most attractive garments, chaperoned by Miss Atkins and a few members of staff, arrived at Shebbear in search of the 'treasure' therein."* Each girl chose a shoe from a pile of boys' shoes to determine their first dance partners but *"there was no need for this method of obtaining partners later in the evening! A return visit was paid by the Shebbearians in February, where*

South playground in the '90s – out of bounds to boys in the '50s.

*we undertook a very exhausting Conga to supper."* Such two-leg social evenings became a regular fixture. In 1957 West Buckland boys became the beef-cake. Fraternising was clearly being encouraged with anyone in trousers except, of course, the boys next door!

Jennie Davies has this to say about fraternisation. *"We were a very social group in my year. Half of our gang went to school on the other side of the hedge but Miss Atkins forbade any contact with those 'reprehensible' boys at BGS. I regarded the dances with West Buckland boys as a dead loss. We used to go to all the local hops so we always had plenty of partners!"*

Thirty-nine of the girls who left school in 1953 met up fifty years later in one of the best-attended single year-group reunions of all time. One of them, Pauline Cox (née Screech) made a commemorative cake.

In 1954 the term 'Head Girl' replaced the previous description of 'Senior Prefect'. The Sixth Form Society had talks on Tudor Devon, Anglo-American relationships, and Justice. One wonders if Rachel James took part in the latter debate. She was one of the leavers in 1954 and a decade later she became the youngest female Police Inspector in England.

March 2003 Reunion of the 1947-53 girls.

*Margret Tamlyn, Enid Sanders, Christine Doble, Margaret Uglow, Anne Docking, Joan Smale, Joyce Oke, Aileen Palryman and others waiting for the Queen on Taw Vale (picture from North Devon Journal).*

In 1955 a Sixth Form group visited the Houses of Parliament. Gym-slips were abolished as part of the uniform. Marjorie Newsham left in 1955 after five inauspicious years. She was the daughter of Arthur Newsham, who taught French at the Boys Grammar. Marjorie admits to being hopeless at French and she gave it up after two years. *"I got just 3% in my second year French exam."* Her father didn't scold her, believing that everyone has different strengths. Marjorie left at 16 and concentrated on raising a family. Years later, her son Philip achieved a BA and a PhD in French and is now a Senior Lecturer at Galway University. The linguistic gene had simply skipped a generation.

In May 1956 the school turned out en masse along Taw Vale Parade to greet Her Majesty the Queen. Joan Sanders was chosen to present a bouquet to the Queen in the Pannier Market. Margret (sic) Tamlyn left the school in 1956 and became a testament to the school's new-found success in grooming scientists. Her Friends Reunited entry says: *"I worked on the Human Genome Project, being in at the start and seeing it through almost to completion, including being in the team that completed the sequence for the first chromosome. I am now known as Gretta Hall."* Such name changes make career tracking of girls very difficult.

The 1956 magazine abandoned its traditional cover with Greek Goddesses in favour of a motif that would change each year. The following edition had a girl playing tennis, designed by Felicity Halfpenny in Antigone blue. The tradition of reflecting the colour of each year's top House would never change.

The 1958 *Alpenant* recorded the retirement of three long-serving teachers. Miss Harris (English) had been very much involved with the magazine and the library and she was leaving along with her long-time housemate Mrs Plaister (Maths). Miss Cowie (Geography) had been Senior Mistress for her last eleven years. 'O.G.A. News' reported that Mrs Margery Hughes (née Oliver) had received the Freedom of the Borough of Barnstaple, the first woman to be so honoured. At Easter a party of senior girls went youth hostelling in the Netherlands. There was a new designation for long-established crafts – 'Domestic Science'.

The Girls Grammar School may have had Physics on the curriculum since the beginning of the '50s, but it didn't claim expertise in the subject. Jennie Davies and two friends wanted to study it at A' Level but they were told: *"'Ladies don't do Physics'. The official excuse was that the school lacked the equipment. We became obstinate and insisted. In the end we had to cycle up to the Technical College several times a week, although the Boys Grammar had an excellent Physics department right next door."* Jennie became a Physicist at the Meteorological Office. Later she did research on navigation for the Royal Navy and also worked for the Army

THE ALPENANT

THE MAGAZINE OF
BARNSTAPLE GIRLS' GRAMMAR SCHOOL

No. 29                    JULY, 1957

RECENT APPOINTMENTS

TEACHING

Sybil Warren at the Girls' High School, High Wycombe.
Mary Richards at Bristol.
Hazel Squire at Bristol.
Peggy Thornton at a Secondary Modern School in London.
Thecla Shutter in London.
Thora Body at a Primary School in London.
Freda Westcott at Exmouth.
Monica Pester at Tiverton.

NURSING

Diana Ball at Guy's Hospital, London.
Janice Hookway at Torquay.

ACCOUNTANCY

Judith Webb.

INFANT CARE

Rosemarie Ewens.

CIVIL SERVICE

Patricia Davies, Deirdre Day, Angela Kingdon, Angela James (London), Ann Laity, Juliet Davy, Shirley Palmer.

BANK

Marion Squire, Pearl Seaward, Celia Body.

LIBRARY

Mary Squire at Ilfracombe (County Library).

HAIRDRESSING

Mary Thorne.

DENTIST'S RECEPTIONIST

Pat Hayman.

SHOPS AND OFFICES

Pat Blackmore, Diane Bosence, Janet Brailey, Yvonne Balment, Brenda Chamberlain, Elizabeth Curtis, Irene Cook, Sandra Dymond, Janet Gaydon, Beryl Groves, Rita Ingram, Robina Keys, Hilda Holmes, Pat Holman, Pat Huxtable, Cynthia Keys, Yvonne Jones, Susan Johnston, Elizabeth Langbridge, Christine Ley, Pat McWhir, Susan Parker, Marie Passmore, Helen Pring, Marion Oatway, Nancy Pert, Sylvia Vanstone, Shirley Squire, Mavis Rigler, Barbara Richards, Elizabeth Webber.

at the time of the first Gulf War. Perhaps ladies can do Physics after all. There were high fliers in other disciplines too but the lists of Recent Appointments that appeared each year in the *Alpenant* showed that the overwhelming majority of girls were still entering traditionally female careers in teaching nursing, the Civil Service, shops and offices.

By the end of the decade, the school had only had two headmistresses in 49 years but then Miss Atkins announced her retirement. She offered a spiritually uplifting sermon on happiness for the school magazine: *"The happy man or woman has a mind stored with the beauty of Art, Poetry, Music and Nature and a desire for seeking after truth. Perhaps even more important is the heart, full of warm feeling and sympathy, eager to help. It is this corporate spirit which leads you to work for the common good – 'sic nos non nobis'."* Miss Atkins remains the longest serving Head Teacher and her successor, Miss Barbara Tinker, had a hard act to follow.

*Staff (from left) include Miss Johns (P.E.), Miss Reid (Geography), 1 un-named, Miss Peacock (Secretary), 2 un-named, Miss Boyle (Biology), Miss Brokenshire (Scripture & Latin), Miss Atkins (Head), 2 un-named, Mrs Martin, Miss Williams (History), Miss Cowie, Mr Harris-Morgan (Chemistry), Mrs Thoday, Mrs Harding.*

## Miss Elsie May Atkins M.A.
## Headmistress, 1934-1959

Born in Surrey in 1896, Miss Atkins was educated at a County Secondary School for Girls in Fulham. She got a pass degree and a Diploma in Secondary Education from Bedford College in 1917. Later she studied part time for an honours degree and then an M.A. in History at Kings College and the London School of Economics. Her teaching career began in Ludlow and continued for 15 years in Wimbledon before she moved to BGS in 1934.

At BGS she taught History and Latin but was especially interested in careers guidance during a period when the range of careers for women was widening. The Alpenant allowed more than its customary few words to mark her departure: *"Miss Atkins' clear vision of what ultimately matters has guided the school through the rough and smooth of the years. With her gifts of sympathy and understanding she has always been approachable and ready to give friendly consideration to our problems. She will be greatly missed by us all."*

When the 1951 intake met for a reunion 50 years later their notes were written up for the school archive. Their career paths followed common patterns - two thirds of them going into teaching, nursing or secretarial work. These are among their magical memories of school life in the 1950s...

*"Getting lost on the first day when I couldn't find the Lynton bus... Two detentions for talking in the first term... Hated the uniform... those awful brown hats, brown gym shorts, brown knickers and brown plimsolls... Playing flying saucers with our berets in the top drive... Joy Snell's beret flew down the railway embankment and we couldn't reach it... Loved the dinners, especially roast potatoes and treacle pudding... Joan Batchelor's tomato sandwiches... Breaking a window with a tennis ball and the embarrassment of having my father come in to measure up for repairs... Sandra Lake falling over and breaking her arm... Flitting*

*around like fairies in modern dance... The Misses Cowie on their bikes... Miss Cowie's wig... Sitting cross-legged on the floor for assemblies... Neatness points... Hair ribbons and hair slides had to be brown or black... No sling-back or peep-toe shoes... Getting told off for kissing my future husband at the bus stop... Throwing notes to the boys wrapped around stones... Mr Frizzell burning his gown on an electric fire... Mrs Harding knitting while dictating Latin... Trembling outside Miss Atkins' office, waiting for the light to go on before entering... Listening to the funeral service for King George VI on the Hall wireless... Walking in a crocodile to the cinema to watch Romeo and Juliet...Barbara Hamling sobbing loudly throughout the death scene... Hazel swallowing a drawing pin... Single sex compartments on the train... Sitting under the trees on a sunny day... Sitting on the bank cheering for our Houses on Sports Day... Getting soaking wet in driving rain along Ladies Mile... Doing homework on the bus... I was sure that I would never wear my skirt as short as Janet Mills, but before long we were all doing it... Floating berets down the river on the last day at school..."*

Despite the continuing prohibitive conditions for meeting the opposite sex in the 1950s, girls and boys still seemed to find mates across 'the gap' and there are plenty of BGS couples approaching their golden wedding anniversaries in 2010.

*BGS couples still together in 2003: Adrian Saunders and Pam Isaac, Bruce Yendell and Judith Hoyle, Chris Harwood and Susan Betts.*

# BOYS GRAMMAR SCHOOL

Drama had never formed an important part of school life for BGS boys, as it clearly had done for BGS girls. But a new era began in 1950 when the Dramatic Society put on four performances of Eden Philpott's three-act comedy *Devonshire Cream*, produced by 'Dai' Williams and 'Woffles' Westcott with staging by 'Chisel' Thoday. These three masters become the mainstays of boys' drama until the early 1960s. Typically, Messrs Westcott and Williams would each rehearse half a play and the whole thing would come together in the latter stages. Before long the boys were invited to attend a performance of *Romeo and Juliet* at the Girls Grammar School. Perhaps the sexual ice was thawing ever so slightly because in 1951 the boys performed *The Ghost Train* by Arthur Ridley and there were two mixed matinees. Did this provoke the hormonal prank of painting a bra on the hall roof?

At Speech Day in 1951, Mr Haywood showed his frustration with the 11+ system: *"In spite of all the assertions put forward by the statisticians and psychologists that the County Test is as near perfect as possible, in my opinion the first year forms have been of a lower standard as a whole than they were before this Test was introduced."* He was none too pleased with County budget cuts either because there had been no money for prizes at Speech Day until the OBA stepped in with funding. A year later the Sixth Form was at its largest ever but the school as a whole still had capacity for a further 90 boys whereas most other Grammar Schools were apparently full to overflowing. There were far fewer pupils than at the Girls Grammar next door.

*Form 5L Pyramid, July 1952. Bottom row from left: Terry Hope, David Fry, John Heyworth, John Gooding; Next row: Ken Jones, Ken Bowden, Keith Thorne; Next row: Ken Slater, John Guest; On top is Barry Price and looking on at the right is Michael 'Spike' Hughes.*

John 'Nobby' Norman became a pupil in 1953 and his school reports show just 14 in his first year class. Music was not a subject deemed worthy of inclusion on the report form. Drill had metamorphosed into Physical Training (P.T.). John can describe every detail of the cross country route over which he usually headed the field but he admits that he was *"petrified"* of swimming at Rock Park Baths. He was also rather afraid of 'Brig' Bradley. John was not alone in having these twin phobias.

In the first full inspection of the Boys Grammar since 1937, Ministry of Education Inspectors paid a 4-day visit in February 1953. They seemed to feel the school had turned an important corner since the mid '40s and they heaped praise on the man they thought deserved much of the credit, Mr E.T.L.R. Haywood: *"In some institutions there is a doubt as to who is in charge. Here every phase of the work and life of the school bear the stamp of the Headmaster's benevolently uncompromising outlook. The virtues of hard work, good manners and sound domestic economy flourish, along with a respect for scholarship and for the potentialities of the individual. The school has risen to an outstanding position under the present vigorous direction, and promises to improve still further in the near future."*

There were no longer any boys boarding. There were two parallel forms in each of the first three years and all boys followed the same curriculum. German was being introduced in Year 4 for the most able 50%, and the rest would drop Latin, leaving French as their only foreign language. Science and Maths were taught to graded 'sets' from Year 4 and the weaker set did General Science, which included Biology. Engineering Drawing had been introduced into Sixth Form and all Sixth Formers had lessons in R.E., General English, P.T. and Public Affairs. With a 35-strong Sixth Form, the average age of leaving was now 17 years 1 month. Inspectors said that the Head had given the Sixth Form *"status and a well-planned curriculum"*. In the previous three years, sixteen boys had gone on to university.

*History teacher and librarian Jack 'Woffles' Westcott in the old boys' library before refurbishment.*

There were 15 full-time masters, the four most senior of whom had joined the staff before 1922. The Inspectors pulled no punches: *"As a body, they are not well-qualified. Of the twelve men teaching academic subjects, there are two graduates with 2nd class Honours, three with 3rd Class, 1 with 4th class, four with pass degrees, and one without a degree."* The main Latin teacher (Mr Taylor) only had a fourth class degree and doubts were expressed about the quality of Latin teaching. But most of the staff were described as *"hard-working and loyal"* and a few were singled out for praise. *"The teaching of Art has been for 42 years in the hands of one man (Mr Smith) who has brought some bracing Yorkshire air into this Devon school."* The Physics laboratory was well-equipped and included much valuable equipment of Mr Cheetham's own design and construction. Inspectors said, *"He is a skilful teacher and a good experimenter, and the results achieved have been most creditable"*. Inspectors noted that there was no longer an orchestra. Because there was so little Music on the timetable, it was suggested that opportunities should be provided for listening to music, either live or recorded.

Inspectors thought that a large capital grant was needed to properly refurbish the library. *"The room gets crowded during lunch hours and boys have to sit on the floor."* Around 4,200 books were in the process of being catalogued under the Dewey system, but many of them needed re-binding or replacing and there was a need for more shelves. The annual County grant to the library was just £37.

*The 1954 boys' cohort in 1960. David Winchester, Terry Ford, Roy Hallowell, Philip Shelton, Stewart Bateman, John Whitefield, David "Fishy" Brown, John Born, Paddy Haughton, Richard Chamings, Harold Murch, Paddy Murphy, Richard Whalley, Nigel Willoughty, John Eastman, Roger Bowden, Alec Godfrey, Tony Summers, John Ruffle, Ian Collier, Ron Chapple, Brian England, Brian Sampson.*

Finally, the report described the overall ambience of the Boys Grammar School: *"The visitor is immediately conscious of an air of alertness and efficiency. During the breaks between lessons, pupils move with a sense of purpose. The mid-day meal is a dignified occasion. Discipline outside the classrooms is in the hands of Prefects who have certain privileges and the power to award sensible punishments. The tradition of reasonable behaviour is so firmly established that punishments are rarely necessary."*

At the end of the summer term of 1953 Mr Fred 'Doggo' Critchley retired from teaching after 38 years. His nickname came from the fact that he bred terriers. He had two degrees from Manchester (B.A. in English and M.A. in French) and had spent a further year at the Sorbonne, a rare thing in the early twentieth century. In retirement he remained active in the OBA and always secured discounts from his accountant, solicitor and car mechanic, who were all Old Boys. When his death was announced in the 1969 Bardian, Mr Newsham wrote of him: *"A man of very wide interests, Fred Critchley organised the athletic and swimming sports for many years. In the staff-room, he daily delighted colleagues with his rapier-like wit, his sense of fun and his constant good humour."*

We know more about what eventually happened to the boys' intake of 1954 than about any previous year hitherto because 39 of them wrote up their CV's for a reunion in 2003 organised by Ron Chapple. 8 became teachers, lecturers or headmasters; 8 followed engineering careers of one sort or another; 5 went into accountancy, banking or finance; 3 joined the armed forces; 3 went into business or management; 2 became ordained ministers; 2 became policemen. There was an architect, a solicitor, a journalist and one of the first ever I.T. consultants. Only 11 spent most of their working lives in Devon. A few individuals followed less conventional paths. Ian Collier became an actor, working at the R.S.C., on Broadway and in film and TV roles. He says, *"I was never a star but just about earned a living"*. Anthony Butler had already been a cartographer, a professional musician, and a management consultant before he became the world's leading expert in dystonia. Geoff Gould retired from banking and became a children's entertainer. Then there was Nigel Watt, who said: *"I left school before they threw me out!"* Nigel had a globetrotting life with stints as deck hand, miner, dustman, crocodile hunter, deer culler, printer, advertising agent and manager of a South African provincial newspaper. Eventually, he settled in New Zealand where he became Group Divisional Manager for 13 companies with 2,500 staff.

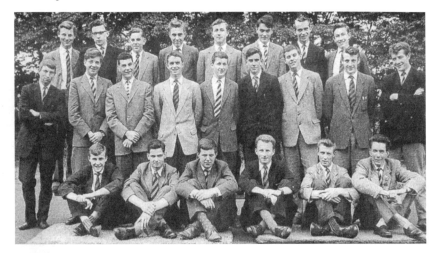

# First grammar school reunion a big success

IT MAY look like a bit of scuffed grass to the rest of us but to these ex-pupils from Barnstaple Boys Grammar School, it is forbidden turf.

When they were there they risked detention or worse if they stood on this strip between the boys' playground and the girls' canteen.

And it has taken more than 40 years for these old 'boys' to enjoy a bit of rule breaking.

Thirty-seven former pupils – most of them from the 1954 intake – got together again for what was the first reunion of any class from the boys' grammar school.

Also with them were three former teachers Ken Doughty, Geoff Smith and Brian Williams.

Many of them still live in the South West but others came from further afield including two from Ireland and one all the way from Canada. They met first of all at the Barnstaple Hotel to get to know one another again.

One of the 1954 student leavers was Ronald Laramy from Croyde who became a journalist for Reuters and was shot dead in Saigon in 1968 while covering the Vietnam War.

1954-5 saw the appointment of three staff who would become towering giants

*The 1954 boys' reunion in 2003. Standing on the narrow strip of grass between the boys' playground and the girls canteen, which was out of bounds in their day.*

in the school for decades to come – Ken Doughty (Art), William Benson (German) and John Charlesworth (Maths). The latter was taking over from Mr 'Jan' Shercliff, who had died after 33 years at the school. Mr Doughty replaced Allan Smith who had taught Art for 38 years and would forever be remembered by pupils for asking them in his Yorkshire accent, *"'Ave you dun yer aart 'omework?"* Ken Doughty brought a different regional flavour, as Paddy Murphy recalls: *"He was from Hampshire and we were baffled by his inclination to launch into a strong Scottish accent whenever he became enervated or angry! Ken's corduroy jacket, pastel shirts and ties contrasted with the greys and sombre hues of his colleagues."*

Paddy Murphy, later a schoolteacher himself, remembers Headmaster Haywood as a distant figure except at assemblies, *"though we all knew the registration number of his Landrover, STA 613, and we took cover whenever we saw it if we weren't wearing our caps."* Then there was Arthur Newsham who regularly snagged his trailing gown on the classroom door handle. But Paddy's favourite story is of timed races around the physics lab on hands and knees, while Mr Cheetham was having a snooze. Martin Ash recalls Mr Cheetham pinching two terminals during an electricity experiment and saying *"Now boys never touch these two terminaeeeeeeeeeeeeeeeee!!!"* Martin adds that *"after a long enough period for us to be thoroughly amused at his misfortune (probably only a second or two) someone had the presence of mind to throw the switch."*

*Robert 'Diddler' Cheetham.*

The best prank Frank Morris remembers was when a group of fifth formers put small mounds of sifted earth on the cricket square overnight. Next morning Mr Haywood sent for the groundsman and got into a frenzy about the mole-hills. *"Mr Baker was later able to report that he'd managed to sweep the earth away with no consequent damage. The 'moles' were never discovered!"* Among the motions debated by the Rock Society around this time was 'This House prefers Mrs Miller (Marilyn Monroe) to Mrs Beeton', which was carried by 40 to 3.

Mr H. J. 'Jerry' Martin, Music and Maths teacher, retired in 1956 after 40 years, an all-time record for a BGS teacher. The school grand piano went with him because it was his own instrument. Apparently, he had bought the piano second-hand from Nicklins for the bargain price of £25 but didn't have room for it at home.

## Harold James ('Jerry') Martin
## Longest-Serving Teacher, 1916-1956

'Jerry' Martin came to BGS direct from Teacher Training College. When asked by a pupil what the H. J. of his name stood for, he replied *"Hezekiah Jeremiah"* and this led to his nickname of 'Jerry'. For a record 40 years he gave his life to the School. He was a non-graduate but very versatile, teaching English and Latin in addition to his main subjects of Maths and Music. He ran the School Orchestra, the Chess Club and the Photographic Society and was Housemaster for Kingsley. Dai Williams said, *"Everyone had immense respect for him."* When his death was announced in 1965, the Bardian said, *"He will be remembered for that incisive quality of mind which quickly seized on the essentials of any situation and so clarified the position for all."*

*Jimmy Isaac.*

One of the new entrants in 1956 was a lad who went on to international success as a boxer. Jimmy Isaac was already West of England schoolboy champion at the age of 11 and he easily won the annual BGS trophy for best boxer. *"One year, on school finals day, the Guest of Honour called me over to the ringside after the first round and asked me to take it easy on my opponent. So I did and just won on points."* Jimmy went on to become Junior ABA champion of Great Britain, twice NABC champion of England, and twice ABA finalist. He represented England eight times in international competitions. Jimmy admits he was not a star pupil academically: *"I had many detentions for failing to do homework. In fact, I had the cane five times from Mr Haywood."* Another punishment came after a gym lesson: *"We were in the changing rooms making a lot of noise when a passing teacher who pronounced his 'r's as 'w's shouted: 'If you don't keep quiet I'll come and 'thwow' you out'. A boy called David Tamlyn replied 'Come and 'twy' it'. He didn't own up so we all had a detention!"*

BGS had another sporting legend in the making at this time. David Shepherd was also no saint: *"I loathed cross country running and I used to cadge a lift back from Bishops Tawton whenever I could. One Saturday I had time to spare in Newport before a rugby away game. I was only 16 but I went into the Rising Sun and bought a pint of beer. I was just lifting my glass for the first sup, when Woffles Westcott, our History teacher, came over and whispered, 'It's surprising what you see in public houses...and surprising what you don't see.' He never reported me."*

*1956 1st XI. Standing from left: Max Norris (scorer), John Norman, Brian Parfitt, Tony Molland, Vivian Greenslade, Wilkes, David Rowe, David Shepherd (then a 4th Former). Sitting from left: Jimmy Dodds, Brian Gregory, Derek Harris, Danny Evans, Ian Taylor.*

## David Shepherd M.B.E.
## Star Pupil, 1951-59

David Shepherd came from Instow. Bideford Grammar was nearer but all his friends had been to Barnstaple, which *"was reckoned to be a better school."*

David picked up his first cricket bat when he was 3 or 4 and he was already in the BGS first XI by the age of 13. *"My cricket masters at the Grammar School were Dai Williams and Basil Hargreaves. I owe them both a lot for all the time they gave up after school hours, coaching us and accompanying us to matches. In Geography lessons, Basil used to allow us to check the Test Match scores on the radio."* David became Head Boy in his final year, by which time he was also Captain of Kingsley and Captain of the first teams for cricket, basketball and rugby. In the 1959 cricket season he topped the batting and bowling averages and established a new school record of 973 runs in one season with three matches still to play.

When D. R. Shepherd left school, he played first class cricket for Gloucestershire from 1965-1979. 'Shep' then went on to become one of the game's best-known umpires, officiating in 92 Test Matches, 172 one-day internationals and three World Cup finals. His trademark was a superstitious hop when the score passed 111 or one of its multiples. He was widely regarded as a true gentleman. In 2007 'Shep' attended a reunion of the 1954 BGS first XI at the Imperial Hotel. He died in October 2009 after a long battle with cancer.

1958 brought an overdue increase in pupil numbers. John Bradbeer was one of the new first-years. He remembers that each form had monitors: *"The board monitor cleaned the blackboard after each lesson and then beat the board rubbers against a pillar in the corridor. There was also a chalk monitor who had to fetch chalk from the office and an ink monitor who had to keep the inkwells in all the desks topped up."*

Former pupil Brian Williams joined the staff in 1958. At his job interview Brian met Mr Haywood and Alderman Dunning. Haywood told Brian he would be expected to coach rugby and cricket and play the piano at assemblies as well as teach. *"Alderman Dunning piped up: 'Headmaster, Mr Williams is a married man with*

two children – is he to have no time at all with his family?'" But that was how it was in those days. Every Master was expected to make significant contributions to the extra-curricular life of the school.

The GCE O' Level results were quite satisfactory in 1958 but the Head declared that, *"there were more weak vessels than usual. It is obvious that some parents have not troubled to see that their sons were doing their homework."* It seemed that Mr Haywood's glass was always half empty. The Chief Education Officer for Devon said in his Speech Day address that BGS had *"the highest academic standard of all the Devon Grammar Schools".*

In August 1958 'Fritz' Benson started a School Exchange with Ravensburg in Germany, one of the first such exchanges between the two countries. Mr Benson had studied at nearby Tübingen and fell in love with the area. Over the next 40 years, hundreds of boys formed friendships with boys from the Albert Einstein Gymnasium.

Chris Harwood enjoyed his schooldays in the late 1950s despite vivid memories of *"the jugs of awful tea at West Buckland after rugby games… freezing cold open corridors… hopper windows collapsing on boys' heads… board rubbers being thrown at us…"* John Norman remembers that six boys each morning and six at dinner time were used as 'rolling squads' for the cricket square. Peter Hallett, writing on Friends Reunited, admitted: *"Yes, it was me who smashed the roller. If they wanted to roll the cricket pitch, they should have got a bloody horse!"* Peter and John both left in 1958. On his final day John Norman collected the cricket trophies for Best Bowler and Best All Rounder. He says, *"BGS was a terrific school and I still feel very privileged to have spent five years there."*

Preston Isaac on the other hand was only too pleased to leave BGS on his sixteenth birthday to work on the family farm. 21 years of farming paid for his hobby of collecting old things. Then he started the Cobatton Combat Collection and the hobby became an earner when 30,000 visitors a year flocked to see it. Preston's interest in military history began at BGS and it was his Geography teacher, Basil Hargreaves, who inspired him: *"At the end of term 'Bas' would tell us about his time in the Desert Rats, frying eggs on the track guards of a tank."* Now Preston has one of the largest private collections of militaria anywhere in the world, including several tanks of the sort that 'Bas' served in.

Mr E. T. L. R. Haywood retired in April 1959 after 16 years. He is still the longest serving Headmaster. Mervyn Dalling recalls: *"there was immediate silence when he came into view."* Mervyn was in Mr Haywood's Economic History class in the Sixth Form and found that he was *"not really the fearsome character he had previously appeared to be."* Haywood had once made Mr Westcott stand to attention along with a class of boys and Brian Williams says: *"the staff was more terrified of Haywood than the pupils were."* Ken Doughty described Mr Haywood as *"a large and somewhat intimidating man, red-faced and irascible, and extremely impressive in his gown, which he always wore. He distributed the monthly pay cheques Army-style from a table in the staff room. On one occasion I marched smartly to the desk, saluted, accepted my cheque and returned to my seat, much to everyone's amusement, Headmaster included. All in all, I liked him."*

*Preston Isaac.*

# E. T. L. R. Haywood, B.A. M.A. B.Sc.
## Headmaster, 1943- 1959

Mr E. Thomas Lancelot Reed Haywood shunned the limelight and there is no known photograph of him during his tenure at BGS. He had two degrees in History from Cambridge and another in Economics from London. At Cambridge he was hockey Captain. He played cricket a few times for Somerset. He came to BGS from Stowe where he was Head of Modern Studies having also previously taught at Cheltenham College.

Mr Taylor wrote this retirement tribute in the *Rock* magazine: *"Under Mr Haywood's hand the School has won a place unequalled in the County. The Headmaster's qualities of courage and integrity and the high standard he has always demanded of himself and others have made a powerful impact on the school. He set a praiseworthy example too in his vigilance over the spending of public money and few schools have been run more economically. Never seeking easy popularity, giving short shrift to red tape and mediocrity in any cloak, his manner could at times be most forbidding, but beneath it lay a real humanity."*

*Boys' Staff, 1959. Standing from left: Wilfred Potter (supply teacher), Arthur Gunn (English), John Charlesworth (Maths), Brian Williams (English & Economics), Ken Doughty (Art), Bill Hodges (Latin), Peter Popham (Maths), Geoff Smith (Geography), Alan Moore (P.E.), William Benson (German). Sitting from left: Edward Watkins (Biology), Harry Bradley (Chemistry), Dai Williams (English), Charlie Taylor (Latin), John Mollison (Head), Robert Cheetham (Physics), Arthur Newsham (French), Jack Westcott (History), Lesley Thoday (Woodwork).*

Charlie Taylor took over as acting Head for one term until Mr J. E. Mollison commenced in September. After 16 austere years without staff photographs under his predecessor, Mr Mollison immediately arranged to have some snaps done!

The final story of the decade belongs to a humble pupil. Mervyn Dalling kept a diary for much of his schooldays at BGS from 1953-59. 30 years later it formed the basis of a scrapbook he produced for his niece, Clare Masters, who was researching a class project at Park School on *"What the school was like in 1960"*. By the mid 1990s, Mervyn had retired from his Civil Service career and one day he met his former teacher Brian Williams in a pub in Landkey. They got chatting about old times and Mervyn was inspired to expand his earlier scrapbook into a fuller account of his time at the Grammar School. When he next met 'Pussy' Williams, at the Ring O' Bells in 1999, Mervyn wore his school cap and gave his old master the first copy of his printed diary, saying, *"Please sir, here is my history homework, albeit 40 years late!"*

This is not the place to quote at length from a manuscript that is deposited for anyone to read at The North Devon Studies Centre. It is a work of exquisite detail as the entry for Tuesday 8th May 1956 shows: *"Salad for dinner to enable kitchen staff to join the entire school as we all walked together down Park Lane and across Rock Park to Taw Vale. We all lined up along the pavement outside Taw Garages to see the passing motorcade of Her Majesty the Queen and Prince Phillip."* The following snippets will give a final flavour of the 1950s - and of the late 1940s and the early 1960s too, so ingrained were the rituals of BGS life…

*"Pupils were always addressed by their surnames and there were many whose Christian names you never knew… It was a school rule that a pupil raised his cap to masters if he saw them out of school… Each bike in the cycle sheds had to have the allocated stand number painted on the rear mudguard… There were leather punches in the woodwork room for embossing your name on your rugby boots… There was a drinking fountain by the steps to the playground and white 'out of bounds' lines on the playground around the staff room… Charlie Taylor said Grace in Latin before dinner ('Benedictus benedicat') and after dinner ('Benedicto benedicatur')… There was a rota of tables for going up first for second helpings… The hymn at the start of each new school year was always Hymn 333 Part 1: 'Lord behold us with thy blessing, once again assembled here.' Then, on the last day of each summer term came Part 2 of the same hymn: 'Lords dismiss us with thy blessing…'"*

Mervyn's own final Assembly came in July 1959. His 1990s printed diary ends with these words: *"I can honestly say that I was proud to be a pupil of BGS and, to this day, I am still proud to have attended this school."* He is by no means alone in that sentiment.

*Mervyn Dalling in 1954.*

## CHAPTER 7

# *SEXY SIXTIES, 1960–1969*

THE 1960S was a decade when youth was in the ascendancy. British society was becoming ever more equal, more open and more affluent. Children were much less likely to accept being 'seen and not heard'. It was the decade of the Beatles, the contraceptive pill, Mods and Rockers and student demonstrations. At Barnstaple Grammar School 54 years of separate-sex education finally came to an end and there were one or two quite sexy consequences. By the close of the decade school rules and hairstyles were beginning to be relaxed, there was more camaraderie between teachers and pupils, especially in the sixth form, and more opportunities for academic pupils of both sexes in Higher Education.

Two new Head Teachers had started in September 1959 and, to their credit, Mr Mollison and Miss Tinker were soon supporting an event which was to act as a marker for the liberated sixties – a Barnstaple Student Rag Day. A group of BGS girls and boys were the prime movers for this unprecedented event in April 1960 and the whole community got behind them. Among the headline activities was a local auctioneer selling off slave girls at the Albert Clock and a tiddleywinks match in Cross Street between Mr Mollison and his opposite number at the Secondary Modern, Mr Blacksell. Martin Ash was Ken Doughty's first A'

*First Barnstaple Student Rag Day, 1960. Martin Ash heads this procession on a tricycle.*

Level artist and one of the Rag Day instigators: *"Part of my job was to make huge banners for the Square, which were hung at first floor level at 5 a.m. Despite heavy rain, the whole thing was hugely successful in raising money for charity and became an annual event."* Jennie Davies takes up the story: *"We challenged Bideford Boys Grammar to take our mascot, which they duly did during a flour-bomb fight in the rain. We had bath and bed races from Braunton and Instow. We invaded shops on kids' tricycles. We put potassium permanganate in the toilet cisterns at the bus station, which turned the loo water purple. We added soap powder to the fountain in the Square."*

Something else that brought boys and girls together was the first ever combined Grammar School orchestra. But the *Rock* and *Alpenant* magazines continued serving two largely separate communities for a few more years. Although the girls' dining hut was tantalisingly close to the corner of the boys' playground, the boundary was patrolled by prefects. Communication between lads and lasses was still strictly forbidden. The *Rock* Editorial in 1961 hinted at change: *"It has seemed somewhat Victorian in outlook that we have been so near geographically and yet so far away socially. Discussion groups and lectures will undoubtedly enable both schools to enjoy the benefits of co-education."* Although the A Level R.E. group was a forerunner in 1962-3, mixed sex classes wouldn't fully come to pass until 1964. Courting among BGS pupils was still carried out clandestinely or at the Ice Cream Parlour on the Square. Vicky Tudor is among those who remember *"mitching from school to meet friends at the back of the I.C.P. with its juke box and knickerbocker glories."* Many Sixties courtships began with a knickerbocker glory!

In 1960, at the penultimate boys' swimming gala to be held at the Rock Park baths, Cook of Raleigh broke the record in the 'Plunge', with a dive plus underwater swim of 49'8", smashing Hallett's previous record by over 7 feet. The fête launched a fundraising campaign for the construction of the school's own swimming pool. There was a competition to win a new Austin Seven car by estimating the exact distance it would travel on one gallon of petrol. Around 35,000 entries were received and Mr Mollison set off for Exeter with a rally driver to find the answer. The car spluttered to a halt just past Lapford on the return journey, after 57 miles, 1,593 yards and ten inches. Former pupil Albert Verney guessed this precise distance and won the car. The school made £700 profit. The actual digging of the pool required a considerable amount of muscle power from gangs of senior boys during free periods and after school hours.

In September 1960 Jennie Davies was awaiting security clearance for a job at the Met Office and called at school to see old friends. Miss Brokenshire was acting Head in Miss Tinker's absence through illness and she asked if Jennie could possibly help out by covering Miss Tinker's O' Level Maths classes for a couple of weeks. As she says, *"This just couldn't happen in today's world!"*

The 50th anniversary of the founding of the school was celebrated with a Golden Jubilee Thanksgiving Service. Boys got new style uniforms, designed by Ken Doughty, with black and gold blazers and matching caps and ties. With grey flannel trousers and white shirts this was a very smart outfit and, apart from a loathing of caps, boys had far fewer uniform complaints than girls. Girls' uniforms remained brown, including an unflattering thick brown skirt and a brown beret, which had to have the badge showing, though it could easily get lost in big hair or come off when riding a bicycle. Diana Overill speaks for the majority when she says, *"the brown uniform was 'ugh' and when I tried to shorten*

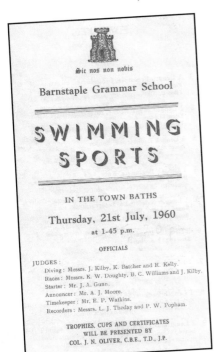

**Sic nos non nobis**

Barnstaple Grammar School

# SWIMMING SPORTS

IN THE TOWN BATHS

Thursday, 21st July, 1960
at 1-45 p.m.

OFFICIALS

JUDGES :
 Diving : Messrs. J. Kilby, K. Batcher and R. Kelly.
 Races : Messrs. K. W. Doughty, B. C. Williams and J. Kilby.
 Starter : Mr. J. A. Gunn.
 Announcer : Mr. A. J. Moore.
 Timekeeper : Mr. E. P. Watkins.
 Recorders : Messrs. L. J. Thoday and P. W. Popham.

TROPHIES, CUPS AND CERTIFICATES
WILL BE PRESENTED BY
COL. J. N. OLIVER, C.B.E., T.D., J.P.

*Boys' caps - 1959 (left) and the new design for 1960.*

*4th year girls in their more flattering summer uniform, 1962. Back row from left: Joanne Thompson, Julia Cornish, Jennifer Flynn, Elizabeth Prest, Susan Francis, Janet Purser, Carol Williams, Jacqueline Halfpenny, Monica Dix; Front row: Heather Moore, Sally Saunders, Vicky Tudor, Ann Partridge, Deborah Dawson, Pamela Barrow.*

*my skirt or wear a bow in my hair I got told off."* Joyce Hill adds: *"The effort that staff and prefects exercised in making sure we weren't breaking the uniform rules was unrelenting."* Vicky Tudor goes further: *"Miss Outen once hauled me down to the toilets to scrub make-up off my face and then she forced me to remove my frilly petticoat. I still find it difficult to wear brown."*

The girls' first teams for tennis and hockey went the whole of the 1960-61 season without defeat. The boys had their Speech Day in the Queen's Hall for the first time. Mr Mollison and Miss Tinker were both doing 'new broom' acts. Three of the old girls' huts were demolished and the boys' library was refurbished. Improvements were being planned for laboratories and new desks were ordered. Rubie of Raleigh broke the Cross Country record by completing the course in 31 minutes 36 seconds. In athletics, David Motion's 96'4" discus throw and Mike Rubie's 2'7.2" for 880 yards were new records. In the boxing finals, Rubie, Isaac and Motion all beat boys who were a stone heavier than themselves.

---

## Extracts from a letter to all parents of new boys, 1961/2

A proper pride in his appearance is a sign of a boy's regard for his school, as well as of self-respect. I should like your help with a few details:

**Buttons.** May I remind you that these should be black.

**Socks.** Please will you see that your sons have enough grey socks. Socks of other colours can quite spoil the appearance of the uniform.

**Shoes.** Too many boys lately have come to school in very pointed shoes, which are quite unsuitable for use during the normal day.

**School Rules** are essential permanent regulations and every new boy will be expected to know them after his first week in school, when he will be examined on them.

**Ball-pointed pens** are not allowed, except for rough work.

**Homework** may not be done at school without permission.

J. E. Mollison, Headmaster.

---

Trevor Hill remembers his first day at the Grammar School in September 1961 as a frightening prospect. *"The printed school rules led me to anticipate a forbidding regime of discipline. That first morning, we were each allocated a numbered peg in a cloakroom with a wire basket underneath for stowing sports kit. Tampering with another boy's kit carried a penalty of three lashes with the cane by the Headmaster. Going near bicycle sheds during school hours and talking in the corridor between lessons could incur similar penalties. A mental picture formed of a Headmaster who spent his entire days caning little boys, their pert bottoms protected only by a thin layer of grey flannel."*

Another first-former, Russell Bass, vividly recalls a caning he received from Mr Mollison for an offence that began with forgetting his gym kit but was then compounded by sheer cheek and daring. Russell was duly summoned to the Head's study and the episode merits quoting at length because it is brilliantly written and will resonate with every male reader who's ever been caned... *"I was very scared. The extremely tall, patrician-*

*looking Mollison came out from behind his desk carrying his chair. He turned it round, signalling me to put both hands on the armrests and bend over. 'Jem' suddenly vanished. Still clutching the chair, I looked around me. Where the hell had he gone? And then I saw him, or rather 'it' - a thunderbolt incarnate! He came briskly out of the stationery cupboard where he kept his rattan switch, his black gown billowing behind him and his arm outstretched, holding the cane, which to his credit was below the shoulder and therefore legal. He was speeding towards my short-trouser-covered buttocks to make a perfect hit. Thwack! It does make a noise and it does hurt. But thank God for that chair to hold and squeeze. Tears were already forming when he returned to take his second strike but this time he went only as far as the stockroom door, allowing just enough distance between my bum and his long bony hand to make the blow truly count. I blinked furiously, anxious to keep back the welling tears, now aware of the pain from the first strike more than the second. I feared more but that was it, just two strokes. I remember standing up and saying, 'Thank you, Sir.' I remember Jem's face as I closed his study door behind me. His jaw was firm, his lips pressed, his nostrils slightly flared. But there was no malice in his eyes. He nodded, almost as if I had done my duty."*

Russell Bass came in by regular service bus every day from Croyde and has kept his bus pass as a memento. Bus boys often had long days unless, like Gerry Potter, they adopted special measures: *"We used to leave school at 4pm and run like hell down Park Lane, through Rock Park and Taw Vale to try and catch the 4.10 bus to Braunton. More often than not we missed it."* Nowadays dedicated school buses line up at the school entrance and pupils board at leisure.

*School bus pass.*

Throughout the 1960s new teachers were still expected to contribute to the extra curricular life of the school and the clubs reflected the staff's own interests. David Rowe set up a Fishing Club. Fred Lee became the lynch-pin of the annual Ten Tors expedition. The Folk Dance Society flourished under Alison Grant, who played an energetic concertina. The Judo Club ended with the departure of 'Archie' Moore.

For two girls, out-of-class activities had other connotations. In the summer months Peggy Slade used to skip classes and go down to Rock Park, where she took off her school uniform and sunbathed. Vicky Tudor had a different pastime: *"I used to move my desk around the class and jump out of windows…I later became Head Teacher of a large Primary School in Surrey!"* Other girls were pure sugar and spice. Monica Dix only got one detention in the whole of her school career, for writing notes about another girl in class, though she regularly got away with warming pasties on classroom radiators.

At the girls' prize-giving in 1962, Miss Tinker expressed disappointment that some girls with good O' Level results had decided not to stay on. *"Sixth Form and further training is worthwhile, including for those who intend to marry."* The Prizes were presented by Dr Joyce Youings, an Old Girl who became the first female Professor at Exeter University. She stressed that there were far better opportunities than in her days. In reality, however, gender equality in the workplace was still some way off and women's careers were more often curtailed than merely interrupted by marriage and children, which was the main aspiration for many leavers. Even so, six girls passed three or more A' Levels and nine girls passed eight O' Levels. Among the subject prizes was one for 'Health and Personal Hygiene' - not something that would have been contested too hotly by boys!

The 1962 *Alpenant* reported on the Boys School production of the *Imaginary Invalid* in which, *"the female parts for the first time in history were played by girls from our school. This is quite the most outstanding example of female emancipation locally since December 14th 1918 when women got the vote."* Simon Blacksell played Argan, and Christine Eckley gave an *"extremely witty, polished and provocative performance"* as Toinette. The situation was reciprocated when nine boys took part in the girls' production of 'A Midsummer Night's Dream'.

The school doctor visited in January 1962 and all boys were checked for descended testicles. There were now 392 boys, a record number. The school hero was John Born – Head Boy, Head of Fortescue, Captain of 1st XV Rugby and Captain of 1st XI Cricket. John also topped the A' Level results chart and went to Cambridge.

At break times and after lunch boys let off steam in intense sessions of touch rugby, returning to classes bathed in sweat. At mid morning break everyone had a small bottle of free milk topped with a layer of cream which often became a frozen plug in winter. Not everyone liked school dinners but Trevor Hill loved them: *"My favourite was shortbread (known as 'concrete') served with custard of all shades from chocolate brown to bright pink and lemon yellow. The desserts made school worth turning up for. We would vie with one other for second and third helpings and engage in inter-table prune-eating contests."*

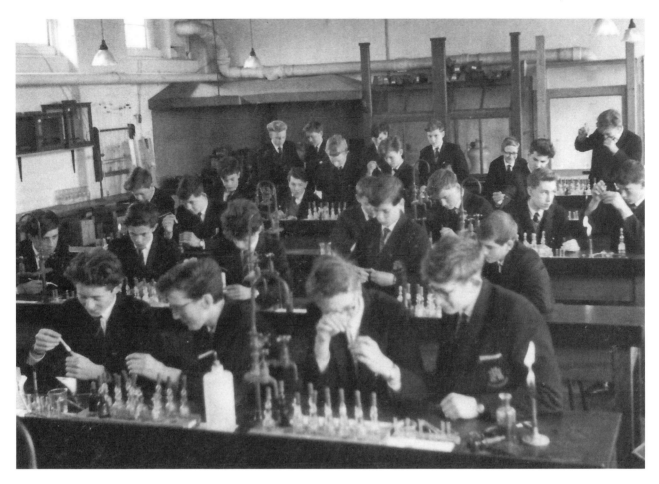

Playground bullying was rife. One particular boy would just walk up to younger pupils and steal their caps or slap them in the face. Prefects might intervene in a playground fight but they turned a blind eye to minor bullying and some even contributed a little random persecution of their own if they caught you in some petty infringement of school rule, such as entering an out-of-bounds area to retrieve a ball. Alan Mackie recalls: *"Prefects used to point their finger at you and say, 'Five to two' – meaning go and see them at that time. You had to line up along a wall and they would hand out essays on ridiculous topics like 'The sexual life of an orange'."*

In January 1963 thirty-eight North Devon schools closed because of frozen pipes and lavatories during two weeks of the worst snow in living memory. Two girls from Lynton were brought into Barnstaple by car and stayed in town for three weeks. The *Rock's* editorial began with a proud boast: *"We never closed, though on many mornings the boys and staff had good reason to regret our open corridors. The news that these are shortly to be enclosed gave some comfort."* This was the use of *"shortly"* in the Devonshire sense of *"dreckly"* - ie: 'not for at least 6 years'!

The 'Mollison Pool' was opened by Jeremy Thorpe M.P. as part of the School Fête in May and work began on the new Science Block, which would have three laboratories each for boys and girls. Mr Mollison left in July to become Headmaster at Varndean School in Brighton. Howard Meadows, an Oxford man, was appointed to replace him.

*Mid 1960s Chemistry class.*

*(Left) Aerial view of school before swimming pool, new hall and science block.*

*(Right) Setting up the pool for its first ever gala, 1963.*

# John Evelyn Mollison, B.A. M.A.
# Headmaster, 1959-1963

Born in 1916 and educated at Winchester College and Clare College Cambridge (Classics & History), Mr Mollison served in the Royal Artillery throughout World War Two, rising to Captain. He taught for 10 years at Winchester College, where he was a House Master, before moving to BGS in September 1959.

At BGS he taught Latin, History, Divinity, Current Affairs and French. He was a traditionalist without being stuffy. 'Molly' (or 'Jem') made quite an impact in a short time. He started the link with the Careers Advisory Service, introduced Parents' Evenings, welcomed the growth of the Parent/Teacher Association, increased the choice of subjects that could be studied, fostered links with other schools and the wider community, encouraged the Duke of Edinburgh's award scheme and was the prime mover in getting the swimming pool built. As Ken Doughty said, *"He brought a fresh routine and ideas and he was very popular with staff and boys alike."*

1963 was the first year that Bill 'Fritz' Benson produced the school play, beginning a run that would continue uninterrupted until 1984. There was a mixed cast for Shaw's *The Devil's Disciple*. Joyce Hill can remember the after-school rehearsal on 22nd November 1963, when Colin Hockridge rushed in to announce that President Kennedy had been shot. *"At first Fritz didn't really hear what Colin said and told him off for interrupting."* It was the last play to use the old boys' hall because a new and bigger hall was about to open on the girls' side and it would soon be shared. The original 1910 Assembly Hall was converted into three classrooms with space left over to widen the corridor and that is how it stayed until the mid 1980s.

*(Left) New Hall 1964.*

*(Right) Hall in use as the girls' gymnasium.*

Before long there would be an end to the rituals of single-sex morning assemblies. Most boys from 1941-1964 will remember the routine as if it were yesterday. Boys filed into the Hall and stood in neat rows by form class, with the youngest at the front and prefects keeping order at the sides. Once in place, the masters would file on to the stage wearing their gowns. The hollow space beneath the wooden floor amplified the noise of their marching feet. Everyone thumbed through worn hymn books to find the hymn of the day. Between prayers there was always a Bible reading by a pupil. The victim of the day would wait, trembling with fear, for the cue to approach the lectern and get their tongue around the 'haths' and 'thous' and 'saiths'.

*The old boys' Hall.*

Then the door at the front would be opened to usher in the dozen or so boys, mainly Roman Catholics, who had been waiting outside in the cold corridor. Pupils sat cross-legged on the floor for the Head's daily announcements. When dismissed, boys stood respectfully until the masters had filed out before proceeding, without talking, to their first lesson.

1963 brought more staff changes than usual at the girls' school but the magazine made no great fuss about it. The number of long-serving spinsters was dwindling and Joyce Hill reflects that, *"They must have been rather special women to win through to university in their day. In many of them I sensed a fierce belief in our potential."* Anyway, it was goodbye to the Latin teacher who used to teach a double period and go out for a smoke in between. And it was goodbye to Miss Irene Johns after 36 years as a P.E. teacher, an exceptional achievement by any standards. Miss Tinker wrote the briefest but choicest words of tribute in the *Alpenant*: *"It is difficult to think of the school without Miss Johns."* Girls now had a male Music teacher, Alcwyn Rogers, who took a party to hear Verdi's Requiem at Exeter Cathedral. A newly-formed Debating Society met to discuss democracy, patriotism, marriage, ghosts and education. A Careers Advisor came to interview senior girls and there was the first mention of Parents' Evenings.

The *North Devon Journal* announced that BGGS was giving up Riversvale Hostel at the end of July. The school's catchment area had shrunk a little and transport links had improved, so there was no longer a need for boarding facilities. There was no mention of the prevailing gossip that boys had been caught spending the night. One girl was allegedly expelled and another girl was supposedly transferred because her parents thought BGGS was a 'den of iniquity'. On the other hand, perhaps imaginations had run wild since the arrival of a young female English teacher, Miss Perry, who was prepared to discuss *Lady Chatterley's Lover*.

Sex was a subject boys talked about a lot in the changing rooms, where their manhood was most visible. Trevor Hill recalls: *"By third year and fourth year there were fewer and fewer of us whose voices hadn't broken, so to speak, and who couldn't therefore join in the dirty talk with any sort of conviction. Showering after games was a rather embarrassing time and some of us kept our underpants on to conceal our deficit. It didn't fool anybody. Being a late developer is a miserable experience."*

In February 1964 co-education proposals and plans to abandon the 11-plus exam were being seriously considered by Devon County Council and the Governors of all four Barnstaple Secondary schools. The Girls Secondary Modern at Ashleigh Road had been replaced in 1963 by a new Girls County Secondary at Chaddiford Lane, which became amalgamated under one Head in 1966 with the Boys County Secondary School at Derby Road. In July 1963 'Charlie' Taylor was one of a few staff to jump ship before the advent of co-education at Newport. It was hard to imagine him teaching girls. Physics teacher 'Diddler' Cheetham was retiring too after 23 years.

John Bradbeer was a pupil from 1958-65 who went on to a career in Higher Education, training graduates as teachers. His comments about teaching at BBGS therefore carry some weight: *"There was a lot of variation, far more than would be acceptable today. The school carried a few poor teachers and, considering that it had the top 25% of local boys, results should have been better. Only five out of 32 managed to obtain an O-level pass in Latin."* Marilyn Mabbott reports a similar case on the girls' side: *"Miss Williams was a History teacher who knew an immense amount but was unable to communicate except by monologues. Only seven people passed History O' Level out of 100 in our year."* John Bradbeer thought the curriculum was lop-sided too. *"We did essentially nineteenth century Physics, with a huge emphasis on heat, electricity and magnetism but nothing at all on the atom. Linguists did no Biology after second year. Music hardly featured on the timetable at all."* Geoff Smith was among the very best teachers and he helped John to record the highest mark in England for Geography in the Cambridge A' levels of 1965.

In 1964 the last ever edition of the *Alpenant* announced: *"In September, the Girls Grammar School will cease to exist as a separate foundation after 54 years."* The process of integration would be gradual. The outer shell of the joint Science Block was complete though it had reduced the girls' playground area, stopping netball. The really good news for everyone was that girls could now use the boys' swimming pool.

Considering that generations of boys had pined to see more of the girls, the last ever edition of the *Rock* didn't show much relish for the impending changes. *"If life in a Co-ed school of 800 seems a little less colourful, a little more like every other school, and without any 'tradition and unique way of life', it is for those of us who remain to build a new school of which we can be proud."*

*Miss Johns.*

*(Left) Science Block prior to completion, 1964.*

*(Right) Second Form Camp, 1964, with Mr David Rowe (left) & Mr Ron Daniels.*

As if to sweeten a bitter pill, a Tuck Shop was opened in 1964 and was run by senior boys under the supervision of Mr Charlesworth. Howard Meadows played a blinder at the last ever boys-only Speech Day. He said that during the upheavals of the past year, *"the boys continued to display that phlegmatic resilience that is so characteristic of the British schoolboy. Come floods, freeze-ups, or, as now, come females, he remains remarkably unshaken."* Mr Meadows went on to scotch apparently widespread fears that standards were bound to drop when the two schools were united.

The stress of the impending changes is said to have been a contributory cause of the departure of Miss B. Tinker at the end of July. She remained an enigmatic character. Mr Meadows became overall Head of the combined Barnstaple Grammar School, with two deputies, Mr Newsham and Miss Brokenshire.

### Miss Barbara Tinker
### Headmistress, 1959-1964

Miss Tinker was formerly at Queen Elizabeth's School, Barnet. Her five years at BGGS included the building of the new Hall and Gymnasium. She taught Maths. Miss Brokenshire wrote the customary understated 'Valete' in the final *Alpenant*: *"Staff and pupils will long remember Miss Tinker's warm friendliness, enthusiasm and infectious gaiety."* After a year of study at Leicester University on the Psychology and Sociology of Education, Miss Tinker moved into Teacher Training.

*(Left) Ten Tors 1964 with (from right) Steve Uglow, Dave Dyke, Colin Hockridge and Colin Tyzack checking the map.*

*(Right) The first girls' Ten Tors Team, 1965: Marilyn Mills, Caroline Hodges, Elizabeth Somerfield, Jacqueline Jones, Marilyn Campbell and Jennifer Hoyle.*

In 1964 a boys' team took part in the Ten Tors Challenge, spending a weekend hiking *"50 miles across the bleak and desolate terrain of Dartmoor"*. This trail-blazing team had no supervising teacher and their preparation consisted of a couple of hikes up Codden Hill. Thanks largely to Mr Fred Lee, girls and boys have taken part in the Ten Tors right through to the present day, with only two breaks — one through industrial action and the other after an error over entry forms.

Miss Joyce Stanley, Head of English, oversaw the 1965 fusion of the former *Rock* and *Alpenant* magazines into the first volume of a new magazine known as *the Bardian*. Its cover showed the symbols for male and female and the editorial declared: *"The barriers are down! No longer do the neighbouring schools live separate existences. The boys and girls have joined not only in schoolwork but also in games and clubs."* The first combined Speech Day was held in the new Hall and the whole school was integrated except for the two Fifth Forms which were doing different syllabuses for GCE. Miss Brokenshire's term as Deputy Head was short-lived. She retired in 1965.

## Miss Amy L. 'Betty' Brokenshire B.A.
## Pupil, Teacher and Deputy Head

Miss Brokenshire's association with Barnstaple Girls Grammar School began as a pupil from 1919-1925. Then she went to Reading University, where she got a B.A. in History and a Teaching Diploma. She taught in Bath before joining the BGGS staff in 1946, serving for 19 years as a

teacher of History, Scripture and Latin. In her final years she became Senior Mistress and Deputy Head.

The *Bardian* magazine carried retirement tributes from three Heads she had served. Miss Atkins said, *"Miss Brokenshire's great interest in the welfare of girls and her knowledge of further educational opportunities made her invaluable as the school's Careers Mistress. Many old girls owe their success to her wise guidance."* Miss Tinker said, *"She made a tremendous contribution to the life of the school."* Mr Meadows added, *"I might have expected to find her set in her ways, forever looking back at 'the way we used to do it', but this was not so. No-one was more ready to break new ground than Miss Brokenshire. I quickly learned that along with her gracious manner went a firmness of purpose which stood no nonsense. Miss Brokenshire has been a great servant of the school."*

On the announcement of her death in 1973, aged 69, the *Bardian* recorded that she had been President of the Old Girls Association for several years and that she had also held office in the North Devon branch of the N.U.T. Rumours circulated that she took her own life by walking into the River Taw but there is every reason to believe that her death by drowning was entirely accidental.

Miss Brokenshire was replaced as Deputy Head by Miss (later Dr) Alison Grant. Miss Grant recalls her first Sixth Form class: *"the girls wanted to be called by their first names but the boys still preferred their surnames"*. The new *Bardian* magazine had a suitably Co-Ed cover but continued the tradition of naming boys by surname-plus-initial. The Devon Rugby Sevens Cup was won by the Colts team of D. Knight, N. Facey, K. James, M. Pill, T.W. Hill, R. Prowse and M. Slocombe. It was one of the greatest sporting achievements of the era. T.W. Hill was Terry Hill, not the author. First names have their uses.

The July fête in 1965 included a boys' wrestling tournament in one of the still unglazed quadrangles of North Building. Fête profits were to go towards glazing the corridors, *"a project of the highest priority as anyone who has walked through those Arctic wind tunnels will appreciate."* So they kept saying!

The new joint Science Block was opened and the joint Debating Society discussed inter-racial marriages. The merger between the sexes brought gains on both sides but Alison Grant believes that girls did rather get absorbed into a boys' school, losing their house names, their London University Exam Board, their female Head Teacher and their brown uniforms - though this latter was clearly a plus point. Miss Grant had to work against the male-dominated culture and fight for a more equal partnership. She admits to having been *"a bit of a dragon"* and was more than a match for chauvinistic male colleagues and badly-behaved pupils alike. She says: *"Bad behaviour didn't suddenly arrive when we became a Comprehensive. There was often trouble in the cloakrooms with smoking and stealing property. The girls were worse than the boys. I always had plenty of confiscated cigarettes in my desk. I remember once there was a spate of shoplifting Latin dictionaries from W. H. Smith. Howard Meadows asked at assembly for anyone who could throw light on this to see him privately and a large queue of pupils formed outside his door to confess!"*

Jeremy Patt started in 1965 and remembers *"getting the whacks from Headmaster Meadows after just ten days at school, earned with Andy Lane for a chalk-throwing battle in class."* Gill MacDonald, another 1965 starter, was proof that girls can be more 'advanced' than boys. She recalls that in her second year the tutor system changed and there were pupils from every year in each tutor group: *"We had Sixth Form boys in the same room as us! We were often given 'impositions' from the prefects on ridiculous subjects like 'The inside of a ping pong ball' but we didn't mind as this was an excuse to see the prefects we fancied when we gave our works of literature back to them."*

*Mixed Choir, 1965.*

*Jennifer Farrar story from* North Devon Journal.

In March 1966 the front page of the *Journal* carried the headline *"School bans girl because her hair is too long"*. The story was picked up by the *London Evening News* the following day. It concerned 15 year-old Jennifer Farrar whose father was quoted as saying, *"The rule is archaic and the school is completely unjustified in enforcing it."* The *Evening News* reporter took Mr Meadows' side of the argument: *"I sympathise with him. He is hired to instruct females. Doing that, whatever their ages, is an awesome business."* Mr Meadows explained in a TV interview that there was **no** school rule governing the **length** of a girl's hair but, for safety and hygiene reasons, *"Hair reaching below the edge of the blazer collar must be fastened back"*. Jennifer was back in school with her hair in a band the morning after the TV report.

Among other disciplinary incidents around this time was the one recalled by Chris Wright on Friends Reunited: *"Someone stole some sodium from the chemistry lab and dropped it in the boys' toilets in the old girls' school. It filled the bottom corridor with caustic fumes."* One wag said it was 'only a flash in the pan' but the subsequent investigation was taken very seriously. The perpetrators remained anonymous for 41 years until one of them revealed at a reunion that the sodium was wrapped in newspaper to delay the explosion, which gave them time to get a solid alibi.

Peter Turner began a Friends Reunited discussion about the anarchy which disrupted the final assembly of 1965. Someone had sprinkled an unstable compound of nitrogen all over the New Hall floor making it crackle underfoot. Michael Floyde seemed confident that *"the culprits got the cane on their last day at school."* But did they ever catch the villains who put drawing pins on the hammers of the school piano, making it sound more like a harpsichord? Such pranks were certainly more creative than the usual end-of-school rituals of dunking Head Boys in the swimming pool and throwing berets and caps in the River Taw.

By 1966 the 11+ exam was widely seen as an imperfect instrument that led to terrible inequalities. Within many families there were siblings attending different schools with vastly different prospects of gaining life-changing qualifications. The Head Boy in 1966, Michael Townsend, perfectly illustrated how the 11+ exam could make premature judgements about individual potential.

---

### Michael Townsend
### Head Boy, 1966

Michael was unique in BGS history. He became Head Boy despite failing the 11+ exam. He says: *"I had been useless at Maths but Mr Blacksell arranged for me to transfer from the Secondary Modern as a late developer at the age of 15."* After just one year at BGS, Michael passed O' Levels in 6 subjects, including R.E., English and History, which he went on to study at A' Level. He was an extrovert - standing as the Liberal Party candidate in a Mock School Election, composing an operetta with his friend John Wren, and starring as Madame Arcati in Blithe Spirit. For the latter role, *Michael confides: "I was sent to get advice on costume from the School Secretary and came away with a tweed twin-set!"*

After a Divinity degree in Manchester he worked as a Methodist Minister before becoming a superintendent of Methodist Churches in 1994 and writing books on religious subjects.

*Michael Townsend in Blithe Spirit, 1966, far right as Madame Arcati.*

---

Those who finished exams in July 1966 had a varied programme of activities laid on including nature study trips to Braunton Burrows. Biology seemed to be getting out of hand with the announcement that a house had been built to accommodate creatures useful for lessons, including 100 rats, 30 rabbits, 20 guinea pigs, 20 mice and a chinchilla. Ken James won the Senior Cross Country and went on to represent South-West Counties at the National Schools Cross Country Championships. Boys' first names were being used in the magazine now, a clear indication that things were becoming soft and that standards were indeed dropping as feared! Only in rugby reporting was the manly surname-only tradition upheld.

One of the rugby coaches, Brian 'Pussy' Williams, left in 1966 to take up an overseas teaching post in

*Rugby 1st XV, 1967. Back row from left: Nick David, Alan Davidson, Brian Spiegelhalter, Chris Wright, Peter Cornwell, Norman Facey, Ricky Knight, Martin Gillard, Steve Jenkin, David Southcombe; Front row: Michael Slocombe, Ken James, Colin Webber, Alan Mackie, Geoff Cresswell, Dennis Knight, Martin Donovan.*

Singapore. Brian had been an outstanding pupil at the school in the 1940s and then became universally popular as a teacher of History, Economics and English. The *Rock* said *"There was hardly an out-of-school activity he did not support, and many which he organised. His cheerful, gregarious personality will be missed."* Among the goodwill messages he received was a Bon Voyage card from four fourth year girls who said they would miss his 'gorgeous smile' and 'fluttering eyelashes'; the message continued: *"Oh Pussy, oh Pussy, what can I do, I just can't live if I can't chat up you!"*

Considering that pupils no longer had to provide any of their own learning materials, Howard Meadows' accounts books for the year 1966-7, show surprisingly small sums being spent for a school of more than 800 pupils. Just £1,092 went on 'textbooks', with the biggest spenders being English (£210), Maths and Physics (£130 each) and Geography (£120). A mere £740 covered 'equipment', of which Sports and P.E. accounted for £190, Chemistry and Physics £85 each, and Biology £70. And £624 went on 'disposable materials', where the biggest costs were incurred by Chemistry (£140), Art (£120) and Domestic Science (£100).

In 1967 Tony Pratt and Dick Amery began teaching careers that would have a profound influence on the Park School over the next 30 years. Mr Amery joined BGS as a lab technician and then filled in as a teacher of Physics when Mr Evans fell ill. He recalls: *"Alderman Dunning was the Chair of Governors who appointed me to the job I'd actually applied for in Biology. He was notorious for spoonerisms and said at my interview: 'I see you have applied for this Bibliography job'!"* Two pupils with very different memories of Dick Amery were later to become teachers at Park School and therefore his colleagues. Gill Hevingham (née MacDonald) recalls that *"nearly everyone fell in love with Mr Amery. Then a girl called Sarah came into the Sixth Form from the Marist Convent and stole his heart, damn it!"* Chris Ley says bluntly: *"Dick Amery made me cry when I was 11!"*

Tony Pratt remembers the pressure to contribute to the extra curricular life of the school: *"Howard Meadows was as interested in my ability and willingness to take on the running of the Under 15 Rugby team as he was in my qualifications as a Geography teacher. Winning matches was important. Members of staff were expected to turn up on Saturdays to referee or take teams away. Outdoor activities were also high on the list of priorities and my wife and I were 'persuaded' to take twenty students to camp on Dartmoor two weeks after getting married."*

---

## Alan J. Mackie
## Pupil 1960-67, Teacher 1971-2010

In sport in 1967 Alan Mackie reigned supreme. At the athletic sports he personally won the 100 yards, 220 yards and javelin events as well as captaining Raleigh House to a clean sweep of most of the honours that year. He was Captain of the 1st XV Rugby, a star bowler and batsman for the 1st XI cricket and a fair competitor at every sport he played. It was a fitting climax to seven glorious years as a pupil.

In September 1971, Alan returned from three years at St Luke's College in Exeter and a year teaching in Kidderminster to become a member of staff in the P.E. Department and a tutor of Fortescue House. In 1972 he sustained a knee injury at rugby which ended his playing career but he was promoted to Head of P.E. in 1975. His hilarious accounts of staff sport were a frequent highlight of *Bardian* magazines in the late 1970s and early 1980s and he was Secretary of the Old Bardians Association in its final years.

In 1987, Alan moved away from PE to become Coordinator of Personal and Social Education. He organised the school work experience scheme and introduced residential experiences with Year 10 students. In the 1990s he became a School Governor and Head of Drake House. Somehow he's also managed to fit in broadcasting on rugby matches for Radio Devon. In 2010 Alan celebrates a record-breaking 50-year association with the School in a new part-time role liaising with Park's Primary partners regarding P.E.

---

*Alderman Dunning presents Alan Mackie with the Athletics Cup in 1967. Alan's mentor 'Archie' Moore, Head of P.E., looks on.*

Various events of 1967 offered evidence of liberalisation. Jeff Bale described a mixed-sex Lundy Expedition: *"In the evenings we wrote up our logs and then went out for some light refreshment; there is only one place on*

*Mr J. Foster with members of the Lundy Expedition, 1967, including Alan Denning and Peter Stacey (standing left), Jeff Bale (standing right), Helen Rideout (sitting left) and Mary Fourt (sitting right).*

*Lundy for this* (the Marisco Tavern), *the boys arriving first and always the last to leave."* A party of 22 players had a short rugby tour in Paris during which they lodged in the red light district of Montmartre and actually went to the Folies Bergères. Among performances the *Bardian* reviewer found worthy of praise in 'Fritz' Benson's production of *Arsenic and Old Lace* was Kelvin Jones's portrayal of Teddy Roosevelt, *"whose intrepid cavalry-charges across the landing, were best appreciated from backstage!"* Any fifth or sixth year boy would have been more likely to pick out Cilla Hodges' performance as Elaine Brewster, who rocked one shapely leg over another while coyly uttering the line, *'You used to tell me I have nice legs, and I have too'*.

One Sixth Form girl became pregnant and she and her boyfriend both left school to have the baby. Remarkably few relationships between pupils had this outcome. A more discernible effect of co-education was a clear reduction in the prevalence of bullying among boys. The presence of girls undoubtedly had a softening effect on the more aggressive male behaviour and there were fewer playground fights. But high-spirited behaviour continued. David Burnell recalls, *"In the playground we used to play 'pill tick' in which you threw a tennis ball at people. Innocent parties got hit and windows got broken, leading to ball confiscation and punishments, including 'six of the best' from the Head."* Jeremy Patt was caught making noises with a ruler in the library by 'Rollo' Mackintosh and had to write four sides on 'The intellectual stimulus of twanging rulers'.

The 1967 Plowden Report on Primary School Education recommended the abolition of the 11+ exam to free Primary Schools from the emphasis on good results. Comprehensive Schools and Middle Schools became 'the next big thing'. Within a year, there were plans for a new Comprehensive School for 11-16 year olds at Pilton and this raised doubts about whether BGS could retain its Sixth Form.

The *Bardian* Editorial for 1968 focused on the expansion of the House system. *"In the past it tended to come alive only for games and competitions, but House assemblies now meet each day to cushion newcomers against the shock of the large school we have now become."* The Heads of House were Mr Thoday (Drake), Mr Doughty (Kingsley), Miss Reid (Raleigh) and Mr 'Dai' Williams (Fortescue). Raleigh House decided to spurn all the namby-pamby cushioning nonsense and take competition seriously. Their cup cabinet overflowed as they won everything in sight across all sports – boys and girls, junior and senior. Ken James and Helen Glass were always in the limelight as Raleigh Games Captains.

Godfrey Welchman and Trevor Hill wrote accounts of school trips to Ravensburg and Spain respectively and they both ensured that the boozy truth was withheld. Five years earlier it would have been impossible to even imagine a week's beach holiday in Spain for a school party of 16-18 year-old boys and girls. But nobody got pregnant and everyone learned several new phrases, including 'cuba libre' obviously! Philip Osment in the title role of 'Hamlet' was said to have *"captured the audience's imagination from the very first scene"* while David Spiegelhalter made *"a handsome and virile Laertes"*. Six out of eight school teams were successful on the Ten Tors walk. After a decade of false dawns, there was a photograph to prove that work on the

*(Left) The north corridors are finally glazed by PTA volunteers, 1969.*

*(Right) Staff Leavers, 1969. Back row from left: Mr Payne, Mr Clarke, Mrs Chandler, Mr Davis, Mrs Jenkins, Mr Durrant, Mr Bradley. Front row from left: Mrs Thoday, Miss Hamilton, Mrs Durrant, Mrs Clarke.*

glazing of the corridors in North Building was finally under way. And Miss Beatrice Boyle retired after 23 years as an inspirational Biology teacher at BGS.

There was a flush of eleven staff leavers in 1969. They included Mrs Thoday, Mr Durrant and Mr Bradley. Girls knew Mrs Thoday as a kindly form mistress and one class can recall a particular Geography lesson when her dentures fell out onto the table in a demonstration of how sheep chew grass! Boys remember Brian Durrant as a slightly bohemian English teacher. Harry 'Brigadier' Bradley had been a Chemistry teacher at BGS since 1945 and a pupil at the school from 1921-27. His nickname came from a prominent US Army Officer, Brigadier Omar Bradley. 'Brig' coached athletics and Colts rugby for many years, was Head of Kingsley for a time, Head of Science and President of the OBA. His lifetime contribution to the school was immense.

By the end of the Sixties girls' uniforms had become more attractive, with grey skirts and jumpers instead of brown. It was the end too for baggy brown P.E. knickers, which featured in many old girls' memories, like this one from Gill MacDonald: *"My friend, who shall be nameless, once attempted a handstand and forward roll off the horse and left her brown knickers behind as she came off the horse into the forward roll. Mrs Winfield was not amused but the rest of us were in stitches for the rest of the lesson."*

Various developments in the 1960s ensured that academically able children had more options now than at the start of the decade. LEA's offered maintenance grants from 1964 onwards to support students away from home. In 1965 the Labour government accepted targets for the expansion of Higher Education recommended by the Robbins Report. Before long there were as many female undergraduates as males.

*1st XI Hockey Team, 1969. Back row from left: Glenda Bater, Lesley King, Sarah Jewell, Jane Chudleigh, Jay Thomas, Eileen Symons. Front row: Diana Westmoreland, Janet Franks, Rosemary Chubb (Captain), Beverley Squire, Christine Hockin.*

Teachers rarely get to find out what happens to their pupils more than a few years down the line, but reunions and history books are rare chances to put that right. The author's year group of boys from 1961-68 held a reunion in 2007 and the record of what happened to them career-wise is the most complete for any year group to this point. Tracing the girls has proved more difficult so this is only one half of the picture, but here is what happened to the 59 boys... 35 stayed on at school to do A' Levels and all bar one of that subset went on to some form of Higher Education, the overwhelming majority becoming graduates. 23 out of 59 have spent a large part of their working life in Devon. Their careers represent a broad range and some have had multiple careers, but counting each person just once for their main line of work: 7 became teachers; 6 became directors of major British companies - including B.T., I.C.I, and Rover; 6 set up their own businesses; 6 became civil servants, including one who was a Home Office Director and authored several government reports; 5 became engineers, including two who run major civil engineering contracts at home and overseas; 4 became farmers; 4 went into pure finance or banking; 3 are in real estate, including one who owns a chain of estate agencies; 2 became professional musicians and experienced chart success; 2 became policemen; 2 became university professors. Among the one-offs were a Fleet Street journalist, a Hollywood photographer, a Christian website designer, a Finnish-English translator, a social worker, a nurseryman, a carpenter, an I.T. consultant, an area sales rep, a school caretaker, an Ordnance Survey surveyor, and a BBC television producer.

*Just like old times. Rogues of yesteryear from the Class of '61 waiting outside the Head's study in 2007!*

Many Sixties pupils have been successful and haven't shouted about it. Martin Ash went on to study at the Royal College of Art, where he became a member of the Bonzo Dog Doo-Dah Band. Angela Manning became a travel writer, specialising in books about historical sites. Roger Cockram, now a well-known potter in Chittlehampton, studied Marine Ecology in Portsmouth and was one of a group of divers who helped find the wreck of the *Mary Rose*, using probes made of bean-poles tied together. Among several who went into politics, Malcolm Prowse was Leader of North Devon District Council for 16 years from 1991-2007 and Ricky Knight was a leading Green Party candidate at the European Parliament elections of 2009. But in the decade of the Robbins Report it seems fitting to end with eight Sixties pupils who went on to become distinguished University Professors:

■ **John Aitken,** Laureate Professor in Biological Sciences, University of Newcastle, Australia. John was a late developer who had to re-take A' levels. He became a world expert on male human reproduction.

■ **Steve Uglow,** Professor of Criminal Justice, University of Kent. He played a pretty young woman in the BGS production of *School for Scandal*. He has been a Home Office consultant on subjects such as the use of voice recognition evidence and the visual recording of police interviews.

■ **Jeffrey Bale**, Professor of Environmental Biology at University of Birmingham. From school field trips to Lundy and Crow, he progressed to research in polar regions, becoming a specialist on insects and climate change.

- **Michael Slocombe,** Principal of Trinity College, Adelaide, Australia. He was Head Boy in 1969 and went on to a Ph.D. in Nuclear Physics.
- **Malcolm McCrae,** Professor of Biological Sciences, University of Warwick. He joined BGS in third year and was put in the 'B' stream because he hadn't done Latin. He is now a specialist in virus pathogens.
- **Richard Balment,** Emeritus Professor of Zoology, University of Manchester. Played 1st XV rugby but Miss Boyle and Lundy field trips kept his focus on Biology. He's a specialist in endocrinology, with 170 publications to his name.

**Joyce Hill**
Emeritus Professor
of Medieval Literature,
University of Leeds
At BGS 1958-65.

Joyce left BGS with the open prizes for English, French and Latin. As a world authority on Anglo-Saxon literature and the Icelandic sagas, she has over 150 publications to her name. Joyce has had advisory roles in many organisations including the Research Council, the Disability Rights Commission, the Equal Opportunities Commission and the Campaign for Racial Equality. She became the first female Pro Vice Chancellor of Leeds University.

**David Spiegelhalter**
Winton Professor for the
Public Understanding of Risk, University of Cambridge.
At BGS 1963-70.

Grandson of long-term Chemistry teacher Cecil Spiegelhalter. David gained four A' Levels and left BGS with the open prizes for Maths and Physics. He has gone on to become a leading authority in the use of statistics, particularly in the field of medicine. David was elected Fellow of the Royal Society in 2005. In 2006 he received an OBE for his contribution to the Bristol Cot Death Inquiry and his work on Harold Shipman's victims.

# INTERLUDE

# *EVER ARTFUL*

*'School from the Riverbank' by H. Ridge, 1914.*

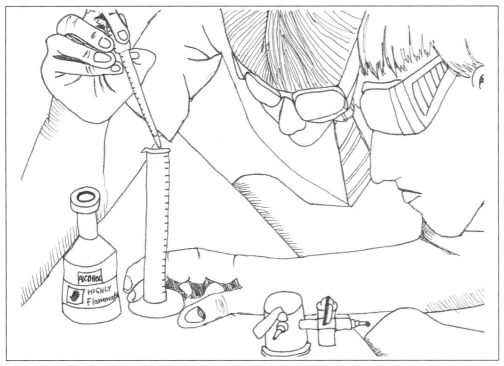

*'Experimenting with Alcohol' by Phoebe Kent, 2009.*

# School Commandments

Thou shalt not always noisy be
Or in the book thy name thou'll see.
Thou shalt not loiter after four,
Or play behind the form-room door.
Thou shalt not shirk in lesson time,
But start work when the bell doth chime.
Always be straight, play not the fool,
But be a credit to the school.

**R. Holland and B. Bale, 1936**

*Peter Lawrence,
1983
(later an award-
winning TV
producer).*

**Save Our School!**

*'Summer Exams',
Peter Davey,
1963.*

SUMMER EXAMS                                    P. Davey, 6th Form

# The Mathematical Problem

I sit with bowed head and wrinkled brow,
Racking my mind and wondering how.
At last a light comes through the fog,
Out with my tables, look up the log,
Divide by two, times by four,
Find the square root and add two more.
Good, that's number twenty done...
Now for number twenty-one.

**Steven Uglow, 1961**

———— ❖ ————

# The Classroom

The classroom is dismal and dull.
All day there's a constant lull,
Of people, voices, pencils and pens,
Of children calling to their friends,
The teachers are scolding
And telling us off.
Desk lids are banging,
The boys are getting rough.

**Patricia Sutherland, ID, 1965**

"The Art Room"                    K. Jones, VI

*'The Art Room',*
*Kelvin Jones,*
*1967*
*(later a*
*Hollywood*
*photographer).*

# Past Hysteric!

Berwick Coates was Head of History at Park School from 1971-1986. This selection from his book *Past Hysteric* is reproduced here with his permission. All entries are taken verbatim from essays and exam papers written by pupils at Park School.

Q: How might you improve the defences of a castle?
A: Get a dragon.

Q: Which town in Spain was famous for its swords?
A: Wilkinsons.

Q: Who pioneered a cure for malaria in Africa?
A: Dr Livingstone, I presume!

Some ships in the Armada didn't get very far because they were shot down.

*"They're drinking tea, I tell you!"*
At Pearl Harbour on 7th December 1941 was the Boston Tea Party.

The English divide foreigners into two – those they dislike and those they hate.

Q: What did men use to build prehistoric huts on Dartmoor?
A: Their hands.

Q: What does 'Christ' mean?
A: Christ means if something goes wrong.

Q: What was Hitler's nationality?
A: Jewish.

*Katherine Price, 2009.*

*(Left) Nicholas Kelly, 1976.*

*(Right) Sarah Spencer, 2009.*

*(Left) Unattributed, 1983.*

*(Right) John Sendall, 1966.*

# Ever Sporty!

Flappers

Flopper

Old pool gala

New water sports

Soccer makes a comeback

Home straight unchanged

New netball
courts

All-weather
cricket

Floodlit tennis

# The Essence

They tried to keep them apart,
The boys and the girls,
But it was not to be.
A quick kiss in the playground,
A tennis ball full of notes
Lovingly thrown over the wall.
Suddenly there was a swish of skirt,
A soft flowing laugh.
They had come, had the girls,
To change everything.

**Kate Spear, 2009**

*Maddie Muirhead, 2009.*

*3-D Art -
Barnstaple In
Bloom, 2008.*

# The Old Tree

I hear the sounds of chatting,
I see grubby shirt tails flapping
And ties hanging low.
Phone ringing,
Music blaring loudly.
But it wasn't always this way…
Well turned out gentlemen
In smart blazers and caps…
Memories carved into my bark.

**Megan Jones-Dellaportas, 2009**

# CHAPTER 8

# PARK LIFE, 1970-1984

THE 1970s brought the greatest single transformation in the school's history during which it was re-branded as The Park School and restricted to taking 11-16 year olds, who were to be selected by where they lived rather than on their IQ scores. Comprehensive education, in which all children from an area attend a common school rather than being divided by ability, was a long time coming. Labour won a large majority in the 1966 general election with a clear mandate for 'comprehensivisation' but they did not compel LEAs to convert. In fact, four years passed before legislation was drafted and then Labour lost the 1970 general election. It was not until the 1970-74 Conservative government that the number of children attending comprehensive schools surpassed those at selective schools for the first time.

In 1970 the first purpose-built Comprehensive School in Devon opened in Ilfracombe. Another was being planned at Chaddiford Lane in Pilton where, by 1972, both of Barnstaple's County Secondary Schools would be combined into a mixed sex school catering just for pupils aged 11-16. In 1969, a Sixth Form Centre was being planned for the area, to be located where Sixth Form teaching already took place, at Barnstaple Grammar School. Howard Meadows fought hard to retain that plan but the outcome of a long battle was that neither Newport nor Pilton should have the advantage of catering for the over 16s, who would all transfer to the North Devon College at Sticklepath. Although the changes would not come into effect for two more years, Mr Meadows resigned as Headmaster of BGS in 1970 and took the vacant Headship of St George's School, Harpenden - a Grammar School which was also about to go Comprehensive, but which was preserving its Sixth Form.

## Howard J. Meadows, M.A.
## Headmaster, 1963-1970

Born in 1923, Mr Meadows' studies for an M.A. in Modern History at Pembroke College were interrupted by military service in Italy and Israel during World War Two. He gained an Oxford

blue at rugby as a hooker and was later a Devon rugby referee. He taught in Canterbury and at the Naval Colleges of Dartmouth and Jervis Bay (Australia) before joining BBGS as Head in September 1963. A year later he became the first Head of the combined co-educational school. His wife June subsequently joined the staff to teach Sixth Form studies.

Mr Meadows' tenure marked a difficult period in the school's history but he brought in curriculum modernisation in Maths and Science, fostered the development of music and singing and laid the foundations for co-education. Howard was a tall man with penetrating eyes and *"not an easily approachable man"* according to one colleague. Pupils were also wary of him. In 1985 Mr and Mrs Meadows returned to live in Barnstaple, where Howard died of a heart attack in 1989.

Another member of the senior staff left in 1970. Mr Newsham took early retirement for health reasons, having served the School for 29 years, latterly as Senior Master, a role which was now taken on by Mr 'Dai' Williams.

## Arthur 'Crown'/'Baldy' Newsham B.A. Teacher, 1941-70

Arthur Newsham was born in 1909 and was appointed to Barnstaple Boys' Grammar School as a French teacher in January 1941. For years he was in charge of administering boxing, athletics, and cross country, as well as coaching and refereeing rugby. He was Chairman of the Devon Schools Rugby Union. He was also a good cricketer and the first team match against Mr A. Newsham's XI was an annual fixture. He was Head of French and Head of Drake House when the two schools amalgamated in 1964, but he renounced both jobs to become Senior Master.

Mr Newsham lived in one of the two school houses, Taw View. When he died in 1981 his family donated the Newsham Prize to be awarded each year in his honour for all-round academic achievement.

The new Headmaster, Mr James Morgan, had been Deputy Head at a Secondary Modern School in Totnes which had undergone the changeover to a Comprehensive. Governors trusted him to steer through the troubled waters of the coming transition. Staff and pupils soon warmed to their new leader. Pupils dubbed him 'Peanut' because of his balding head but he was also widely known as 'Jimmy'.

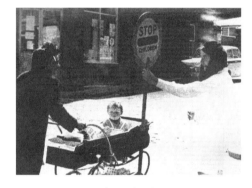

*First work experience trial, 1970.*

Sports Day events went metric in 1970 resulting in a whole raft of new records. The Mile race would never be run again and J. Padden of Fortescue became the first holder of the 1,500 metres record with a time of 4'56. The school swimming pool was kept in use throughout the summer holidays with parents organising a supervisory rota. In a work experience trial four girls took over the duties of Lollipop Ladies at Cyprus Terrace Infant school.

William 'Daddy' Hodges died suddenly in May 1971 at an evening cricket match. He had just returned to the pavilion after batting for the School against the Old Boys. He had joined BGS in 1955 and was Head of Classics and Raleigh House Master. Barry Jackson took over Raleigh in a year when Mr Morgan introduced the practice whereby 'pastoral care' became the responsibility of Heads of House. Parents of first and second year pupils attended an evening meeting with the new 'House Tutors'.

In 1971 the P.T.A. gave the school a minibus which soon became much-used.

Among a burgeoning list of school trips was a ski trip to Austria, a Geography Field Trip to Pembrokeshire,

*The P.T.A. was having a heyday and their Donkey Derby was one of many fundraising successes.*

BARNSTAPLE GRAMMAR SCHOOL P.T.A
GRAND SUMMER DRAW No 21247
Excellent Prizes: STEREO RECORD PLAYER
RADIO : : £5 PREMIUM BONDS : : and others
Draw to take place Friday 7th July 1972, at the NEW HALL,
Barnstaple Grammar School, at 9.30pm approx.
in aid of P.T.A. funds to purchase equipment for the School
Promoter: Mrs. P. J. Holland, Upcott, Roundswell, Barnstaple.
Promoted under the Betting Lotteries
and Gaming Act 1963.          TICKET   2½p   EACH

*Fifth Form archaeologists
at work with David
Burnell standing (left).*

and an archaeological dig at a Bronze Age barrow near Bratton Fleming, run by Miss Grant who had to take a special test to drive the minibus. David Burnell remembers leaving his packed lunch in a storage tent at the dig but *"by lunchtime a dog had eaten my sandwiches!"*

The raising of the school leaving age to 16 was introduced for the 1971/72 academic year. Schools retained 60% more 15 year olds than were staying on voluntarily across the board, though the difference was less marked in Grammar Schools. The school used extra capital funding to build the so-called RoSLA block in the north playground which was used for Domestic Science and Textiles. The Art Department has moved there in more recent years.

In May 1972 the photographers for that year's all-school panoramic photo discovered that two boys had made offensive hand gestures which had to be blacked out. Boys will be boys... Robert Hughes writes

*The 'RoSLA' building,
opened in 1971.*

on Friends Reunited: *"I believe I have the privilege of being the last person in our year to attend 'D', after I got caught smoking in the bogs by Dill Clements. I ended up in detention on the last day of term."*

A new Comprehensive era began in September 1972 with 839 pupils and 54 teachers. The newly-named Park School took in 182 eleven-year-olds. James Bracher was one of them: *"There were still Sixth Formers around and it seemed like a Land of Giants to me coming from Braunton Primary."* There were 89 'giants' in the upper Sixth Form but the Lower Sixth form transferred to the North Devon College, where Mr Doughty and Mr Evans commuted to teach A' Level courses, while two staff from the college taught part-time at the school.

It is surprising that such an upheaval did not involve a new-look school magazine but the good old *Bardian* continued to serve. The words *"Park School, formerly Barnstaple Grammar School"* appeared on the inside cover. Although the change was a major event in school history, the 1972 Editorial said: *"it has not been the only one of importance. The miners' strike early in the year gave the girls the longed-for privilege of wearing trousers to school. It also enabled some of us to skive homework with the sometimes legitimate excuse of a power black-out."*

Moyra Milton was a pupil in the last ever Grammar School intake from 1971 to 1976. Her younger brother started the following year in the first Comprehensive intake. They were the great grand-children of the 1910 Clerk of Works, James Hill. Moyra continued through into Fifth Form in a class of wholly-selected pupils and, although she and her brother had the same teachers, she feels that *"they may have tried harder for the Comprehensive pupils to make the new system work"*. Moyra moved to the 'Tech' for her Sixth Form years and speaks well of that transition: *"We were pleased to be treated as more grown up"*. Moyra's daughters, Rebecca and Jenny Milton both subsequently attended Park Community School, becoming the fourth generation of James Hill's descendants to attend the school which he built.

Ann Richardson had joined BGS in 1966 and she took A' Levels a year early in July 1972. She won the French prize in her final year thanks to *"a brilliant French teacher, Miss Barbara Morrish."* Her Sixth Form English teacher was Michael Grey, who became an authority on Bob Dylan. *"One day he turned up wearing pyjamas and slippers having been off ill the day before!"* But it was another English teacher, Paul Adams, who first suggested that Ann might become a writer. *"It was the first time I'd considered the possibility."* Years later, under her married name of Ann Cleeves, she did become a successful writer.

## Ann Cleeves (née Richardson)
## Star Pupil, 1966-72

Ann Cleeves is an established novelist. Her Shetland Quartet – *Raven Black, White Nights, Red Bones,* and *Blue Lightning* – has received wide critical acclaim. At the 2006 Awards Ceremony of the Crime Writers Association she won the Duncan Lawrie Dagger for *Raven Black.* Her short story *The Soothmoother* was broadcast on Radio 4 and *Hidden Depths* is to become a 2-hour ITV drama starring Brenda Blethyn as Detective Inspector Vera Stanhope. But Ann's first ever published work was a piece for the 1968 *Bardian* entitled 'Off To The Front'. It contained a first sentence which she now thinks ought to have been edited:

*"In the crisp November morning, every noise and outline could be clearly heard and seen: the sound of the men's boots on the platform as they stamped their feet, trying to keep warm, the broad country voices as they talked, not about the adventure that was just beginning for them, but about the village news and gossip, as if what was taking place was a dream and that soon, after an interlude of fantasy, they would come back to the reality of village life, to their family and friends."*

David Burnell and Ed Tuohey were in the very large last Sixth Form in 1972. They had to wear jackets and ties – no jeans or trainers – but otherwise they had plenty of freedom and scope to abuse it. *"We gambled at three-card brag and poker, even though only 'bridge' was allowed. When staff came in to check on us, we had to drop the cards on the floor and hide the 'pot'. Some of us made surreptitious visits to the Liberal club in town to play snooker."* Ed recalls: *"The common room was a great place - there were always a few courting couples but it was all tame stuff. The cigarette smoking was a far greater danger."* Science students enjoyed some pretty edgy experiments according to David: *"In Physics we used rifles for measuring the speed of a bullet. In Chemistry, with just a lab coat for protection and no goggles or gloves, we made*

*The last ever Sixth Form, 1972-3. Hair was no longer a guide to gender.*

*poisonous gases like nitrogen dioxide and ammonia, and used carcinogens like benzene and xylene. In Biology we propagated geraniums, raised chicks from eggs, and dissected toads."*

James Bracher, a pupil from 1972-77 can remember *"no real bullying"* in his time, though he then goes on to say: *"One boy was once taped to a pillar outside the new Hall. Oh, and Phil Mac and I hung one lad on a peg in the Raleigh cloakrooms by the back of his blazer...We also once nailed a dead frog to the desk lid of a girl called Christine Rogers... Then there was a dead budgie which flew into a tutor room window - I think Heather Bolt may have been on the receiving end of that one... I felt sorry for Maths teacher Mr Beer whose form re-arranged the desks so that the whole class would be facing outwards in a circle with his desk in the middle."* Quite clearly there was no real bullying!

Throughout the entire period of his tenure, Headmaster Morgan kept a daily diary of school events peppered with his personal comments. This is what he wrote about Park School's first tentative steps: *"The first year with a Comprehensive intake has gone quite successfully, but the biggest problem has been mixed ability teaching. However, I am sure it was the right decision and not only for the children as it made most staff meet all kinds and types."*

The rapport between staff and students had already improved dramatically since the mid Sixties. In a few well-known cases this was an understatement. Science teacher Dick Amery says: *"What can I say about my romance and marriage with a pupil in 1970? Having been happily married for nearly 40 years, the decisions we took have been vindicated. Sarah interrupted her education but she later went on to be a successful Primary teacher."* The Amerys seemed to catalyse other relationships - beginning with P.E. teacher Keith Summers and Head Girl Teresa Walter in 1977, then Steve Boreham with Lynne Sobey.

When the School lost its Sixth Form, Fifth-Formers became House Captains, Games Captains and Prefects, with David Priest as Head Boy and Mandy Reardon-Smith as Head Girl. The Fifth also faced the prospect of being guinea pigs for a handful of new hybrid GCE and CSE examinations, and it fell to them to edit the 1972-73 *Bardian* magazine.

Some altruistic extra curricular activities had sprouted. 'Wombles of Park School' was a group keen on recycling, whose members had collected six tons of paper, netting £100 for school funds. Fourth and fifth year students did Community Service on Wednesday and Friday afternoons as part of the Social Education programme. This involved house visits, shopping, gardening and DIY jobs. Some pupils assisted at local care homes and hospitals, while others helped with a Council housing survey. In the 'One Way Club' pupils got together at lunchtimes to sing or talk in groups with the aim of *"making the 'LIVING JESUS CHRIST' known throughout Park School."* Fund-raising schemes included a sponsored sew-in of soft toys and a sponsored beach clean at Crow Point. The latter was organised by Mr Pratt, who also designed a raft to enter the Barum Belle Raft Race from Umberleigh to Barnstaple. June Rice won the senior girls' Cross Country, then came second in the Devon Championships and took part in the All-England Championships.

The staff list for 1973-4 showed 40 male teachers and 18 female teachers. Miss Stanley and Mr Benson were now also teaching A Level classes at the College. Among staff characters fondly remembered from this period is History teacher Berwick Coates, who had a book published in 1971 called *A Level History* and promptly found himself stranded in a school with no A' Level courses. Maths teacher Ram Harijan reputedly began every lesson with the words *"Right, er, get your books out"*. He drove a bubble car and boys once left it upside down in the middle of the rugby pitch. Rosie Bracher recalls Ken Doughty as: *"fiery and frightening, but we all thought he was great, even when he completely lost it, like when someone hummed 'I don't like Mondays' by the Boomtown Rats."* Rosie's brother James remembers there were *"some lovely old guys still teaching then - Dixie Deans, who seemed as old as the hills, and Dai Williams."* Dixie Deans once compiled a maths test on yellow Banda that got bleached in the sun so the papers were illegible when exam time came! Then there was the Headmaster. Tony Pratt says that one of Jimmy Morgan's idiosyncrasies was *"his mispronunciation of new canteen foods - yoghurt became 'yogart' and pizza became 'piatzza'"*. Sixth Formers once advertised Mr Morgan's Volvo for sale in the *Journal* and his secretary started receiving enquiries.

The Editorial for the 1973-1974 *Bardian* said: *"Huddled in dim classrooms with the doors wedged tightly shut, we have survived many power cuts this year and also two General Elections."* Two teams of each sex successfully completed the Ten Tors Challenge. The review of Mr Benson's production of Ibsen's *The Dolls House* said: *"emasculated of its Sixth Form, the school lacks the sort of maturity that can bring out the nuances of character"*. This criticism did not throw 'Bill' off course and his productions went from strength to strength.

---

### 'Bill' Benson Drama Productions

1970 *The Caucasian Chalk Circle* (Brecht)
1971 *The Crucible* (Arthur Miller)
1972 *Charley's Aunt* (Brandon Thomas)
1973 *A Doll's House* (Ibsen)
1974 *Twelfth Night* (Shakespeare)
1975 *See How They Run* (Philip King)
1976 *Importance of Being Earnest* (Wilde)
1977 *Pools Paradise* (Philip King)
1978 *The Ghost Train* (Arnold Ridley)
1979 *Wait Until Dark* (Frederick Knott)
1980 *The Farmer's Wife* (Eden Philpotts)
1981 *Night Must Fall* (Emlyn Williams)
1982 *A Christmas Carol* (Dickens)
1983 *The Crucible* (Arthur Miller)
1984 *Arsenic and Old Lace* (Kesselring)

---

At Speech Day in 1974 Mr Morgan reported that 60-70% of pupils were being taught from one syllabus and sitting a common exam paper to be awarded grades from the highest GCE grade to the lowest CSE grade. He said: *"Schools today are very different places from the schools of yesteryear. There is much more variety and spontaneity. They are infinitely kinder than hitherto, the aim being the success of each and every pupil rather than the labelling of each child."* According to his Deputy, Alison Grant, labelling did still apply. Pupils were set from Year 3 onwards into seven Form classes according to their ability. The word MUSICAL was used as a mnemonic for distinguishing the forms: 'M', 'U' and 'S' were the top sets, 'I' was borderline and 'C', 'A' and 'L' were the bottom sets.

In the *Bardian* magazine for 1974-1975, Alan Mackie wrote a humorous account of staff sport. *"Early season victories on the hockey field included one over a much-fancied team of boys. Some of the lads took to the field dressed as fairies and played accordingly."* Among staff who had impressed the selectors were *"T. 'bites-yer-legs' Edwards, for his skill when tackling deadly second year soccer strikers."* In tribute to his departing colleague, Mr Daniels, a man of modest height who had reorganised the P.E. department, Mackie wrote: *"He will long be remembered as the only man to do a limbo dance under the staff room carpet."*

Representative sport was still thriving, with many fixtures against other schools as well as continuing inter-House rivalry. 24 records were broken at Sports Day, five of them by just two girls - Mary Reynolds of Raleigh (200m, Long Jump and High Jump) and Wendy Nowlan of Kingsley (100m and 400m). In Chess, the School Team won the North Devon School's league for the third year running and reached the South Western Counties finals.

The first ever two-way School Exchange with Trouville was launched in 1975. There was also a girls' canoeing course near Plymouth and a trip to watch tennis at Wimbledon. Fred Lee remained the backbone

*(Left) School Chess Team, 1975. Back row from left: A. Churchill, N. Dennis, M. Champion; Front row: G. Cole, M. Davis, N. Tiller, J. Rice.*

*(Right) Under 14 Netball Team, 1975. Back row from left: K. Wilkey, K. Middleton, J. Holm, S. Payne; Front row: S. Ridd, S. McManus, S. Turner.*

of Ten Tors preparations and James Bracher recalls: *"We would start with a few road walks around Chittlehampton, just getting used to following routes and maps before going on to more serious navigation by compass and graduating to moorland. On one outing it was so bitterly cold, Roger Delaney and I decided a small fire was in order. A gust of wind took it and we came close to torching acres of Dartmoor."*

Mr Morgan commented in his diary on the slow progress in meeting the challenges of Comprehensive education. In January 1976 he wrote: *"HM* (Headmaster) *attended meeting on mixed ability teaching at the Teachers' Centre. Would it be unkind to say the blind leading the blind? There appears to be very little knowledge about mixed ability teaching."* In July he struck a more positive note: *"I feel the gradual change to Comprehensive has been the right decision, by giving staff time to prepare for each year's problems. Some, unfortunately, are still looking backwards instead of forwards – but we shall persevere."*

In 1976 the last Grammar School pupils left and Park School became entirely Comprehensive. It took pupils from the immediate neighbourhood including Newport, Landkey, Bishops Tawton, Sticklepath and Forches. But Rosie Bracher explains how catchment areas could be manipulated: *"My brothers and I lived in Raleigh, which was in the area for Pilton Community College but our parents had registered us at our grandparents' house in Newport in order to get us into Park. Dad took the view that all the old Grammar School teachers were at Park so his kids were going there."*

A sunny Sports Day produced 27 new records including one by W. Paterson of Fortescue who broke the javelin record by two metres with a throw of 43.91m, having already won the event at the Devon Schools Sports. Miss S. Brigden (later Mrs Edmonds) became the first female teacher to play for the Staff Cricket Team in the annual match against the students. An Electronics Club was formed and music seemed to be diversifying, with a Wind Band, a Clarinet Choir, a String Ensemble and a Guitar Club.

Gone were the days of keeping 16 year-olds at school with tempting post-exam activities - now there was just a Leavers' Service for departing Fifth Formers at Newport Church. The 1976 exam results were published in a single list of *"successes gained by pupils at GCE O' Level or at CSE Grade 1"*. Thus defined, 8 boys and 16 girls managed to pass in 8 subjects. At Speech Day there was concern about the *"dismal exam failure"* of a few pupils.

## The Rise and Fall of The Old Bardians Association

The Old Boys Association was founded in 1918 with an annual subscription of 12½ pence and it took the name 'Old Bardians Association' in the 1930s. OBA whist drives, cricket matches and dinners were all enthusiastically supported in its heyday. OBA fund-raising provided the Cricket Pavilion, the Rolls of Honour boards and many ad hoc gifts of great benefit to the school. On the girls' side the first *Alpenant* magazines of the 1920s had news of old girls but not of an actual Association until 1934. The two Associations combined in 1964. They helped to foster a spirit of belonging to a body of people united by a common experience. But by the 1970s such sentiments had become unfashionable.

The gradual decline began in the 1950s. Many members took life membership and the invested money did not provide sufficient income to run the Association. Fewer leavers joined in the 1960s. The loss of the Sixth Form sounded the OBA death knell and 1972 brought the last School v Old Boys rugby match - to continue would have meant an unequal contest with Fifth Formers. In 1973 the practise of putting Old Bardians News in the school magazine was abandoned and members received a newsletter instead. By 1976 only 30 people attended the annual dinner.

The minute book for June 5th 1976 shows how the committee discussed termination. Harry Bradley was thanked for trying his best to resuscitate the OBA against the odds. Secretary Alan Mackie sent a letter to all Life Members advising them that the future of the Association was in jeopardy and announcing a Special Meeting in September to discuss its probable closure. He wrote: *"There have been disappointingly few school leavers who wish to join and attendance at social and sporting events has been very low. We understand this is not unusual in 11-16 schools."* Mr A. Verset-Suys, an evacuee pupil in 1914, replied: *"It may have to go by the board like so many things of our youth"*.

The OBA's final social event was a skittles evening in July 1976. At the Special Meeting in September, Jack Prowse and Hazel Bradley proposed that *"the inevitable decision to wind up the Association be made"*. This was carried and the meeting discussed how to spend the Association's funds. The last line in the minute book reads: *"The Bardians terminated at 8.42 pm, Wednesday September 29th 1976."* Jimmy Morgan's diary for 1984 confirms that the OBA Trust Fund of £731.86 was paid into an Investment Account and that interest would be used for school amenities and welfare purposes.

The *Bardian* magazine was still helping to unite the current pupils of Park School, and the 1976-77 edition contained an amusing article by R. P. on the subject of lunchtime detentions. *"We offer to all pupils of the Park School the opportunity to spend a lunchtime — though not necessarily one of their own choosing — closeted with a senior member of the teaching staff — though not necessarily one of their own choosing. 'D' Soc. meets regularly every weekday in Room 52. A large number of members are unable to resist coming at least once a week and some have tried to gain admission three times on the same day. Best attendance record is 38 times in one term!"*

The four Houses now had well-defined bases within the school, with Kingsley and Drake in North Building and Raleigh and Fortescue in South Building. When the North Hall kitchens were refurbished pupils from Kingsley and Drake had their meals supplied by Braunton School. The under 15 rugby team won the Devon Cup, the final of which was played at Barnstaple Rugby Club. Stand-off Billy Patterson was the rugby hero of the late '70s; he played for Devon Schools and was a regular trialist for the South West team.

To cope with the larger numbers the annual swimming gala was now being split into Intermediate (Years 4 and 5) and Junior (Years 1-3). Julie Smith wrote a report for the *Bardian* on a week of camping and orienteering on Exmoor in July for 8 boys and 10 girls accompanied by Mr and Mrs Amery. Mr R. Chugg, an Old Boy and former Mayor of Barnstaple, attended his last Governors' Meeting as Chairman.

In 1977, only 12 pupils attained 8 O' Levels or CSE Grade 1 passes. There were no subject prizes awarded at Speech Day, just lots of Form prizes, including 30 prizes for Fifth Formers. The emphasis was no longer on being best. Mr Morgan's diary entry for Speech Day revealed some inside information: *"Guest of Honour was Professor Charles Thomas of Exeter University, who is Chairman of the BBC Regional Advisory Council. Half way through the afternoon he asked for a ten minute break for a smoke. All the platform party went outside and stood around looking lost. The school with parents remained seated. We do not want such nonsense again."* The *Bardian* merely said: *"After a short break the guest speaker began his address."*

In the 1977-78 academic year 24 girls went on a hockey tour to Holland. Three Fifth Formers (Julie Drake, Christopher Keeling and Jonathan Rice) won the North Devon Junior Chamber of Commerce Public Speaking Contest. A club for Mastermind (the pegging logic game) met twice a week and offered prizes of chocolate bars; Nicky Squires won the inaugural knockout championship. An Autumn Fair involved staff, pupils and parents in various fund-raising activities. Mr Bailey was the hero of the afternoon as the target for wet sponges. The event raised £1,094, some of which was used to purchase canoes, a display cabinet, and a concrete runway for long jump. The Schools Traffic Education Programme (STEP) introduced a two-year CSE course on the Principles of Motoring and a ten-week social educational course. The first crunch came when *"a fourth year girl scraped her way along the corrugated iron next to the tuck shop. She ended up with the moped on its side and the horn blaring."* The system whereby the school had two dedicated full-time groundsmen was changed to a service provided by a pool of LEA groundsmen who were scheduled by rota. Mr Morgan's diary for 30th June 1978 wrily recorded: *"Sports Day. 17 new records established. Perhaps the new groundsmen have a different measuring stick."*

In July 1978 Dai Williams retired after 38 years of service. 'Bill' Benson became Senior Master and Tony Pratt took over from Mr Benson as Head of Fortescue.

## David Albert 'Dai' Williams B.A.
## Teacher, 1940-1978

'Dai' Williams was born in 1916 and educated in Pontardawe and University College, Swansea, where he gained a B.A. in English, History and French. At Grammar and Park he taught English and French and was Senior Master from 1970.

On July 14th 1978, people associated with his 38-year career at the School met in the Hall to help him celebrate his retirement. Former pupils, colleagues and Headmasters came from far and wide to be part of a 'This is Your Life' style entertainment. There was a tribute from David Shepherd, Gloucestershire cricket captain, who was at BGS when 'Dai' was Master in charge of cricket. Dai had often umpired, usually in a cloud of pipe smoke. Few teachers get such a send-off but 'Dai' Williams was a much-loved character. Mr Morgan said, *"I cannot speak too highly of the devoted service Mr Williams has given to the school, where he is respected equally by staff and pupils."*

When he died in 2004, his family donated a commemorative bench to the school. Former pupil Ron Chapple said at his funeral: *"There may be many in Wales but at Barnstaple Grammar School there was only one Dai Williams."* Dai's broad Welsh put-downs will remain in the memory of those whom he taught... *"Who did your homework then, your Granny?"*, *"This place stinks - open the pong hatches!"*, and *"If you don't pull your socks up, all you'll be good for is gobbin' and thatchin'."*

One school story from 1978 was symptomatic of a particular mood. A boy who had been sent out of class for persistent misbehaviour was subsequently caught distributing racist National Front pamphlets that he had obtained from his father. The pamphlet was entitled 'How to Spot a Red Teacher' and declared *"Commies have infiltrated our schools. They are trying to indoctrinate you with Commie ideas. If you get lessons in 'social studies' then you are probably being fed a diet of Marxism."* Headmaster Mr Morgan wrote to the boy's father and to the Area Education Officer who fully supported a course of action to defuse the situation.

On a lighter note, Rosie Bracher recalls her part as Peggy in Fritz Benson's 1978 production of *The Ghost Train*. *"The part called for a passionate kiss in Act 1 with the character of Charles, played by a handsome boy called Sean Grice. I had never kissed a boy and so I asked my friend Alison Williams what was required and, when the moment came during rehearsals in front of the entire cast, I French-kissed a very surprised Charles. Sean and I had to go to Mr Benson's office one lunch time so that I could be taught how to 'embrace my fiancé in the correct 1920's manner'!"* Six months later, Rosie says the kissing experience came in handy when *"I lost my heart to Jean-Marc who came with the French Exchange."*

Deputy Head Alison Grant has a wealth of good pupil stories. One winter after a snow-fall when roads were disrupted, two Fourth Form boys from Lynton trekked across the edge of Exmoor and arrived at school about 3pm, just in time to set off home again. That same day there were pupils from Forches who didn't make it in. Alison says that neither school canteen was as popular as Newport Chip Shop. One Fifth Form boy was a serious danger to others but *"fortunately we discovered the home-made petrol bombs he hid along the school drive before he had chance to use them"*. Many pranks were harmless, as when the Pope visited Britain in 1982 and pupils hung a large banner on the south building which read, *"No Hope Pope, We've Got Benson"* – meaning 'Bill' Benson, who had been ordained into the Church of England in 1979.

There were several staff departures in 1978-1979. The *Bardian* said: *"The departure of each person removes some special jewelled qualities which go to make up the kaleidoscopic pattern of our life together."* Collaboration between students and staff led to a successful first ever 'Fifth Form Revue'. Raleigh beat Drake in the final of the first Junior General Knowledge Quiz. And Speech Day was held in the evening for the first time which allowed more parents to attend.

*Rosie Bracher (right) with Adrian Baker and Michaela Watts.*

The 1970s ended with the best exam results since the school went Comprehensive, placing another generation of boys and girls on the road to success. They would be following in the footsteps of some of Park School's earliest progeny who were already making their mark on the world. Geoff Bateman went to work for the Environment Agency and would gain an OBE for services to the environment. Rosie Bracher trained as a solicitor and would run her own business in Barnstaple specializing in family cases, returning as a Governor of Park from 1996-2001. James Bracher, according to his sister, got *"one of those well-paid jobs in industry that you don't exactly know what he does but involves a lot of travelling abroad!"* Sarah Gunn started a PR business in Plymouth. Robert Tyres entered the world of Formula 1 motor racing, initially as a mechanic. Philip McEvansoneya became a lecturer in Art History at Trinity College, Dublin. Steve Hawkins became a Professor. Adrian Baker became a gynaecologist. Andrew Crisp got a high-powered job with British Aerospace and now travels the world selling military hardware. But among a lot of high-flying '70s students, Vivienne Cox has perhaps flown higher than most.

## Vivienne Cox
## Star Pupil, 1968-75

Vivienne was Head Girl in 1974-5. She shone at music and all sports, representing the school at hockey, netball, tennis and swimming. But it was Fred Lee who sparked her academic interest.

Vivienne went on to read Chemistry at Oxford and then began a career with the Chemicals division of BP. In a 28-year career with BP she became their highest ranking female, as Vice President of Gas, Power and Renewables. Her last role at BP was to set up and run the Alternative Energy business arising from her interest in climate change issues. In 2007 she was awarded the Business Woman of the year award. Vivienne retired from BP in 2009 and is now a non-executive director of Rio Tinto Plc and of the privately-owned company Climate Change Capital. She is married with two daughters.

An excellent witness to the final years of James Morgan's tenure as Headmaster is Ian King, a pupil from 1978 to 1983, who went on to become a journalist and is now deputy business editor of the *Times*. Here is a lengthy but insightful selection of Ian's thoughts on the development of the school during that period...

*"When I started at Park in 1978 it still had the feel of a Grammar School, partly because many of the teachers from that era were still working there. By the time I left the atmosphere had changed to that of a Comprehensive School. Many things contributed to this... At the outset it seemed quite an austere place and I can remember Mr Morgan wearing a gown and a mortar board at assemblies. He was not doing that by 1983... In my first year, the boys did just one term of cookery and needlework before reverting to the more traditional subjects of woodwork and metalwork; by my fifth year, the younger boys had much more opportunity to enjoy the former disciplines... A number of younger teachers made their mark, including Simon Pearson, who taught Art in a very relaxed manner. I can't ever recall studying a Shakespeare play, which would have been a staple in Grammar School days. Miss Wootton tried alternative approaches in Drama — in one lesson she took off her shoe and pretended it was an ancient relic, the Holy Dido, before which we had to genuflect. Martin Bosworth, the Head of Music, would invite us to bring in pop records for discussion. Berwick Coates and Tim Edwards discussed current affairs with us in History lessons and encouraged us to take an interest in the news... By 1983, many of the teachers who had taught me in my earlier years had left the school - Miss Stanley (English), Mr Pumfrey (Physics), Mr Clements (French), Mr Gomes (R.E.) and Mr Jackson (Art)... In my final year, there was an 'It's A Knockout' competition, based on the popular TV show of the time, which was far more fun than the annual Sports Day."*

Three new Inter House Trophies were on offer for the first time in 1979-80 — an Overall Rugby Cup, a House Work Trophy and an Overall House Shield. Fortescue won all three, along with several other honours. 41 pupils took part in the Ravensburg Exchange, the largest number in its history. Alison Grant, Deputy Head, began a year's secondment to Exeter University to complete her doctoral thesis on early North Devon Ceramics.

Helen Fry was a pupil at Park School from 1978 to 1983. After a B.A. and then a Ph.D. from Exeter University she has since had several history books published. Helen attributes much of her success to the excellent teaching she received at Park School, particularly from Berwick Coates and Alison Grant whose Ph.D. inspired her. Helen would have preferred Park School to have had its own Sixth Form.

Ian King doesn't think that all of the changes at Park in his time were for the better. *"We were permitted to study only a maximum of eight GCE O' levels, whereas in the Grammar days, able children would have been encouraged to take more than that. It was a disappointing example of the 'one size fits all' mentality... The changing intake contributed to greater indiscipline in classes and this definitely intensified during the later years I was there. There was much less respect shown to teachers by pupils, who became far more aware of their rights. It was also the dawn of the era when parents, on learning that their child had been disciplined at school, might complain rather than simply shrug and say 'it serves you right'... One pupil, a skinhead, used to turn up at school wearing earrings, Dr Marten boots and only a very vague approximation of the school uniform. In previous years he would probably have been sent home... I found it absolutely liberating going to the North Devon College for A' Levels because the quality of teaching there was, by and large, much better. Even though we were streamed at Park from the second year onwards, there were still people in the top stream who had no real desire to learn and who just spoiled things for the rest. There was none of that at the College. We all wanted to be there."*

Park's staffing level and its equipment, furniture and book allowances were all below national averages in 1980. Exam results were dismal. Only eight pupils passed eight subjects at GCE/CSE Grade I, only seven pupils passed in seven subjects, and only ten pupils passed in six subjects. Mr Morgan said that exam success wasn't everything and pointed to the wide range of extra-curricular activities on offer. Some parents voted with their feet. Jean and Alfred Crisp's son Andrew was a pupil at Park and they were both active in the Parent Teacher Association. But the Crisps' two youngest children went to Pilton because, when their turn came, *"Park was having a dip in standards"*. Mike Canham goes further. He is the current Chair of Governors at Park Community School, having arrived in Barnstaple in 1972 as Head of Maths, Science and Computing at the North Devon College. He speaks with some authority when he says: *"The school had a poor reputation. Pilton had newer buildings, better funding and a succession of charismatic Heads."* Mike believes it is easier for a Secondary Modern School to turn into a good Comprehensive than for a Grammar School to do so. Both of Mike's daughters attended Park School.

Emma Canham has some frank recollections of her early schooldays: *"The toilets at Park School introduced me to every swear-word I have ever encountered; graffiti on the walls and doors made eye-opening reading material. Just getting into the toilets required some nerve because you had to run the gauntlet of the smokers who spent a lot of time in there."* Bad behaviour seems to have been rather rife. *"There was great excitement when a boy with a grudge decided to leave a home-made bomb in the middle of the main school drive one afternoon. The police were called and the whole of the North building was evacuated. The 'bomb' turned out to be just a shoebox with batteries and a few wires sticking out of it."*

Corporal punishment was still in force for boys but, rather than Mr Morgan meting it out, the job fell to Bill Benson. Alison Grant says, *"As a Christian, it probably hurt Bill to do it. After he'd given a boy a thrashing, he'd tell him to come back to his office at 1pm for a counselling session."* He used to ask a colleague to witness his canings. Tony Pratt once witnessed the classic 'book down the trousers' technique. *"After the boy had been caned, Bill asked him to take the book out, and then he caned him again. He didn't have a great back-swing but he made up for it with a very deft wrist action."* Dr Grant says the main sanction for girls was detention but they begged for corporal punishment, which was over and done with more quickly.

In January 1980 a cash cafeteria system began for school dinners, with hot meals and hot snacks in the canteen, and soup, chips, cold snacks and drinks in the old Hall. By February Mr Morgan reported to Governors that the system was unsatisfactory and he wrote in his diary: *"A balanced diet has gone. It is chips with everything — usually a cream doughnut. There is no check on how pupils spend their money. Many spend it on sweets coming to school."* But Emma Canham was one pupil who was very clear about what she thought was the best school dinner: *"freshly cooked chips in a hotdog roll with grated cheese, a little lettuce and finished off with lots of salad cream!"*

The *Bardian* for 1980-81 said: *"Inflation has meant that the form of this magazine and even its very continuation has been questioned."* There was a plea to support the advertisers who were supporting the magazine. There were

two new woodwork rooms, a refurbished science laboratory, a new art room and a new secretarial office. Among educational trips, there was one to Italy and one to the Ford factory at Bridgend. There was a water polo team called 'Park Otters', a Tai Chi Club and a Dance Club. The intermediate school swimming gala was held for the first time at the Barnstaple Leisure Centre and from now on the school pool would get less

*Park Otters water polo team.*

*End of term caper, 1981.*

*New Sports Hall in use (this photo is from the 1990s and shows Graham Sloman taking a Year 8 group for basketball).*

*Geography Field Trip, 1981, with school minibus and Miss Jayne Freeman far right.*

use because the civic facility was superior. At Speech Day, the Head mentioned *"the 2% of pupils who make no attempt to learn and who try to prevent others from learning"*. He asked for a Special School locally for such maladjusted individuals.

Bob Blincow arrived on staff in 1980 and was responsible for starting up competitive football. *"I asked about the possibility at interview and I was informed that Park was a 'rugger' school. I already knew that because I was previously at Hele's School in Exeter and we had just beaten Park in the Devon Cup! Jimmy Morgan was very supportive though Alan Mackie, Head of P.E. and a firm rugby man, was sceptical."* One sport that was not for the faint-hearted was skiing. Dick Amery remembers: *"On the 1981 ski trip we drove 2½ hours each way every day by coach to find snow, having already driven 28 hours across Europe to get there. The worst skiing injury happened on a later trip, when my daughter Rebecca broke her leg."*

In 1981-82 a large new Sports Hall Complex was completed as a facility not just for the school but for use by the whole community outside of school hours. The girls' hockey team won the North Devon tournament. A new course in Computer Studies was incorporated into the curriculum. Barry Jackson, Art teacher, set designer and Head of Raleigh took early retirement and Mr Amery succeeded him as Head of Raleigh. New group activities included a Surf Week at Croyde in July and a two-day history course at the Athenaeum. There was a newspaper report on the thriving work experience programme organised by Mr Charlesworth: *"Each autumn, around 150 pupils in their fifth year are integrated into the labs at Yelland Power Station or work in High Street stores, local garages and a wide variety of other businesses from Primary Schools to plantations."*

**Cape Cod Tim...**

THE CAPE AND ISLANDS' DAILY NEWSPAPER

Vol. 48, No. 88                                    Thursday, April 12, 1984

## Barnstaple visitors enjoy Barnstable

HYANNIS — Ferried from one event to another in a shiny red double-decker bus and four-wheel-drive vehicles, 20 students from Barnstable's British sister city toured the villages of Barnstable yesterday.

The students and their nine adult chaperones from Barnstaple, England, crossed the Atlantic last week as part of an exchange program.

Last February, after a year of exchanging letters, 33 students and 11 adults from the Barnstaple Middle School visited Barnstable, England. Yesterday, the Cape Cod town returned the favor.

Selectman Martin J. Flynn was presented with a British Union Jack by Brian MacBeth, headmaster of the Park School in Barnstaple. Barnstable officials, in turn, gave commemorative plates and buttons with the seal of the town to every student.

Then the group was sent to Barnstable Village for a tour of the Barnstable County Complex, the Sandy Neck reservation for a four-wheel drive excursion and to Centerville for

*Bardian* magazine Number 19 for 1982-83 was the final ever issue. Its report on Speech Day was beautifully crafted: *"All those chairs! And tickets! The flowers! Would it be warm enough? Would the orchestra hit the right note? Would anyone actually come? We need not have worried. The hall was full, the music sweet, the speeches comprehensive, hard-hitting in places, and always expertly introduced. The guest speaker, Captain R. V. Holley RN, succeeded in being relevant and kindly and exceedingly humorous. He admitted he liked girls and he actually kissed the Head Girl!"* In other news, pupil numbers stood at 980, 136 fewer than 3 years previously. 26 Park School pupils plus ten staff and parents participated in an exchange visit with Barnstaple's twin town in Massachusetts. And the fifth form had a designated social area in the new Sports Hall, with coffee machine and table tennis table.

In February 1983 County Inspectors produced the first Inspection Report since 1953. It made several recommendations for change: *"The standard of internal decoration is generally poor in the north building and the overall impression is one of drabness. Provision in some of the older classrooms is unsatisfactory, with desks of uneven height covered in graffiti... Parts of the school environment will have to be made more attractive and stimulating as an encouragement to learning... The predominantly didactic teaching style in the school is not always effective as a means of engaging some average and academically low-ability pupils... The curriculum requires more coherence within it and an improved balance of subjects for some pupils in years 4 and 5."*

An information pack sent out to parents in 1983 referred to a 'Unit for Specific Learning Difficulties' designed for approximately twelve pupils with a qualified tutor. The overall streaming policy was spelled out in detail: *"In their first year the majority of children are placed in mixed ability teaching groups, while some who have experienced difficulties with reading and/or mathematics receive remedial education."* In subsequent years children were placed in three different teaching groups dependent upon their ability in English, Maths and French. There was a wide range of options in fourth and fifth years and most pupils followed a course leading to C.S.E. and/or G.C.E. examinations. The information pack also mentioned that a fully qualified nurse was in school every day.

Emma Canham describes a nightmare third-year camping trip to the Lake District at Easter 1984: *"The trip got off to a bad start when the trailer being towed by the school minibus had a flat tyre, causing a long delay at the motorway services. We eventually arrived at the campsite in the dark, looking forward to a hot meal, but the gas canisters for the cookers were empty, having not been checked before we left. It was a Bank Holiday weekend and there were no shops open to change them... As the week wore on, the weather deteriorated, culminating in gales. We girls were woken up in the middle of the night when our big tent took off, leaving our belongings blowing across the field in the dark. One of my friends became hysterical, throwing mud at the teacher's tent. Someone else tried to run away and was eventually found waiting for a train at the railway station. Salvation finally came when we were allowed to stay at a nearby hotel for the last two nights."*

In 1984 Jimmy Morgan's Senior Staff consisted of Dr Alison Grant as Deputy Head for girls, Reverend William Benson as Deputy Head for boys, John Charlesworth as Director of Studies responsible for curriculum and timetable, and four Heads of House responsible for pastoral care - Jonathan Baxter (Drake), Tony Pratt (Fortescue), Ken Doughty (Kingsley) and Dick Amery (Raleigh). It was an extremely experienced team with a leader who had been in post for 14 years. In July, Mr Morgan retired.

## James W. Morgan B.Sc.
## Headmaster, 1970-1984

Mr Morgan had been a Battle of Britain pilot in World War Two. He has been described as 'the last of the Gentlemen Heads'. Looking back over his 14 years, some say he managed the transition to a Comprehensive School skilfully, as a gentle process of evolution rather than revolution. Others argue that he held on to old traditions for too long. But everyone who knew Jimmy Morgan spoke very warmly of him and with genuine respect – he was a very nice man, if a little out of date in some respects...

Tony Pratt: *"Jimmy Morgan was never seen around the school other than in a dark suit and highly polished black shoes which would squeak as he rocked back and forth. His manners were impeccable. He was always polite, hard-working, approachable and fair. He was a man of the old school in every sense of the word."*

Ken Doughty: *"A superb chap whom I grew to like all the more as time passed. A natural gentleman, he constantly increased the respect one held for him. His leadership style was firm, courteous and kind with total and complete integrity."*

Chris Ley: *"Jimmy Morgan had a true passion for the school. He was very much a Grammar School Head and much of the Grammar ethos remained after the school went comprehensive. He had a presence which is difficult to describe. You could sense him in the staffroom even when you couldn't see him. At the whole-school assembly when he retired, Bill Benson was in tears."*

Sadly, Mr Morgan's retirement was short-lived. He died before the end of the 1980s.

Mr Morgan's diary covers his entire tenure and offers insights into what Headmasters do for a living. There is an entry for most working days, always beautifully hand-written with a fountain pen. Mr Morgan probably used the log as an aide memoire though it's not clear whom he intended to read his terser comments. Perhaps the diary became a release valve. There are two clear trends over 14 years: more and more of HM's time is spent on meetings and training days, often away from Barnstaple, preparing for the next curricular or organisational initiatives; and there is a strong sense that the school gradually became less insular and more responsive to broader political and social changes. But the diary isn't all serious. Some entries have already been quoted. Here is just one more per year to give a fuller flavour...

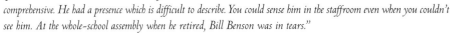

## Extracts from 'Jimmy' Morgan's Diary

*Dec 15 1970: Fifth and Sixth Form Dance held in New Hall. Employment of Securicor guards with dog prevented any problems with gate-crashers.*

*Feb 9 1971: Sixth Form debate with outside speakers. Mr T. Keigwin, the Tory candidate, was rather upset by the 'liberal' views of the students and refused to stay for tea. Rather a petty attitude.*

*Oct 13 1972: Chairman of Governors, Chief County Adviser and HM dealt with a continual feud between two members of staff by telling one of them that he must accept the authority of his Head of Department. (After further disciplinary meetings over three years, the teacher concerned moved to another school. Mr Morgan's comment then was: "No regrets, but much sympathy for the other school.")*

*Apr 11 1973: HM attended meeting with Divisional Education Officer and Archdeacon of Barnstaple to discuss recent press reports containing gross exaggerations of the sexual behaviour of Sixth Form students.*

*May 8 1974: Mr Slocombe from Divisional Office came to discuss the siting of a Sports Hall. (This shows the long lead time on major capital projects – the new Sports Hall would not be completed until 1982.)*

*Nov 15 1975: HM attended a meeting at Braunton Road Motel entitled 'What's Education For?' He is still puzzled.*

*Apr 5 1976: Easter Concert. The standard was embarrassing. (This eventually led to the appointment of a new Head of Music and to what Mr Morgan regarded as a significant improvement thereafter in the standard of school music events.)*

*Mar 11 1977: Interviews for Head of Science. This was a real marathon. Physics, Chemistry and Biology need welding into a new Department. Also, new courses need to be introduced. We interviewed a national field but by 7pm there was a unanimous decision to appoint Mr F. Lee – an internal candidate.*

*Sep 4 1978: Autumn term began with a record staff of HM + 61.5 teachers. Also record pupil numbers – 1,116. You can feel the pressure in corridors, halls and even in the playground. CSE results are rather disappointing.*

*Dec 3 1979: Staff meeting to discuss reallocation of 2nd and 3rd year pupils. Still too many 'nice' girls staying in top band. We need to be more ruthless.*

*Apr 23 1980: Staff meeting to discuss the idea of setting up a unit for children with Specific Learning Difficulties. Very strong opposition. Staff suspicious this will just involve more behaviour problems in school. I think the idea has good potential. HM to visit other units and report back at next staff meeting.*

*Nov 19 1981: Duke of Edinburgh Awards Presentation evening at West Buckland School. 20 of our pupils received silver awards and 25 bronze awards. One former pupil gained a gold award. A new record and the result of hard work by Mr R. Amery.*

*Dec 16 1982: Meeting at Area Office. There is now an imbalance in numbers between Park and Pilton Schools. Park is dropping while Pilton is rising. A slight change in the catchment area would solve the problem but there seems little chance.*

*Mar 24 1983: Governors received an oral report from Mr Silvester, HMI, on the recent school inspection. Adverse report on the general standard of decoration and upkeep of school building and grounds. Teachers stay too long (perhaps they like the school) and too many men. House system praised. Pastoral system very caring.*

*Sep 1 1984: I leave with very mixed feelings. It has been a great school to work for with so many pupils gaining tremendously from their time here. There have been all kinds of very enjoyable occasions with pupils, staff, parents and governors. It has been a very full-time job, very rewarding and interesting and I have felt it a privilege to serve such a school. But I am now looking forward to following some of my own interests and hobbies. I wish the school every success in the future.*

In 1984 someone with a good camera took some nice photographs which ended up in the archive cupboard. A few of the best ones merit inclusion here before we move on to a new era with a new Headmaster.

*Derek Slade in a science lab.*

*View across north playground towards Park Lane. From 2008 this view has been obscured by the building of the support and study centre for special needs in this playground.*

*Scene from* Arsenic and Old Lace *in 1984, with scenery and costumes reminiscent of the 1967 production.*

*Sports Day field from science block.*

*Ken Doughty in his element.*

*Girls-only swimming lesson in Mollison Pool, which is now looking rather shabby around the edges.*

# CHAPTER 9

# A GOOD SHAKE UP, 1984-1997

IN SEPTEMBER 1984 Arthur Hodgetts replaced Jimmy Morgan as Head Teacher. Mr Hodgetts had experienced Comprehensive Education at first hand as a pupil in the Midlands and had taught for 17 years in four different Comprehensive Schools before coming to Park. Anyone hoping for a new broom to sweep away the last remnants of the Grammar School would not be disappointed. He had a clear vision of what he felt needed to be done and was prepared to sacrifice his own popularity to achieve it. But how much the incoming Head can personally take the credit (or the blame) for the many changes in the school during his 13 year tenure is not a straightforward matter, because this was a period of great upheaval in education nationally. Mr Hodgetts inherited a school that was somewhat in the doldrums and his own Headship was not at all plain sailing. But by the time he left office in 1997 Park School was proclaimed as a beacon to others. By then too, the job of being a Head Teacher in an English Comprehensive School had been radically transformed.

For the sake of clarity, in this chapter the big issues of the period will be dealt with first. The biggest issue was the raft of Education Acts passed by the Conservative governments of the 1980s, culminating in the 'Baker' Act of 1988, which changed the landscape of British secondary education.

---

## The 1988 Education Act and Its Consequences

Sometimes simply called 'Baker', after Education Secretary Kenneth Baker who introduced it, this Act was the most important education reform since 1944. It was presented as giving power to schools but it actually took some powers away and gave them to the Secretary of State. The power of LEAs was seriously weakened. The main initiatives were as follows:

- **The National Curriculum.** Teachers and schools would no longer decide what to teach. Instead, they had to deliver courses whose content was prescribed by legislation.
- **Testing and League Tables.** Each pupil was to be assessed across a myriad of 'attainment targets', which proved unworkable and had to be reduced. League tables of exam results would be published and parents would, in theory, be able to choose which school they wanted their child to attend. A public service turned into a market. Some schools became reluctant to take pupils with learning difficulties because they brought down average scores.
- **Religious Education and Collective Worship.** Although other faiths were to be acknowledged, every day had to start with a 'predominantly Christian' act of collective worship. The definitions provoked plenty of argument.
- **Local Management of Schools (LMS).** Previously, schools controlled only their budget for books and materials. Under LMS, schools were given control of almost the whole budget, though staff costs accounted for much of the total so any scope for changing spending priorities was limited. Budgets were to be based on pupil numbers so schools had to attract pupils. Many believe the Act's real purpose was to

---

> push the blame onto schools when budgets were cut, as they were in six of the next eight years.
>
> ■ **Governing Bodies.** More parents were added to school governing bodies, which would now have legal responsibilities for implementing the National Curriculum, determining school policy on sex education, acting as an appeal court on disciplinary matters and controlling the school budget. Heads would often look to their Governors for management expertise on such things as employment law and buildings maintenance. Governors were to produce an annual report and hold an annual parents' meeting. But it was not clear how unpaid volunteers could be held legally accountable.
>
> ■ **Ofsted.** The 'Office for Standards in Education' would be a quango employing private contractors to inspect schools and publish reports. It was established in 1992 with Chris Woodhead as Chief Inspector of Schools. Ofsted inspections quickly caused stress and resentment among teachers, especially when Ofsted reports were used as a basis for 'naming and shaming' so-called 'failing' schools.

During Mr Hodgetts' time as Head wave after wave of new government initiatives left him and his staff navigating troubled and stressful waters. The role of computers took a quantum leap and Park introduced GCSEs, more residential activities, Personal and Social Education, GNVQs, Records of Achievement, and a National Contract for Teachers to include 1265 hours of 'directed time'. One colleague credited Arthur Hodgetts with an extraordinary ability to keep up with all the latest vagaries of legislation and regulations.

In 1985 the government proposed linking teacher appraisal and performance-related pay. The result was a year of industrial action by the teaching unions. Mr Hodgetts joined the strike action himself as a member of NAS/AWT and this won him a measure of respect from colleagues, though Governors were less impressed. During this period a girl called Sarah Hearn led a student sit-in protesting in part about being disrupted by the teachers' action. After attempts at reasoning had failed Sarah was suspended and, although she carried the argument to the media, Governors upheld her exclusion.

Looking back on the days before the various initiatives outlined above, teacher Alan Mackie observes: *"There was very little stress-related illness among staff and very few courses for staff to attend, so there was very little need for supply teachers or for staff to cover colleagues during their free periods. There was often time during the school day for a game of bridge in the staff room, a game of tennis, or a swim in the school pool. Before the introduction of the 1265-hour contract, people didn't count the hours they worked and many gave a lot of time to extra-curricular activities. After the contract was introduced extra-curricular activities couldn't be enforced and many clubs and societies waned."* The years of relentless change left many teachers suffering initiative fatigue or worse and there were times when a strong camaraderie was needed to keep staff together.

Arthur Hodgetts evoked mixed feelings as a leader of his staff. Some say he was a good organiser and even a visionary, but others were questioning of his people-management skills. Teachers who had been around since the Grammar School days sometimes felt that the Head was dismissive of the school's heritage and that also caused friction with Old Bardians among the Governors. More recent staff knew that change was needed and that the school could no longer continue to trade on its past. David Atton, who arrived in 1986, observed: *"I found a school with a strong core of staff intensely loyal to its heritage at a time of significant change. The old was being swept away but concern fuelled an uncertain confidence for what might be replacing it."*

Mr Hodgetts says: *"Being a Head is not for faint hearts. You get a vision of where the school needs to be and you then have to get everybody there whether they want to go or not."* One colleague admits, *"Some staff were not quite up to the task of delivering a suitable education to the fully comprehensive intake. The staffroom needed a good shake up".* Although Mr Hodgetts did not seek to be popular, one colleague firmly believes that his heart was in the right place and says, *"Arthur was a man of huge vision and deep concern for the students in his care."*

Arthur Hodgetts is the only former Headmaster the author has been able to interview for this book since all of his predecessors died in the twentieth century. Looking back, these were his priorities and his achievements:

**Changing the Punitive Aspect of the School.** *"Within my first term, Bill Benson came to me and said, 'I cane the boys here, Headmaster, what are your views?' I replied, 'I've never caned a child in my life and I don't intend to start now. From that day forward, no child was ever caned again at Park School."* There was no formal policy change, and no edict had to be ordered. Reverend Benson had presumably received permission to follow his heart. The ending of corporal punishment nationally awaited a 1985 judgement in the European Court of Human Rights.

**Adding Rewards for Achievement and Effort.** The aim here was to *"incentivise the majority not just the most able and most sporty pupils."* Trying hard came to be valued as much as winning or getting top grades. Mindful that Park served the most disadvantaged area of North Devon, Mr Hodgetts came up with the phrase 'Excellence and Achievement for All' as a new mission statement. 'Excellence for All' prevails to this day on Park School letter-heads.

**Focusing on Curriculum & Staffing.** *"The vision here was for nine curriculum areas. I appointed Heads to all of them and created coherent teams working together."* Appointing people to key positions is one of the biggest aspects of any Head's legacy and Mr Hodgetts can claim important members of the team that propelled the school forward. As Deputy Heads he appointed Sue McEldon and David Atton. In key departmental roles he either brought in or promoted: Jean Evans-Loude (English), Robert Barber (Expressive Arts), Dave Rowsell (Humanities and Learning Resources), Pat Kivlin (Maths), Peter Elmy (Science), and Bob Blincow (Design and Technology).

**Establishing the School Council.** Each tutor group nominated students to be on House Councils and each House had delegates on the School Council, which met each term with the Head and Mrs McEldon. The students brought up many issues that might not otherwise have been raised – about lockers, playgrounds, toilets etc. It was part of a bigger social process of giving children a say and its culmination came in the late '90s when students from the School Council began taking part in the interview process for all new senior staff.

**Introducing Personal and Social Education (PSE).** This was a national initiative to make part of the curriculum directly relevant to everyday life and citizenship, but schools had some freedom over what to include and how to treat it. PSE at Park initially included sex education, family life and relationships, consumer education and moral education. There were modules taught by form tutors for two periods per week with outside specialists such as health visitors assisting where appropriate. Alan Mackie was a key member of the leadership team in this field having attended a year's course in Exeter.

**Improving Accommodation.** Mr Hodgetts says, *"These were all Tory years, so there were strictures on capital expenditure. Frankly, it was a struggle to get money to paint a classroom."* Given the political climate, setting up the Learning and Resources Centre in 1986, and improving the provision for Humanities, Maths, English and Expressive Arts were all considerable achievements. On top of that an artificial all-weather sports facility was created by bringing in funding from unconventional sources, including the new National Lottery.

**Piloting Local Management of Schools.** Park was one of Devon's Pilot Schools and Mr Hodgetts was on various committees for LMS. He says that around 25% of the budget was flexible and that *"a Head who couldn't get what he wanted under this system didn't deserve the job."* In particular, the balance of genders and ages of staff could be affected by recruitment strategies and gradually more women and more young teachers joined the staff.

❖

The historian writing about the period from 1985 onwards at Park School faces a major limitation, namely that the *Bardian* magazine was discontinued in 1983 and so there was no regular account of the school's events from the student point of view. Governors' minutes had ceased to be colourful and official newsletters tend to present an institutional perspective. To make matters worse, former pupils from the last 25 years have not stepped forward in numbers to contribute anecdotes about their school life, as they did for the 1940s, '50s, '60s and '70s. Thankfully, some key members of staff have been willing to talk and the archive cupboard contains a few gems.

Two attempts were made to re-start a student magazine. An undated copy of *SPLAT!* is in the School Archive from around 1984. It contains a miscellany of creative fiction,

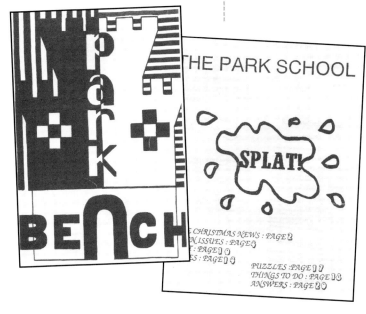

serious articles (eg: on Green issues), cartoons, puzzles and adverts. It was duplicated on white A4 paper and stapled. It didn't last and neither did a 1992 publication, *Park Bench*, which had an interview with the Head in which he said that his least favourite subject at school had been Music.

Soon after Mr Hodgetts arrived, regular hymn-singing came to an end at assemblies, which were House–based and which each child attended three times a week. Dick Amery recalls: *"From September 1985, hymns were sung on special occasions and at the end of term only. The last recorded attempt at House singing by Raleigh was at Easter 1987. It failed dismally. Very few pupils knew the words to 'There is a Green Hill Far Away'."* Reverend Benson's retirement in 1986 may have been a factor but Mr Hodgetts says: *"hymn singing was already withering on the vine nationally and would have come up for discussion when hymn books needed replacing."* Singing and music continued to have a place in the curriculum. Assemblies became less overtly religious despite the legal requirement to provide 'an act of collective worship'. Themes like 'humility', 'faith' and 'tolerance' were evolved to cater for all faiths.

The House system remained the primary focus for pastoral care within the school despite Mr Hodgetts' instincts to replace it by a Year-based system. It has evolved into a much-envied selling point for Park and is perhaps the greatest continuing legacy of the Grammar School era. There was a Merit Trophy awarded every half term for the House whose members earned the greatest number of merit cards – small yellow slips given by teachers for good work or behaviour. Prefects were no longer selected but could qualify by upholding key standards codified in a contract confirmed with their Head of House.

In January 1985 the Admin Committee of senior staff discussed *"complaints from parents about the state of the toilets and about the behaviour of senior girls in the toilets. Younger girls did not feel safe and bullying, real or imaginary, was an issue."* The question of grey trousers for girls had also been raised and it was agreed to amend the uniform rules to include them.

The accounts of the Park School Parent Teacher Association for the year ending July 1985 show around £2,000 in receipts from Discos, Car Boot Sales, a Christmas Dance, a summer Barbecue, and a Fashion Show. Over the years, PTA fund-raising had provided the swimming pool, the minibus, the P.A. system and camping equipment and much else besides. The Tuck Shop closed to avoid competition with the newly-privatised canteen, which now took on the sale of crisps and snacks. Governors' minutes for 1985 noted that this deprived the School Fund of £800 of income which the Tuck Shop had contributed the previous year out of a total miscellaneous income of £2,992.

1985 brought the first edition of a single folded news-sheet called *Park School News*. Mr Hodgetts wrote a piece saying that he hoped to change the *"bleak drabness"* of the school, whose superb site deserved better. He admired the pupils' fast response in collecting £500 in 3 weeks for the Ethiopian Famine appeal and he floated the idea of fund-raising through non-uniform days. He invited everyone to submit their ideas of how Park School could change for the better. A Dance Club was now being held every Monday after

*Park School News (this one is from 1987).*

hours. There was a **mixed** Gymnastics Club on Tuesday and Thursday lunchtimes. A Park School team entered the North Devon Volleyball League and won 10 out of 11 matches. In October a joint volleyball, netball and basketball tour of Guernsey was organised by Mr Mackie and Miss Brigden.

The end of the summer term brought the retirement of Dr Grant after 20 years as a Deputy Head.

## Dr Alison E. Grant B.A. Ph.D.
## Deputy Head, 1965-85

Alison Grant was born in 1928 in Middlesex and studied for a B.A. in History at King's College, London. She came to Barnstaple after a 15 year stint at a mixed Grammar School in Edgware, where she was Head of History.

As Deputy Head and Senior Mistress in charge of the welfare and discipline of girls at the newly co-educational BGS, her organisational duties left little time for teaching. But she took charge of the Sixth Form Society, established a popular lunch-time Folk Dance Society and stimulated interest in archaeology. Miss Grant found Comprehensive Education to be *"better in theory than in practice"*. Mr Morgan had described her as an excellent, loyal and committed Deputy who served the school to her utmost. He was particularly complimentary about the way she tackled sensitive issues – *"firmly but fairly, with thoroughly rational arguments"*.

In view of her Ph.D. thesis on North Devon Ceramics, a beautiful pottery jug inscribed with her name and the school motto was an apt retirement present. She has since written a dozen books, including social histories of Instow, Appledore and Bideford.

Dr Alison Grant with fellow Deputy Heads John Charlesworth and, Reverend Bill Benson in 1984.

Mrs Sue McEldon took over from Alison Grant as Senior Mistress, becoming one of three Deputy Heads, along with Bill Benson and John Charlesworth. Her special responsibilities were for pastoral care, PSE and Special Needs teaching, liaison with parents, and Years 1 and 2. She recalls arriving for interview in April 1985: *"I found myself in a gender time warp. Boys were called by their surnames and the playground was a football pitch, around the edge of which girls gathered in small groups. My own son was a pupil and I had already argued with the previous Head about a letter inviting Dads to 'come and find out about the new computer age' and Mums to 'come and make the tea'. On appointment I determined to work on the equality of girls and to do something about the social and emotional development of all pupils."* In her second year, Sue organised an away-day for staff on 'PSE Teaching and the Development of Emotional Intelligence'. A male-dominated institution was finally getting in touch with its feminine side. The Head of Kingsley had to be told that it was not acceptable to separate girls and boys in assemblies and then punish boys who came late by making them sit with the girls. Sue McEldon says, *"I soon grew very fond of Ken Doughty, who once said to me, 'I think we're getting somewhere with all this sex, drugs and first aid we're teaching. I'm learning a lot myself!'"*

Julie Bennett became a pupil at Park School in September 1985 and she looks back on her early years with a smile. *"Our first year disco was awash with shocking pink regardless of gender. 12 year olds strutted their stuff - boys on one side of the hall rocking Status Quo style and girls on the opposite side swaying to Wham and A-ha. Over the years the fashions*

Sue McEldon.

*didn't improve - puff ball skirts, Miami Vice rolled up sleeves and pineapple hair styles for the girls, and spiked hair and tramlines for the boys. Crazes came and went but none was as contagious as yoyos. Virtually every student was 'walking the dog' or creating a 'cradle'. There was even a lunchtime competition with a panel of judges giving points and comments."*

Park School already had a Counsellor, David Nelson, who was available every day to help with any difficulties pupils might have with lessons, homework, friends, teachers, tests, or home. He worked on bullying and improving attendance and offered pupils a safe place to go if they were feeling low or needed a good cry. The school also now had a Unit at Alexandra Road where some pupils received full-time special help for a term or longer before returning to the main school. Another special unit operating at this time was for students with dyslexia. Anton Eratt, a dyslexic boy with significant reading and writing difficulties, did well thanks to the guidance and expertise of Roger Mullis, who dictated whole novels onto tape for dyslexics doing exams. Anton went on to read Physics at Oxford and now runs his own I.T. Company.

In 1986 it was announced that GCE O' Levels and CSEs were to be abolished and they were replaced within a year by General Certificate of Secondary Education (GCSE) exams. 36 staff attended outside courses at some point in the year. Contributions to the School Fund were doubled from 25 to 50 pence per term. The water supply to the swimming pool was switched off as a result of excessive water consumption caused by leaks. This followed PTA concerns about safety so Governors declared the pool unusable and it was eventually earthed over. There was concern too about the well-being of pupils who were being inadequately supervised at lunchtimes because of the teachers' industrial action.

A 'Welcome Booklet' for all Year 7 starters in 1986 said that about a quarter of all pupils ate packed lunches. The booklet gave sample menus for the school canteen and said, *"If you get free school meals then you can choose any sensible balanced meal up to the daily allowance of 67p, but you are not allowed 'unwise' choices such as five packets of crisps!"* Burger and chips at 51p was still acceptable. Weather conditions for the 1986 Ten Tors Expedition were ranked alongside 1967 and 1973 for atrociousness and only one Park team and one lone individual completed it.

The greatest pupil achievement of 1986 was when a Park School team captained by Stephen McKeever and supported by teacher David Morgan beat 2,901 other teams to win the National Fire Prevention Quiz. One of their trophies, a mounted fireman's axe, was displayed on the wall in Reception and later used during a burglary to break down the door of Mr Hodgetts' office!

In 1986, Bill Benson retired after 31 years at the School. He was replaced as Deputy Head by David Atton, who came from a similar role in Torrington. Head of Drama Robert Barber had already taken over production of school plays. *Bugsy Malone*, with Tim Coles in the title role, involved guns, gangsters, sedans and chorus girls.

*National Fire Prevention Quiz winners, 1986, with axes later used in a burglary!*

## Reverend William G. ('Fritz'/'Bill') Benson B.A.
## Teacher and Deputy Head, 1955-1986

'Bill' Benson was born in 1926 and was educated at Battersea Grammar School and London University. He then did a diploma in Tübingen and three years teaching at Queen Elizabeth's in Crediton before being appointed as a German teacher at BGS.

Among his long term contributions to Grammar/Park are the Ravensburg Exchange, which ran for 40 years from 1959, and the production of school plays from 1963 to 1984. He became successively Head of BGS Junior School (Forms 1-3), Head of Fortescue House, Senior Master and Deputy Head for Staff and Community, responsible for in-service training. Bill was one of the best and most respected teachers of his day and he remained popular even when he became the person responsible for caning boys. After retirement he became Minister at Newport Church for a time, keeping an ongoing interest in Park School. He died in April 2003.

Carol Vanderpeer, the long-term Cleaning Supervisor at Park School, reports tales of a ghost which haunted one of the North Building quadrangles at this time: *"A cleaner working in one of the temporary huts felt something 'rush past her face' and not long afterwards a contractor experienced the same thing in the roof space above the corridor by the quad."* Carol also remembers Tony Pratt and Dick Amery with a broad smile: *"Both worked late and so we always saw them. They were great characters with offices at opposite ends of South Building so they were like bookends — upholding the establishment."*

*Cleaners Val Hornby and Keith Biggs.*

The summer 1988 edition of *Park School News* reported that teachers and pupils faced the new GCSE examinations for the first time. Fifth Formers had regularly challenged *"the flabbier members of staff"* to football matches. Work produced for the Armada celebrations was on display in Barnstaple Library and Activity Days had been repeated by popular request. The new Governing Body had five Parent Governors but the early statutory Annual Governors' Meetings with parents got off to a bad start with hardly anyone turning up, as this amusing memory from Sue McEldon reveals: *"The main Hall echoed to the murmur of Governors' voices only and at intervals the lights, which were noise-activated at night, would switch off, whereupon the Head would stamp his feet loudly to put them back on again! Various things were tried to encourage a better attendance but these meetings were never a sell-out."*

Park had the best results of any school in North Devon in the last ever GCE O' Levels in 1987, but even these were improved on in 1988 with GCSE results well above the national and county averages. It was announced that the school day would finish at 3.20 from January 1989, reducing the lunch time period in order to avoid any loss of lesson time. The Library and Resources Centre would stay open until 4.30.

In 1988, Richard Wakely came straight from a building site for an interview as an assistant caretaker. His clothes and boots were covered in cement dust. The other two candidates waiting to be seen both wore suits and ties. Luckily, Arthur Hodgetts didn't want a caretaker who looked posh but one who could solve practical problems so Richard got the job. He became Senior Caretaker in 1997, and he's still there in centenary year. Looking back on more than 20 years, Richard says: *"When I first came here, the school was really dark and dismal. All the toilets were ancient and smelly and had leaking roofs. Soon afterwards the North Building toilets were gutted and the paintwork was given a facelift. The wooden floors of classrooms*

*Richard Wakeley, caretaker since 1988.*

*and corridors needed stripping and re-sealing every summer holiday and they had to be buffed every night until they were carpeted. When the school took over under LMS our conditions improved. We're jacks of all trades – unblocking drains, building walls, changing light bulbs and tubes, glazing, mending plugs, putting up shelves – and I've been on numerous courses for Health and Safety and DIY."*

In September 1989 Sue Lee was appointed as Head of Drake to become Park School's first ever female Head of House. There were strong internal male candidates but Arthur Hodgetts only interviewed women. Six other female teachers were appointed in the course of the year as part of a deliberate strategy to change the balance of genders within the staff room.

There were plans to create a single new system of General National Vocational Qualifications - GNVQs. At Park, only business subjects were ever embraced under this initiative when it began in 1992 and GNVQs have since fallen by the wayside. Students were now leaving school with a 'Record of Achievement', a document summarising their achievements in and out of school. It included a C.V., a statement negotiated between student and tutor, and a statement of positive achievement from each subject area. A fair number of former pupils from Park School were gaining Oxbridge places via the North Devon College, which took around 75% of Year 11 leavers.

From 1989 the old PTA became known as the Parents and Friends Association. In June they held a fund-raising fête in Rock Park with a Tug of War, majorettes, various sideshows and produce stalls. The highlight was the 'Duck Race', which involved 250 numbered ducks being launched from the Long Bridge towards the main event upstream. The sponsor of the winning duck would win £100 so people gathered on the riverbank to watch. Sue McEldon takes up the story: *"Suddenly, the cry went up from one of the canoeists in the water that the tide was turning. I picked up the finishing post and ran with it towards the now retreating ducks! One duck was well ahead so the winner was easy to spot. But when David Atton announced the result it turned out that I was holding the winning ticket!"*

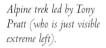

*Alpine trek led by Tony Pratt (who is just visible extreme left).*

There were various opportunities at Park for residential experience – language exchanges, geography field trips, sports tours and ski trips, tutor group visits, and 'adventure weeks' in Years 7 and 11 designed to help develop personal skills and self-confidence. Sue McEldon recalls one particular adventure week at a centre in Lyme Regis where they did activities like climbing, abseiling and canoeing. *"One night, our group leaders informed us we would be bivouacking. After we'd collected firewood and cooked a hot meal, Fred Lee and I busied ourselves helping youngsters find a good spot for rigging up shelters and somewhere in the woods to use as a toilet, which was a real trauma for some. It was dark when everyone was settled and Fred and I bunked down on my tarpaulin and used his tarpaulin as a cover from the rain. Next morning we were woken by a boy wanting to know about lighting the fire for breakfast. Seeing us under the tarpaulin, he said, 'Oh hello, Miss, I didn't know you were sleeping with Mr Lee'. We had been so preoccupied with practicalities that we hadn't given a thought to the way things looked!"*

Julie Bennett became Head Girl in her final year, 1990-91. Nearly 20 years later, a flood of impressions come tumbling back to her… *"In Biology, the horror of dissecting a sheep's eyeball and the collection and counting of*

*Lyme Regis Residential, 1989.*

worms... In Food Technology, making baked beans from raw soya beans, which eventually stuck to the tin and had to be prised off using tools from the woodwork room... the delectable chocolate 'squidgy' from the school canteen, always warm, with caramel and chocolate oozing on top of a shortbread biscuit... pushing unsuspecting fellow students down the embankment... covering text books in your favourite wrapping paper... having a 'jam' at the cricket pavilion with guitars and voices ... the Duke of Edinburgh scheme - eating cold rice pudding for breakfast, loosening the tent pegs of companions to create a flurry of confusion in the middle of the night... Young Enterprise Awards, where I made £1.35 profit... two students who were sponsored to live inside a large display case in the Reception area for a whole day...Bugsy Malone and Oh What a Lovely War were very professional productions, with staff and students dedicating many weekends and evenings to them, motivated by the inspirational Robert Barber..."

Robert Barber himself remembers *Oh What A Lovely War* for the cat that fused the local sub station and cut the lights on the first night. Another early production, *Cabaret*, was inspired by "one brilliant student" but "it turned out that I had many brilliant students so we had a double cast which alternated over the four nights." Revues also blossomed around this time with fifth formers and staff getting together for a fun time.

In 1990, an 'Inspection Review' was put together by Devon County Council and consisted of statements by the Head Teacher, reports by Advisors and a list of points for action. It was the first review since the rather adverse inspection report of 1983. The Advisor reports praised the

*Staff/Student Revue, 1992. Back row from left: Pat Kivlin (Head of Maths), Kerry Reed; Middle row: Kevin Adcock (Counsellor), John Sharpe (Physics), Bob Blincow (Head of D.T.) Helen Munro; Front row: Angie Robertson, Zoe Eckett, Sarah Stocker, Jane Featherstone (R.E.) and Jayne Gayton.*

school's *"significant areas of strength"*, which were: staff/student relationships; the range and depth of experience among teaching staff; the broad and balanced curriculum; the teaching of PSE; work with students with special needs; the House and tutoring system. Areas the advisors thought required further development included: developing consistent policies on marking work and recording achievement; forging links with Primary Schools to ensure continuity; coordinating careers work within PSE; improving the environment of the school, for example by a wider use of displays of student work and directional signage.

Mr Hodgetts' 'Head's Statements' reviewed the changes of the last five years – how the school had responded to various national requirements. The implementation of the National Curriculum was still in the early stages for Maths and Science in Year 7, and other requirements were *"far from clear"*. The school had revised its timetable, changed the structure of the school day, and improved the accommodation for Special Educational Needs. The building stock still required considerable attention – seven separate buildings plus temporary classrooms, dating from 1910-1982, were in a *"fair to poor condition"* and Governors needed

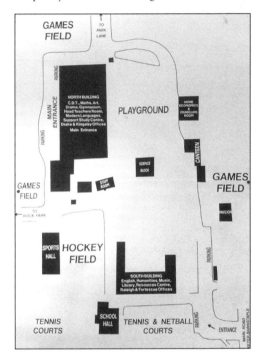

*Plan of the school from mid 1990s before the building expansion.*

additional LEA grants to improve this. The Parents and Friends Association was providing lockers for pupils because normal school finances could not meet the need. Mr Hodgetts threw down a gauntlet: *"The school will exceed its planned admission numbers in September 1990. This is likely to continue and capital developments for expanded accommodation will be essential."*

The School Prospectus for 1991-92 explained all the latest developments to new students and their parents. There was an emphasis on partnership: *"When a child becomes a member of the Park School, so also do the parents. In order to encourage effective learning we seek to forge a partnership between home and school"* Mrs McEldon visited every feeder Primary with a group of Year 7 pupils and a video to introduce prospective newcomers to Park. There was an introductory evening for new parents and then tutors contacted them in the first term to find out how children were settling in.

The old 1st, 2nd and 3rd Year designations were changed to Years 7, 8 and 9, emphasising the continuity from Primary, which ends with Year 6. Since the introduction of the National Curriculum, new terminology was also now in use to describe broad curriculum areas. 'Technology' included Business Education, Craft Design, Home Economics and Information Technology. 'Humanities' encompassed Geography, History and Religion. 'Expressive Arts' included Art, Drama and Music. Some PSE themes – Careers, Health, Citizenship, I.T. and Environmental Education – crossed many subjects. Careers Guidance and a Careers Library were more developed now, with a Careers Coordinator, Sue Edmonds, and another active partnership, this time between the school and local industry.

Everything seemed to be going terribly well...

Then, in 1992, the first league tables of GCSE results were published, based on 'raw scores' and not allowing for calibre of intake. They put Park School in seventh position out of the nine North Devon secondary schools. This formalised a perception among many parents and some Governors that the school was not yet out of the doldrums. Mr Hodgetts says he told Chris Woodhead personally that *"the publication of raw scores will destroy good schools"*.

This is David Atton's take on the situation: *"When other local schools, now 'rivals', were astutely connecting with their communities and developing inviting profiles for prospective pupils and their families, Park allowed itself to become somewhat detached. The league tables confirmed that any lingering loyalty to Park just because it had once been the Grammar School was misplaced. Loyalty had to be earned. The developing nature of the catchment inevitably placed us low in the local GCSE league. Ironically, Park's 'Special Needs Unit for Specific Learning Difficulties' drew children from across the area. If your child had a learning difficulty, Park was the place to go. Unfortunately, the school's academic credentials did not command similar respect, despite a dedicated and talented staff working very hard."*

The School Prospectus for 1992-3 began by saying, *"The school was formed in 1972 on the Barnstaple Grammar School site"* and it stressed the separation from the Grammar School past by emphasising that Park now served the wider community, particularly through the *"Community Sports Centre"*. The school blazer became optional,

another act of separation from tradition. There were now classroom assistants to help *"students with statements of special educational needs"*. There was also a team of technicians and resource assistants providing support for teachers in many subjects. The school budget approached £1,700,000. But none of this changed the statistics regarding results. The table of exam results still showed large numbers of failures in Geography and uninspiring grades for Maths. Boys did significantly worse than girls in English Literature, French, German, and Art and Design and three times more girls than boys took Drama.

In 1992 girls wore blouses in House colours and boys wore a House flash on their blazer or jumpers. A system of full and half school colours were being awarded for many activities. Extracurricular activities were offered at lunch-time and after school until 4.40 pm. Tony Pratt started a group called P.E.S.T. (Park Environmental Support Team) which planted trees, collected litter, opened a recycling area and worked at cleaning up Saunton beach. Sports clubs included weight-training. A student-run shop sold stationery. Andrew Jackson became 'Mr Adventure', taking groups to France for climbing and white-water rafting with a huge inflatable raft provided by the P.F.A. Risk assessments would probably preclude such trips today. A man who had developed the school's spirit of adventure since the 1960s, Head of Science Fred Lee, was diagnosed with a pituitary gland problem which weakened his sight and needed major surgery. He was absent from July 1992 and eventually took early retirement in 1993. Like many a student after a Ten Tors expedition, Fred has since recovered well.

There was a separate 'Upper School Curriculum' booklet for 1992-3 to help pupils entering Year 10 to make their GCSE choices. Most pupils could be entered for exams in nine subjects, including English Language and English Literature, or even ten subjects for able students doing Statistics or Additional Maths. When the booklet went to press nobody yet knew what the new syllabuses in Maths, English or Science would be for the exams in 1994, which were due to be taught from September 1992. But GCSE English would have an examination covering 60-70% of final marks instead of the 100% coursework of previous years. There were detailed descriptions of the syllabus in every area where choices were to be made. For example, the GCSE History course was now very focused on International Relations from 1900 to the present day, with detailed study of the two World Wars, Nazism in Germany, Chinese Communism, the Cold War, and Conflict in Ireland.

The curriculum booklet advised that: *"Decisions about options must not be made on the basis of 'Do I like that teacher?' or 'Is my friend doing that subject?'"* There was also a special plea for girls to look beyond Domestic Science options: *"At the age of 13/14 many girls anticipate a future in which they will only work until they have a family. Yet women are 40% of the work-force and two-thirds of women at work are married and have children under 16. 10% of families have a woman as the sole breadwinner."*

Devon County Council inspectors visited in May 1993. Their report shows that there were 962 students - 529 boys and 433 girls, a gender imbalance that was present in all years. Pupils came from 20 North Devon Primary Schools and none were from ethnic minority groups. Fewer than 25% of pupils came from rural communities and about 25% came from economically disadvantaged areas. 16.4% were entitled to free school meals. 6.5% had statements of special educational need (boys outnumbered girls here by 3:1) and a further 100 pupils without statements required intervention. These latter factors had an impact on the school's overall exam results, which was the downside of being an inclusive school. The percentage of pupils gaining five or more A-C grades at GCSE in 1992 was 30.2%, compared to a Devon average of 37.8% and a national average of 32.4%. English, Science and Maths were significantly below the averages, whereas Modern Languages, Art and History compared favourably.

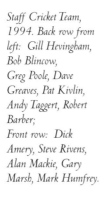

*Staff Cricket Team, 1994. Back row from left: Gill Hevingham, Bob Blincow, Greg Poole, Dave Greaves, Pat Kivlin, Andy Taggert, Robert Barber; Front row: Dick Amery, Steve Rivens, Alan Mackie, Gary Marsh, Mark Humfrey.*

In inspected lessons, the quality of teaching was found to be satisfactory on the whole, with good classroom relationships. There were 58 full-time and 3 part-time teachers and 14 non-teaching staff. The House pastoral system was praised. The Inspectors identified several issues for attention, including the wide variation of standards in Science and Technology. The legal requirements of daily acts of collective worship and R.E. should be met and Health and Safety practises should be reviewed, particularly in the 'resistant material' areas of Technology.

By the time the 1994 'Upper School Curriculum' booklet was published, the choices for Year 10 were clear. English Language and Literature, Maths and Science were compulsory subjects at GCSE. Students then had to choose one Humanities subject, one or two Modern Languages (if only one then also a Technology subject), plus one Expressive Arts subject. Technology had many branches and sub-options. P.E., R.E. and P.S.E were compulsory subjects but did not need to be taken at GCSE. Some students, particularly the most academic ones, would have activity-based challenges for the Youth Award Scheme integrated into their timetable.

Assessment of various subjects at GCSE was now clearer than it was in 1992. English was 60% exam and 40% coursework. Science was 75% exam and 25% coursework. In Maths the most able pupils had a split of 80% exam and 20% coursework. Geography was 50% exam, 30% coursework and 20% individual study. In Art, it was 60% coursework and 40% controlled test.

Two long-serving members of staff from the Grammar School era retired after careers of 39 years apiece. John Charlesworth and Ken Doughty had each contributed more to the school than most Head Teachers.

## Kenneth Walter Doughty A.T.D., N.D.D.
## Long-Serving Teacher, 1954-1993

Ken Doughty was born in 1930, grew up in the New Forest, studied Art in Bournemouth and taught briefly in Dorset before applying to BGS. At his interview, Alderman Dunning asked him what sports he could offer and Ken said soccer, which he admitted was *"not a well-researched choice for a rugby school"*. But Mr Haywood asked him if he could keep discipline and when Ken replied

that he could, the job seemed to be his. He was soon running clubs for badminton and art.

Ken maintained and improved the school's high standards in Art throughout his tenure. His heyday was 1964–1972 - *"between the arrival of the first batch of artistically-talented girls and the loss of the sixth form"*. He commuted to Sticklepath part-time in order to continue teaching A' Level. Ken became a firm supporter of the egalitarian nature of Comprehensive Education and both of his sons were educated at Park. He was a legendary Head of Kingsley House until his retirement. His House Assemblies are reputed to have been hilarious affairs. One Park student recalls: *"I remember him as a cheerful and benign dictator with a great sense of humour."* His drawings and paintings have been exhibited worldwide, including at the Royal West of England Academy and the Royal Society for Marine Artists. Ken Doughty died in 2009 and Pilton Church was packed with mourners at his funeral.

## John R. Charlesworth B.Sc.
## Long-Serving Teacher, 1955-1994

John Charlesworth was born in 1933 and educated at Exmouth Grammar School and Southampton University. He joined BGS as a maths teacher in 1955 but he also managed the tuck shop and the work experience programme. As Director of Studies he took responsibility for the timetable, exams, liaison with the North Devon College and other curriculum matters. His wife Molly was one of the school secretaries.

Mr Charlesworth wrote this in 2003 for a group of 1954 Reunionists: *"What have I done in almost half a century since you left? Aged by at least ten antilogs. Altered my hairstyle —just a wisp of grey at the back. Became bespectacled. Thought a lot about heaven - statistics suggest I will be there shortly so I've been checking it out in advance."*

For the academic year 1994-5 a Register of all students with special educational needs was filed in the school archive. Of the 178 pupils listed, 62 were 'statemented'. Some of their issues were coded by letter but there were comments such as the following in plain English: weak distance vision; disorganised; lacks motivation – dreamer – needs monitoring closely; behavioural problems at Primary School; poor spelling, slow writing; autistic tendency, weak maths; worrier, especially about bullying; generally weak in all areas; emotional, help with reading; auditory sequencing memory weak; hearing impaired, sit near front. The school was a long way from being elitist now. The Department of Education 'Performance Tables' for 1995 showed that Park School had 1,021 pupils. There were 217 in Year 11 and 41% of them got 5 or more A*-C grades at GCSE.

Arthur Hodgetts wrote a letter to parents in which he anticipated *"savage cuts in the funding of many schools nationally in 1995-6"*. From April 1995, this would mean a loss to Park of over £70,000, to be balanced by savings from staffing, text books, equipment for lessons and the maintenance of buildings.

'Park School – It's Brill!' was a booklet written by Year 7 pupils under the guidance of Sue Lee for the 210 new pupils who joined in September 1995. It contained articles by existing pupils with useful tips on getting to know the school system and even a map showing the layout of school buildings and what was where. This was a simply written attempt to integrate children from Primary Schools and suggests a truly caring community. There were notes on merit points: 25 merits = 1 house point and 25 house points = a house badge. There were reassurances, such as: *"Having your head flushed down the toilet by bullies never happens. People just spread these rumours to scare you."* and *"Don't worry about detentions - if you try your best, they are hard to get."* The booklet was a success and was revised by successive Year 7 pupils for several years to come.

Another booklet for 1995-6 was 'Welcome to the Park School – A Handbook for New Staff'. There were now 60 teaching staff, 31 men and 29 women. There was a complicated Daily Duty Rota covering the canteen, various patrols and bus duty. There were detailed notes on all aspects of school life including assessment and marking policies, a health and safety policy, the staff appraisal system, the equal opportunities policy and the homework policy. The cross-curricular spelling initiative stated that to ensure consistency and fairness there should be no more than three spelling corrections per piece of work. Daily contact books gave parents information about homework. On discipline, there was an emphasis on praise and the merit system and on encouraging students to be sensible, kind and honest. When punishment was needed, sanctions included a 'Time Out Room': *"Students should not be told to stand outside a classroom as this leaves them unsupervised."* A teacher sending a pupil to the Time Out Room should *"negotiate re-entry conditions. If a student does not negotiate re-entry, she/he goes to the Time Out Room for the next lesson."*

On the Admin side the school now had an Administrative Officer (Jenny Walsh), a Finance Officer (Pauline Down), six Curriculum Support Staff (of whom four were women), three classroom assistants (including two women) and three female secretaries. Among staff retirees were Joyce Vestey after 25 years as School Secretary and Keith Wheeler after 26 years in the Science Department.

Six of the Governors for 1996-7 had children at Park, others had children who had been at Park and a few were former students themselves. On relocating back to North Devon in 1995, Rosie Bracher had offered to talk to students about her work as a solicitor. After giving a moving speech at a House Awards Ceremony, she was invited to become a School Governor in 1996 when a lot of older Governors left and younger blood came in. She recalls: *"The Head often spoke in language which was impenetrable to me as a new Governor. I remember sitting in meetings and thinking, 'If I, as a post-graduate and a solicitor can't understand this jargon then others must be in the same boat' and so, whenever I didn't understand, I would politely ask for further explanations... I remember the inspection of the boy's toilets which had amazing fungi. The dilapidated buildings were not up to parents' expectations. The school was losing ground to Pilton, whose intake was going up and up. There were real fears for Park's future and concern that its pupil numbers were falling."*

But two bits of major good news were just around the corner. In September 1996 the artificial turf pitch was officially opened by international hockey star Shaun Curley. The project had been jointly funded by grants from the National Lottery, the Sports Aid Foundation, North Devon District Council, and the North Devon Hockey Club and it was designated for community use outside of school hours, which brought outsiders in.

*All-weather pitch.*

Then, in November, a 12-strong team of Ofsted Inspectors looked into every aspect of school life and spoke to a cross section of pupils. They reported that Park was *"a good school with some very good features"*. The strong points included: a house system *"which effectively provides security and a sense of identity"*, a very good Personal and Social Education course, strong partnership with parents, good links to local business and the community, and *"effective teaching at key stages and in all subjects"*. Inspectors found that pupils got on well with teachers and that there was a shared sense of purpose. They found pupil behaviour to be very good and the atmosphere *"calm, considerate and friendly"*. The school was listed in the Top 50 secondary schools inspected by Ofsted in 1996/7. Martin Harvey, Chair of Governors, welcomed the report and congratulated the staff and pupils on achieving it.

In January 1997 all the local papers reported the splendid Ofsted news. The public perception slowly started to turn in Park's favour. Sue McEldon recalls that the school's pastoral work was much admired beyond Barnstaple: *"We were constantly asked to give talks on our PSE courses and behaviour policies. Sue Edmonds was doing notable work on the careers side. We became highly regarded nationally in these areas and I was even interviewed on 'Woman's Hour' about sex education."*

The Park School Prospectus for 1996-97 was a more professionally-presented brochure than it had been in previous years. There were some great photos of pupils making use of modern facilities. The school's purpose was clearly stated: *"School exists to provide the highest quality education possible for all students... to support and*

*The 1996 Prospectus showed off the new technologies.*

*encourage students to learn. . . to play a major role in providing a strong sense of community in students. . . and to promote a positive ethos of an orderly and caring community, with values such as honesty, truth, integrity, teamwork and the building of relationships".* The local authority's admission criteria were spelled out too, showing that the following factors would all be taken into account if the school's quota of places became oversubscribed: living in the school's designated area, attending a contributory Primary School, having a sibling already at the school, distance from home to school (along the shortest walking route), and medical and social issues. In Sport, the prospectus claimed that at some stage all girls and boys did football, cricket, hockey, badminton, basketball and volleyball. Boys also played rugby, while girls also did netball, rounders and tennis.  Extra-curricular activities ranged from an Amnesty International Youth Group to a Homework Help Club after school each day.

The Rover Challenge for Year 11, which involved designing a go-cart, was the enthusiasm of teacher Steve Boreham and Park won the South West and Wales Championships for the fourth year in a row in 1997 with an all-girl team.

*Steve Boreham with 1997 Rover Challenge winners.*

HEAD PREFECTS

| 1972 | Margaret Morris | Keith White |
|------|-----------------|-------------|
| 1973 | Amanda Reardon-Smith | David Priest |
| 1974 | Vivienne Cox | Graham Courtney |
| 1975 | Elizabeth Symons | Philip Sammons |
| 1976 | Philippa Pengelly | Hugh May |
| 1977 | Teresa Walter | Kevin Dymock |
| 1978 | Caroline Bartlett | John Moore |
| 1979 | Tracey Inson | Stephen King |
| 1980 | Anne Harding | Jeremy Mann |
| 1981 | Jayne Hughes | William Hind |
| 1982 | Sarah Brown | Nicholas Mann |
| 1983 | Linda Ley | Richard Harris |
| 1984 | Sophie Dudgeon | Warwick Bailey |
| 1985 | Joanne Drew | Jonathan Brewer |
| 1986 | Marion Loveridge | Richard Butler |
| 1987 | Lucy Greensmith | David Pratt |
| 1988 | Catherine True... | David Lee |
| 1989 | Julie Bennett | Jeremy Richards |
| 1990 | Katie Elliott | Christopher Moakes |
| 1991 | Helen Lacey | Matthew Trigger |
| 1992 | Anna Lifford | Matthew Newcombe |
| 1993 | Kerry Williams | Stephen Moakes |
| 1994 | Samantha Munro | Nicholas Tyrrell |
| 1995 | Rachel Tucker | Jonathan Beer |
| 1996 | Sara Wearne | Oliver Murch |
| 1997 | Kate Hollis/Kelly Nearves | Edward Peers |

A brochure setting out the options available to Year 11 pupils at the North Devon College in June 1997 made it clear that a much wider range of options was open than could ever be possible in a normal school Sixth Form. Subjects available at A' Level included Media, Sociology, and Psychology. Among vocational courses were auto engineering, electronics, plumbing, bricklaying, surveying, catering, hairdressing, leisure and tourism and social care.

Tony Blair's 'New Labour' Government swept to power in May 1997 with a Commons majority of 179. They began by introducing targets for literacy and numeracy in Primary schools and followed this up with the Key Stage framework for attainment targets carrying through into Secondary Schools. Having done battle throughout 13 years of Tory Governments, Arthur Hodgetts retired as Headmaster in July. He had suffered a huge personal setback in 1995 when his wife Pauline died. Having persevered at work until the school was on a firmer footing Arthur now needed some personal space.

## Arthur Hodgetts  B.A.
## Headmaster, 1984-1997

Arthur Hodgetts is the school's only ever Head to have experienced Comprehensive Education at first hand as a pupil. After graduating in Geography at Sussex University he did a PGCE course

in London and then taught for 17 years in four Comprehensive Schools before coming to Park in 1984. His achievements at Park have been thoroughly documented in this chapter.

Mr Hodgetts was 52 when he retired. After a break, he took a travelling Fellowship to America, where he produced a report on Sport in Schools to inform the UK debate. Then for two years he was Co-Director of the Centre for the Study of Comprehensive Schools at Leicester University. Until 2003 he did freelance consulting work, advising Governors on the objectives of Heads.  He still lives in North Devon.

The outstanding Ofsted report of 1996 had been achieved in large measure thanks to the hard work of Mr Hodgetts' two Deputy Heads, David Atton and Sue McEldon, who were both explicitly cited by the Ofsted inspectors.  They would both be staying on to further consolidate the ground that had been gained.

One important task was to make sure that Barnstaple knew what a good school it had at Newport. Education was now a market-place and Park needed to get bums on seats. Sue McEldon attended marketing courses because part of her role was to promote the school in the community.

The job of marketing also fell squarely on the shoulders of David Atton, who had served for eleven years as Deputy Head and now became Mr Hodgetts' successor, as the only internally-appointed Head in the school's 100-year history.  David sums up his predecessor's contribution as follows: *"Arthur set about creating a modern, inclusive Comprehensive School. Under his leadership, important changes were introduced and he set the path for the development of the school we know today, establishing the organisational structure we still use."*

Governor Rosie Bracher's thoughts lead through to the next chapter: *"The LEA was not in favour of promoting Deputy Heads and it was put to Governors as not the done thing. David Atton had quite a shy demeanour but was known as a grafter and when he spoke in interview of his passion for what the school could be and laid out his vision, the Governors were determined to have him. It has since proved to be a good choice. The school has gone from strength to strength."*

# CHAPTER 10

# *ONE HUNDRED NOT OUT, 1997-2010*

IT'S REALLY too soon to write a proper historical account of the period from 1997 to 2010. Pupils from the last thirteen years are too young to be looking back nostalgically on their school-days and they have not come forward to enrich this chapter with their stories. Most staff members of the period are still in post, their role in the overall story still unfinished. But premature though it may be to get any real perspective on the last thirteen years, the process of evolutionary change has clearly been rampant. The biggest programme of building work in the school's history has transformed the site into a modern and integrated campus fit to cope with an equally dramatic 58% increase in pupil numbers, from 920 in 1997 to 1450 in 2009-10. The expansion reflects not just a growth in the local population but also much greater confidence among parents that Park is a good choice for their children.

This improvement in external perceptions of the school's achievements was not a foregone conclusion, as the new Head David Atton knew only too well: *"When I was appointed Head, we were not 'the favoured child' of the two secondary schools in Barnstaple. Pilton Community College had established a fine reputation and successive Headteachers had done an excellent job of developing and promoting it."* But the time had come for Newport's resurgence.

Among secondary schools inspected by Ofsted in 1996-7, Park was listed in the top 50. It also entered the 'Top 100 Most Improved Schools' table, with the percentage of pupils getting five A-C grades rising from 36% in 1994 to 50% in 1997. Then came a listing in the *Observer's* 'Top 1,000', showing which Secondary Schools 'added most value' by comparing pupils' Primary School scores with their subsequent achievements. Mr Atton says, *"Government statisticians had created a measure of success that made allowance for contributory factors such as gender, ethnicity, and socio-economic context. On this basis, Park was an effective and 'high performing school' and we soon became popular and even oversubscribed."*

In 1997 Park was celebrating the 25th anniversary of the first Comprehensive intake when it was re-named 'Park Community School'. The new title had little meaning because the government was renaming many LEA secondary schools as 'Community Schools' at this time. The label brought no extra funding and no new responsibilities. A broader community role, with adult evening classes and youth provision, was no closer to being realised. However, a gradual increase in community use of school facilities began with the Sports Hall and the all-weather pitch, both jointly managed with the District Council. Park has hosted the North Devon Music Centre for many years and musicians use the school on Wednesday evenings to work with county music staff and volunteers. The annual North Devon 'Gang Show' rehearses at Park and the netball courts get good use by outsiders. More recently the school has been able to extend community programmes with its Primary Schools and to offer free Maths and basic I.C.T. courses for local adults.

Mr Atton's first newsletter in 1997 reported on the completion of various building refurbishments. The North Hall and kitchen had already morphed into flexible teaching spaces for drama and music. A state-of-the-art I.T. room gave access to the internet and contained the heart of a computer network which linked the whole school via fibre optic cables. In South Building all the classrooms were upgraded and new ones imaginatively created around the hub of the Library and Resources Centre, whose former architectural splendour had now been restored.

Further accolades were coming thick and fast. In February 1998 Park won the education equivalent of an Oscar when it was highlighted as 'outstanding' and placed in the top 2% of 7,500 schools inspected for

*David Atton (right) and Peter Groves, Chairman of Governors, with the Outstanding Achievement Award, 1998.*

standards and achievement. June brought an announcement that Park would host one of the UK's first Numeracy Summer Schools with pupils from local Primaries spending three weeks doing puzzles and games. In July the government unveiled a network of 75 'Beacon Schools', selected as benchmarks for standards because of their outstanding performance and results. The Park Community School's inclusion on the elite list was all the more remarkable because it served the most disadvantaged district within North Devon. As a Beacon School, Park received £50,000 per annum for sharing the secrets of its success with other schools in the area.

*The cutting below comes from the* Western Morning News.

Such recognition made for regular positive coverage in the local press. The management team was quick to exploit other newsworthy opportunities, like the 1998 Ravensburg Exchange, which celebrated the 40th anniversary of an association that had led to at least one marriage between a German boy and an English girl. 1999 began with a local journalist's dream – a visit by the Chief Inspector of Schools, Chris Woodhead, who was keen to be photographed with pupils at one of his new Beacon Schools. In April, all three local papers showed four members of a 34-strong Science class which won the British Gas 'Powersavers' competition by involving the whole school in an investigation of how energy

# Beacon school initiative dazzles Ofsted's chief

*1.2.99    WMN.*

**JENNY BARNICOAT**

HER Majesty's Chief Inspector of Schools, Chris Woodhead, paid a special visit to North Devon to see one of his "Beacon" schools at work and to gain grassroots reactions to the scheme from participating teachers.

The Park School in Barnstaple gained Beacon status in recognition of the quality of its work and the standards it achieves. Park was named as one of the best in the country by Mr Woodhead, head of Ofsted (the Office for Standards in Education) in his 1998 Annual Report.

Under the government's Beacon schools scheme, schools in the area are visiting Park to share good practice and develop teachers' skills.

Initially the focus is on behaviour and discipline management, testing and target-setting, science and literacy. The funding is used to cover such things as supply costs, travel and resource materials, enabling as many teachers as possible to learn from each other.

Mr Woodhead said he was delighted to be visiting North Devon. He is a former deputy chief education officer for the county.

"To see Barnstaple at the cutting edge of a national educational initiative is very satisfying indeed," he said.

After spending time touring the school and meeting staff and pupils, Mr Woodhead shared an open and frank discussion with representatives from three of the 12 schools involved in the project and Park's two deputy heads who are co-ordinating the scheme.

CLARE KENDALL

● **JUST CHECKING:** Ofsted chief Chris Woodhead discusses what makes the Beacon school so special

savings could be made at Park. Katie Helliwell, Head of Art, made headlines in May when she was named Secondary Teacher of the Year in the regional finals of the first ever National Teaching Awards. Park School's Public Relations machine was on a roll.

---

## Katie Phillips (née Helliwell)
## Award-Winning Teacher, 1994-present

Katie was 23 when she started her first teaching job at Park School and a year later she was promoted to Head of Art. The South West's Secondary Teacher of the Year introduced 3D art and modernised the department. The percentage of pupils gaining GCSE A-C grades in Art rose from 28% to 70% and Park pupils were soon attending 'Gifted and Talented' residential courses. Getting student art out into the community was another aspect she focused on, introducing annual exhibitions at Barnstaple library and outdoor displays for the North Devon Festival and Barnstaple in Bloom. Katie's £3,500 prize purchased printing equipment for the Art department.

---

Projected increases in pupil numbers led to the creation of a fifth House in September 1999, when Chichester House began with just a first year membership. Contrary to popular belief the House was not named after yachtsman Sir Francis Chichester but after the former owner of the land on which the school is built, Rosalie Chichester. Chichester is now firmly established and has since won the prestigious overall activity shield twice.

Gill Hevingham has been Head of Chichester from day one and has seen it grow. *"We weren't able to join in any all-school House matches until the summer of 2003, when we won the athletics shield at our first attempt."* Gill was a Raleigh girl in the late 1960s when, as Gill MacDonald, she represented the Grammar School in five sports and brole the high jump record as the first pupil to use the 'Fosbury Flop' technique. Gill joined Park as a P.E. teacher in 1990 and was Deputy Head of Raleigh in Dick Amery's time. She now also teaches Philosophy, Theology & Ethics, and Child Development. She says, *"I tend to think of Chichester as my House, having been its Head since the beginning, and I'll probably be very reluctant to let it go when I retire."*

Another former BGS pupil is teaching at Park in the twenty-first century. Chris Ley is now Head of Modern Languages, having notched up a total of 36 years at the school, man and boy. Looking back over four decades, Chris concludes: *"The school has changed physically and in terms of ethos during my time. The 'inclusive'*

*Chichester cheerleaders by Rachel Broome, 2009.*

*Gill Hevingham and Chris Ley.*

*Exploring Jewish customs in an R.E. class.*

agenda has presented us with many challenges, but the school has led the way across the county in a number of initiatives, the most notable being the Mulberry Centre." Chris has been a tutor in Fortescue, Drake and Kingsley and says, "I want to try the other two before I retire." That ambition may hinge on whether Gill Hevingham will make room for him in Chichester!

In 2000, students created a large wall-mounted mosaic of the school crest and motto during Activity Week. The Millennium turned many former pupils' thoughts to school reunions and the classes of '51 '58, '62 and '90 were in the vanguard. Five girls played hockey for Devon Schools' teams, the most ever at one time. The Head reminded parents of the jewellery rules and warned that *"piercing on the face or around the eyes"* would not be acceptable. A mock wedding at Newport Church was part of a broad programme of Religious Studies which has gradually come to reflect our more secular and multi-cultural society.

Roger Mullis left after 18 years as Head of Special Needs. Mr Atton wrote of him: *"His dedication, patience and skill have helped many pupils to achieve far more than could ever have been expected or hoped for."* Roger has gone

*Roger Mullis with Tamil children in India.*

on to work with children from Romanian orphanages, asylum seekers, refugees and migrant workers and he says that, *"teaching those with little or no English seems very similar at times to some of my work at Park!"*

David Atton was asked to complete a survey in 2000 about the quality of support provided by the Local Education Authority. His answers showed 'poor' support in a long list of areas: disseminating best practice among schools, help with bidding for external grants, effectiveness of liaison with health and social services, clarity of rationale behind school funding, support for improving pupil behaviour, quality of Special Needs provision, support for pupils with statements, educational psychology support, advice on obtaining value for money from suppliers, support on the planning and control of the school budget, and building maintenance. The only area where he considered LEA support to be 'very good' was catering. That must have caused a few ripples at County Hall.

From the beginning of his tenure staff found the new Head's own supportive nature extremely refreshing and they also liked the sense of humour he brought to daily staff meetings, making every morning start with a buzz. The senior management team now included Tina Marns, who had replaced David in January 1998 as Curriculum Deputy Head, and Sue Lee who, as Assistant Head Teacher, took on the organisation of charity fund-raising, activity days and residentials. Sue kept up her Year 7 responsibilities, introducing individual interviews each June between tutors and all upcoming new pupils and their parents.

By September 2001 the school was oversubscribed, even with two extra classes in Year 7. That autumn a substantial building programme began which would include additional accommodation. A three-storey

*Demolition Site, March 2002.*

*Steel erected for new Link Building, April 2002.*

Link Building would provide covered and disabled access between the three main existing buildings. A successful bid to the Home Office had secured £104,000 to improve security with a closed circuit television system. The County Council opened a 'Park and Ride' car park incorporating half of Pill Field adjacent to the school and including the old railway cutting. The additional access road gave plenty of space for school buses to line up each afternoon – mad dashes across Rock Park to the bus station having become a thing of the past.

At the end of January 2002, a 14-person Ofsted inspection team carried out a week-long review. There were 1,212 pupils, with almost equal numbers of boys and girls, and the proportion of children with statements or special educational needs was above the national average. 90% of parents who responded to an Ofsted questionnaire said they were satisfied with the schooling their children were receiving at Park. GCSE achievements were highest in Art, Combined Science, French, Statistics and some areas of Design and Technology. The least satisfactory areas were I.C.T. and Music, which both needed better accommodation and resources.

The report concluded: *"This is a very good school. Pupils achieve well in Years 10 and 11. In GCSE examinations in 2001, attainment was above the national average in the majority of subjects and well above the average for similar schools. This is the result of good teaching and the very positive attitudes to work that the school generates in almost all of its pupils. Behaviour is generally very good. There are excellent links with the community. The provision for moral, social and cultural education is an important factor in the school's success. The educational and personal support for pupils is very good and some aspects are excellent. . . This is an improving school. It went through a period of thorough self-review upon the appointment of the present Headteacher and it recognised where its weaknesses were. Effective action has been taken, resulting in improved examination results, better teaching, and the raising of the reputation within the local community."*

The *North Devon Journal* reported that Park School's 'Beacon' status had been renewed for a further 3 years. Then, in September 2002, the school achieved Specialist Technology College status, which attracted extra annual funding of £120,000. A one-off capital grant covered the costs of moving Food Technology and Textiles from the RoSLA building to North Building, bringing all the Technology rooms together there.

Park was now riding on the crest of a wave and further major improvements to the fabric of the school soon followed. In September 2003, the new £3 million Maths and Science Link Building was opened, with

*Maths and Science Link Building.*

*Dining Room in use, 2006.*

*Tennis Courts and Sports Hall from staircase of Link Building.*

8 new laboratories, 8 new classrooms and new I.T. suites. The old South Building toilets and the old canteen were replaced by an attractive new kitchen and dining room extension. The Link project was guided by the expert vision of a Parent Governor, Jerry Kent - a local architect who created the unity that Park needed at the heart of the campus. Jerry wasn't finished yet.

It was the end of an era for a long-serving dilapidated hut, because the new arrangements provided for a new staff room.

## The 'Temporary' Staffroom.
## 1964-2003

In 1964, male and female staff moved from previously separate accommodations into a hut which had already seen two previous lives. No matter - it would only be temporary! In 1967, the hut was heated by a one bar electric fire and Tony Pratt recorded a temperature inside of minus 10 degrees. Still, most teachers smoked back then so it felt stuffy! In the 1970s, on his interview day for a P.E. post, Keith Summer was demonstrating his ball skills outside when he kicked a football through the staffroom window. He still got the job! In February 1980, Jimmy Morgan's diary records that the staffroom was surveyed by the County Architect and found to be *"in a pretty poor state"*. Chris Ley says, *"When they put in double glazing, the walls weren't strong enough to support the new window frames."* In the 1990s, teachers recall *"snail trails on the carpet every morning"* and *"holes in the floor through which the wind howled, though we tried to block them up with newspaper"*.

This photo was taken on the day the hut was decommissioned, when staff gathered for a celebratory 'keepy uppy' game to try to beat the record of 423. Clockwise from the empty chair of photographer Bob Blincow are Susan Holland, Chris Ley, Helen Dunn, Graham Sloman, Matt Street, Alan Mackie (explaining strategies), Tony Pratt, Andy Taggart, Ruth McMeechan, Derek Slade and Dick Amery. An annual game of 'keepy uppy' is still held at the end of each Christmas term and in December 2009 a staggering record of 873 was recorded in the new staffroom.

A 2003 Green Paper called 'Every Child Matters' led to the Children's Act of 2004 and the Children's Plan of 2007, put forward by the newly-named Department for Children, Schools and Families (DCSF). The aims were to improve children's educational outcomes and health, reduce offending rates among young people and eradicate child poverty. In theory, families were placed at the heart of the strategies since young people spend only a fifth of their time at school, but that's not quite how David Atton sees it: *"Schools increasingly became required to assume the role of a one-stop solution to every aspect of educational, emotional and social demand. The 'Children's Plan' even prompted the proposal that schools be held accountable for childhood obesity and other measures of personal well-being. The policy of 'inclusion' championed the aim of all children attending the local school, with special schools at risk of closure. But common sense prevailed. Whilst the majority can thrive in the mainstream setting, often with defined additional support, a minority with significant learning, emotional or behavioural needs do still require the smaller, caring environment of more specialised provision."*

One of Park's specialised units was the Mulberry Centre, named after a mulberry tree that grew near the hut where it was first sited. Pupils with challenging behaviour receive special attention here, reporting to the unit every morning and working with specially- trained staff for some of their lessons as well as attending regular classes. Over the years, the unit has helped to bring down the number of pupils permanently excluded to around four or five a year. Mike Canham, Chair of Governors, says: *"Exclusion really is a last resort and the school feels a sense of failure when it becomes necessary. We try many things before we get to this point."* In a wonderfully ironic twist the Mulberry Unit moved in 2009 to the former Headmasters' office in North Building, the very place where naughty boys in former times were thrashed with a cane.

*Mike Canham, Chairman of Governors, and Sue Lee (rear left) at a Drake merit winners' presentation.*

In 2004 Jerry Kent designed the floodlit netball courts, placing Park even more firmly at the centre of the sporting world in North Devon. He was already drawing up plans for a Support and Study Centre for Special Needs students for completion in 2008. New textile rooms and a new Office and Reception would follow in 2009.

*Jerry Kent, whose architectural vision has transformed the campus.*

## Farewell to 141 Years of Experience!

2005 brought the retirement of five long-serving staff who had witnessed many changes at the school and whose own individual contributions had been immense. Collectively, they had served for 141 years.

Tony Pratt (Geography and Head of Fortescue) was leaving after 39 years, during which he had served as a Union Rep, a School Governor and in countless other roles. Looking back on one of the longest teaching careers on record, Tony says: *"At one point, five North Devon Secondary Schools had Heads of Geography whom I'd taught."*

Dick Amery (Science and Head of Raleigh) had two spells totalling 36 years, during which he'd been a doyen of the table tennis club and Lundy field trips as well as managing football and cricket teams. Dick says modestly, *"We all did a lot more additional jobs in the early days."*

Completing a trio of Heads of House was Sue Lee, who wore several hats (Head of Science, Head of Drake and Assistant Head Teacher) during her 16 years, and says that *"being Head of House was a tough job because unexpected problems cropped up constantly."*

Derek Slade had taught Science for over 30 years and Mr Atton paid tribute to a man *"of selfless dedication and intense sense of duty."* Derek first joined BGS as a lab technician in 1968, then sat in on Harry Bradley's A-Level Chemistry classes before training as a teacher in Exeter.

Finally, the School said farewell to Sue McEldon (English, Drama and Deputy Head), a key member of the management team for 20 years who developed the school's pastoral and community dimensions. For Sue, the school she loved *"was and is a true Comprehensive School, which takes a total cross section of society, making it colourful and vibrant."* Mick Cammack took over as Deputy Head.

From 2005 every student was issued with a bar-coded photo-ID 'Smart Card' for borrowing library books and paying for canteen meals. The office can now track what pupils are eating and report to parents on their choice of food and its cost. 'Big Brother' watches in other ways too, with 11 CCTV cameras able to identify escapees, smokers and other miscreants, including anyone in breach of the uniform rules. 'SLEUTH' software helps staff to track and record discipline and behaviour issues, providing an up to date and instantly accessible file on each pupil. A new system called 'Schoolcomms' allows staff to contact participating parents by email or text message when required. These measures all remain in place and are fully explained to new pupils during their induction.

In 2006, Mr Atton had a purge on school uniforms in his newsletters to parents, declaring that *"tee-shirts visible under shirts or blouses, ties not fastened properly, cuffs undone and boys' untucked shirts all spoil what we are seeking to achieve"*. He took an even tougher line on 'hoodies' and baseball jackets, which *"send the wrong messages and*

*Joseph Duhig presents his 'smart card' to canteen cashier Lesley Deegan.*

*Big brother is watching! CCTV control area.*

*Lunchtime in the Library, 2005. This room was the assembly Hall for over fifty years.*

damage our standards and ethos. Please ensure your son/daughter does not return in September wearing one." There was another no-go area too: text bullying' had become a national issue and mobile phones were not to be brought into school.

In November 2006, Ofsted inspectors were back again with a new model of standards. They scored Park 'Good' in terms of overall effectiveness, though this didn't mean it was less good than the 'Very Good' it had achieved in 2002. On the contrary, inspectors noted that standards had risen across all years. There had been significant improvement in the way I.T. was used and in the range of enrichment activities. Inspectors praised the fact that students get involved in decisions about how the school is run and they remarked on their awareness of how to stay healthy through diet and exercise. Another conclusion was that *"the school offers exceptional standards of care to its most vulnerable students."* The transition from Primary School was being very effectively managed. But there was room for further improvement in attendance rates and in ensuring that all homework was planned effectively, set regularly and marked constructively.

School newsletters in 2006 showed how modern and grown-up Park had become. A student 'Anti-Bullying Action Group' was established. A student 'Food User Group' produced information sheets on the impact of a poor diet on health. The school now had 450 computers. There were plans for an observatory for thriving astronomy groups. The Religious Studies department changed its name to the 'Philosophy, Theology and Ethics' department. Students continued to raise impressive amounts for all kinds of charities including: £355 for Amigos International, £1,940 for 'Children in Need', £780 for the South Asian Earthquake Appeal, £600 for a Romanian Orphanage and £1,000 for Lepra.

Among extra-curricular achievements by pupils in 2006, Year 10 singer/songwriter Helen Dennis won first prize in a North Devon competition for her song 'Last Tear'. Ollie Passmore became one of North Devon's top chefs in the 'Young Chef of the Year' Competition'. Katy Rogers and her band 'The Insanity Plan' won the School 'Battle of the Bands' competition. The Girls' Football teams went the whole season without defeat and a Surf Club team came twelfth in the British Championships. There was a major staff achievement too when Robert Barber, drama teacher and Head of Expressive Arts, went to Buckingham Palace to receive an M.B.E.

## Robert Barber B.Ed., M.B.E.
## Award-Winning Teacher, 1986-present

In 1986 Robert Barber became the first designated Drama teacher at Park School and he was soon taking on ambitious school plays and musicals with big casts, like *Oh, What a Lovely War, Bugsy Malone* and *Cabaret.* Before long he became Head of Expressive Arts. In 2000 Robert wrote and co-ordinated a millennium pageant for Barnstaple, involving 14 schools in a performance at Rock Park. His M.B.E. for *"Services to Education and the Community"* followed a National Teaching Award for the quality and breadth of his work, which he received on live TV at the London Palladium in 2003. In July 2010 Robert is due to lead another major musical production, this time to celebrate the impending School Centenary.

In 2007 Park's stature grew still further. The 'Investors in Work-Related and Enterprise Learning Diploma' was awarded for a further three years in recognition of Park's links with community organisations and its commitment to work-related learning. The extra funding for being a Specialist Technology College was also renewed but most schools were now 'specialist' in one subject or another so the government introduced a new status of 'Vocational Second Specialism' (now called Applied Learning). This re-established elite schools with another £100,000 p.a. of extra funding to benefit the whole school and extend community programmes.

There were some exceptional pupil achievements in 2007. Thomas Pearce of Year 8 won a place with the Royal Ballet, Thomas Harris of Year 9 won a Bronze Medal for Weightlifting, Craig Attwood of Year 10 became a member of the Great Britain Target Shooting Team, and Howard Alford of Year 11 won the Historical Association's Young Historian Award for his local history research. A hundred staff and students took part in the annual Fashion Show, organised by the Parents and Friends Association, and Lucy Dymond of Year 9 won the prize for designing the most imaginative outfit.

The Park School 'Portal' (soon to become the 'Virtual Learning Environment') was launched in the summer term, providing an online workspace for students and allowing easy access and transfer of files between school and home. It would enable absent students to keep up with class work and there would also be guidance and resources for exam revision. A Year 7 'Parenting Academy' was launched, offering an *"informative, relaxed and open-minded programme that will help to unravel the mysterious world of the teenager."*

In 2008 thirty-eight 'mysterious teenagers' from Year 10 went on a forensic archaeology trip to Exeter University, which involved DNA investigation of two 'bog bodies'. Park won the 'Investors in Careers'

*Some of the 500 computers in use.*

award, for the high quality of its Careers Education and Guidance programmes. A group of Year 11 boys won the 'Good Schools' Guide' award for the best results nationally in astronomy, a subject promoted by science teachers Andrew Urwin and Phillip Reason. The 'Mount Sandford Shield' was awarded for the school's outstanding contribution to the 'Barnstaple in Bloom' displays around the town, which included giant colourful floral art structures in the Library Square. Finally, the catering staff achieved the top 5-star 'Environmental Health Award' following an inspection of the school kitchen.

By March 2009 pupil numbers stood at 1433, 17% of whom received free school meals. Pupils had come from a total of 27 schools, including the nine designated feeder Primaries. There were 23 students of non UK origin, an indication that North Devon had become a little more cosmopolitan.

Gizmos now in use in labs, workshops and I.T. rooms included 17 interactive whiteboards. These enable a display from a laptop to appear on a high-tech electronic screen on the wall so that teachers and students can create and manipulate text and images, all without blackboards and chalk monitors!

*Park News* reported on the 2009 survey of parents and pupils, which showed widespread satisfaction with Park but listed 'truancy control', 'sociology' and 'school security' among issues that parents were least

*Louise Brierley's 'Product Design' class, 2009.*

*Jack Burch and Thiego Bento doing 'Food Technology', 2009.*

happy with. As if in response, there was news of a forthcoming traffic security system with rising bollards to prevent vehicular access to the site for all but essential users. Ruth McMeechan, Head of Kingsley, retired after 20 years of teaching at Park, and Olga Williams finally handed in her library card after 32 years as an assistant in the Learning Resources Centre.

Among pupil successes in 2009, Edward Pearce (Year 10) and Samuel Meadowcroft (Year 9) were outstanding in the UK Mathematics Trust Challenge, Craig Pike (Year 9) won three events at the South West Indoor Athletics Championships, and Lily Nichols (Year 8) won seven gold medals at the National Stillwater Life Saving Championships. Thirty students attended a wide range of performance workshops at the Devon Mix Music Festival, where a group of them helped to run the 'salsa zone'.

*Head of Music Matthew Street with the school salsa band at Devon Music Mix Festival, 2009.*

Of all the subjects on the school curriculum in 2009/10 the one that will be least familiar to anyone from the Grammar School days is also one of the most popular. PSHEE – Personal, Social, Health and Economic Education – includes useful life-skills and knowledge that was simply never taught back then, except obliquely and unsystematically. The syllabus covers: Citizenship (including the rights and responsibilities of citizens, domestic violence, making 999 calls, first aid); Sex and Relationships (including contraception, parenting skills and gender issues); Personal Finances (including managing a budget and savings); Health (including drugs, alcohol, smoking and cancer); Careers and Work-Related Learning (including work experience placements, writing CV's, interview skills); Social Skills (including friendship, bullying and discrimination); Study Skills (including time management and exam techniques). There are timetabled PSHEE classes each week, mostly taught by form tutors but with some visiting specialists. The co-ordination of PSHEE is the responsibility of one of Park's most versatile teachers, Sue Edmonds. In 2009, Sue became the latest staff award-winner.

## Sue Edmonds (née Brigden)
## Award-Winning Teacher, 1975-present

Sue Edmonds has taught a wide range of skills in her 35 years at Park. She began with Domestic Science *("food and sewing")*, P.E., and a City and Guilds course for pupils with learning difficulties. She also ran teams for hockey, netball and tennis, and was a Deputy Head of both Kingsley and Fortescue. By 1986, she was teaching child development and electronics, believing that *"learning new skills keeps you on your toes."* After a spell of maternity leave, Sue returned as a Technology teacher, which led on to Graphic Design.

She gained a Diploma in Careers Education and Guidance in 1997 and her work in this area now includes teaching Careers modules within PSHEE and liaising with the Careers Service. She arranges a Year 8 Industry Day, a North Devon College Taster Day, and a Careers Options evening for Year 11. She keeps a record on each student, writes their references and organises the annual Leavers' Prom.

In 2006 Sue also became Head of PSHEE. Her handbook for staff on what she calls the *"holistic part of education"* ends with a proverb: *"Teachers open the door - you enter by yourself."* There's another proverb that goes: *"If you want something doing, ask a busy person".* Sue has become one of three UK careers teachers producing resource materials for the DCSF website and she gives briefings in Westminster. In November 2009 she was crowned 'UK Careers Teacher of the Year' by the Institute of Careers Guidance.

In October 2009 yet another Ofsted inspection, with yet another new set of even more demanding criteria, gave the school an overall 'Grade 2' (the latest jargon for 'Good'). Since it was based largely upon raw GCSE results, Park celebrated this result as the best it could achieve. The Inspector's report was full of praise: *"The outstanding care, guidance and support the school provides for its students are significant factors in their development as fully-rounded individuals by the time they leave. Support for all students is exemplary but particularly noteworthy is the time and care devoted to students who are potentially vulnerable or who might otherwise be excluded from full-time education."* Lead HMI Anne Looney included her main criticisms in a letter addressed to all students, telling them: *"We have asked the school to further improve the quality of teaching by getting teachers to work more closely together, share what they do well and ensure that all marking makes it really clear what you need to do to improve."*

Ofsted visits have increased in frequency and they can, in some circumstances, now come without notice. Inspectors have the power to take over a school's management so Heads have to accept that leaping the Ofsted bar periodically is part of what they do for a living. The joy of the job is to help a large and diverse body of pupils achieve their potential. But the incessant drive to raise standards brings the whole staff under intense and continuous pressure, with workloads and accountabilities growing and keeping people late at the office at a time when work-life balance is also being championed.

In 1970 Barnstaple Grammar School had 39 male teachers and 19 female teachers. Many of them were in the latter part of their careers. Today Park has 90 teachers. There are more women than men and it's a considerably younger staff. The actual job of being a teacher has changed too in forty years. In 1970, boys were still being caned. Now every member of staff receives training in Child Protection and has to be cleared by the Criminal Records Bureau before they can be left alone with children. We're a long way from corporal punishment now. Teachers are generally better qualified academically and professionally than they were in the 1960s. But teachers' conditions of service and the pressure to focus on improving teaching and learning standards and examination outcomes leaves less time for contributing to extra curricular activities. David Atton says, *"When I arrived in 1986, the school had a critical mass of staff who regarded Park as 'their school' to be protected and cherished. Today the sense of ownership is not as tangible as it used to be."*

The 'non-teaching staff' has changed even more. Park now has 11 office staff, 30 teaching assistants, 2 cover supervisors, 1 social worker, 5 learning mentors, 21 part-time cleaners, 1 cleaning supervisor, 9 meal-time assistants, 5 library and resource centre staff, 6 technicians and 2 caretakers. There is one non-teaching post for every teacher, and that doesn't include catering and grounds staff provided by outside contractors. The overall ratio of female to male staff at the school is now 2:1 and, due to the age profile, it is unusual if there are not several members of staff on maternity leave.

*Pauline Down, Bursar.*

When Pauline Down joined Park as an administrative assistant in September 1991 there were just three other ladies in the office. Pauline is now School Bursar and Business Manager, a vitally important role that didn't even exist before LMS (Local Management of Schools). When the school started in 1910 the annual budget was a few thousand pounds and there wasn't even a single secretary. Pauline now prepares and controls an annual budget in excess of £6 million and she manages an office staff of eleven. The additional administrative burden has arisen out of new statutory regulations, through more aspects of management being delegated from the Local Authority and because teachers have shed some of their former non-teaching roles. But Bursars are not the only new breed in today's large comprehensive schools.

Everyone refers to Lydia Parish as the 'SWaP worker', which stands for 'Social Worker at Park', but she is strictly-speaking a Community Care Worker. Lydia's training equips her to understand and support children whose performance or behaviour at school suffers from a range of anxieties and problems caused by social factors outside of school - things like domestic violence, parents with mental health problems, and drug or alcohol abuse. *"At any one time there may be 80-100 pupils on my radar. I see more girls than boys, mainly because girls are more willing to talk about their problems."* Lydia deals sensitively with a range of social issues, sadly including cases of abuse, self-harming, exploitation and internet grooming. It can be messy work. Many of her regulars just suffer from poor parenting. And she does have regulars – around 30 pupils whom she sees every week at appointments that can last 10 minutes or a whole lesson. Some of her regulars are bright students and a few are designated 'gifted and talented'. Some are in foster care, some come from homes where custody issues cause anxiety and some have child protection plans to be followed.

Lydia spends four days a week in school, keeping her eyes and ears open, talking to pupils and liaising with teachers. She tries to nip problems in the bud by alerting Social Services to problems at an early stage. She visits the homes of pupils who are having difficulty and also runs a programme to help parents with whatever issues are affecting their children's education. Park and Pilton each now have a Parent Support Advisor, whose role is to help parents to get their children into school and gain maximum benefit from all that it has to offer. Some children are referred to mental health and other professionals. Some pupils live on the fringes of crime and Police Community Support Officers run a drop-in session at the school every Wednesday. To put things in perspective, in 2008-9 Lydia only knew of one case of pregnancy at the school and only one case of a pupil with a drug problem.

*Lydia Parrish, 'Social Worker at Park'.*

At the end of the school's first century, the term 'Community' in its title has some real meaning. This is no longer an institution that dictates terms to its users on a 'take it or leave it' basis. The school reaches deep into the community and the community reaches deep into the school. Six times a year, David Atton attends meetings of the Barnstaple Learning Community, along with the Head of Pilton Community College and the Heads of all the Primary Schools they both serve. The issues they discuss embrace a broad social agenda that goes way beyond education as the school's founders knew it. The society within which the school operates is much more complex than it was.

In most cases the relationships between school and parents have never been stronger. A new generation of parents took over the Parents and Friends Association in September 2009. In an attempt to encourage parental involvement, they are reducing the committee culture by using e-communication and meeting off school premises. They have adopted the more appealing name 'Friends of Park', though legally it is still the P.F.A. and it still has a fund-raising function just like the P.T.A. of long ago.

The next phase of building work has already left Jerry Kent's drawing board and will provide a suite of six new modern languages classrooms in a development being called 'the Street'. This will be on the playground side of the existing North Building classrooms with a covered corridor in between. The top corridor there will become absorbed into the existing classrooms. The plans also allow for a new Graphics department and a Music performance area, both in the quadrangle nearest to the gym, where Modern Languages have occupied 'temporary' huts for longer than most people can remember.

At the end of its first century, the Governing Body of the school consists, as it did at the very beginning, of twenty men and women drawn from the local community who bring a diverse range of skills and experience to the job of keeping a light hand on the management tiller of the school. They include a senior partner in the Brend Group, two lawyers, an architect, a planning officer and a journalist. Their Chairman, Mike Canham, is a retired lecturer from North Devon College, where 98% of Park leavers go if they want to continue their education. Mike's relationship with the Head is crucial: *"David is very hands on but he always consults Governors on important matters. Head Teachers also have a 'School Improvement Partner' - a retired Head or Ofsted inspector who acts as a critical friend. These days, they need all the help they can get. Thankfully, David has a great sense of humour."*

---

## David Atton B.Sc.
## Head Teacher, 1997-present

A native of Lincolnshire, David Atton taught science at three schools before taking a Deputy Headship at Great Torrington School in 1983. He joined Park as Deputy Head in 1986 and

soon established himself as an excellent organiser whose work-rate was second to none. His promotion to Head Teacher in 1997 makes him the only internal appointment to the post in the school's history. With typical modesty this is how he assesses his own performance over the last thirteen years: *"I have sought to lead and manage with and through others, enabling each to achieve more effectively in their particular area than I could have achieved myself."*

One colleague says, *"David is passionate about this school, and everything he does is always very thoroughly thought through."* Alan Mackie, who has observed five Heads at close quarters, writes: *"David Atton is the most committed Head I have known. The interest of the school and its pupils and staff are at the forefront of his dedication. He inherited a school that had diminishing pupil numbers and immediately set about restoring its reputation in the town. David leads by example, he is always approachable and he expects a professional approach in return. He believes in consultation, weighing up the strength of arguments and making what he considers to be the best decision for the school."*

---

As if it weren't enough to lead a large institution with a multi-million pound budget, a challenging brief and a diverse range of customers, David is also conscious that he's a steward of the school's heritage: *"I regard the school as 'held in trust' – to be developed, enabled to be successful, and one day handed on in fine condition to the next generation."*

What the next generation will make of it all one can only speculate. At the end of Park's one hundred years, one thing is certain – the school won't suddenly stand still. The latest projections are for a 50%

growth in the population of Barnstaple by 2026 with an expected further growth in pupil numbers by then of about 14%. Will the town's growth lead to the creation of a third Comprehensive School or will the existing ones expand to cope? Environmental pressures are leading more pupils to cycle to school and thirty more cycle lockers in 2010 may not be the last. One of the latest initiatives is that designated children are to get more 1:1 tuition. One possible future scenario is that more use will be made of 'virtual learning', allowing students capable of independent study to spend less time at schools, freeing up teacher time for those more needful of it. Will Secondary Schools of the future specialise in particular areas of the curriculum, so that children regularly attend more than one school in a given week? Will any of the educational developments of the last hundred years be reversed – a return to smaller schools, for example, with a more homogeneous intake? These are the sorts of issues that school managers may have to consider.

In the years ahead each change of government and each major shift in the social fabric of our society is likely to change the way schools go about their business. Probably, despite threatened cuts arising from the impact of an economic recession, the bar of expectation will continue to be raised. David Atton expresses the view of a seasoned campaigner: *"Will the Park Community School continue in its current guise for the next 100 years? Or even the next 10 years? Probably not. Even if it were advisable, schools like this one will not be left alone to get on with life!"*

The most important legacy of any school is what its pupils do when they leave. Unfortunately, we shall never know what proportion of BGS or Park pupils over the last century have become happy, contented and useful citizens. But there are some positive indications.

In November 2009 the author was asked to present the certificates and prizes at the annual Leavers' Evening. What an extraordinarily mature and good-looking group of 16 year-olds filed before him that night. They had been responsible collectively for the school's best ever results at GCSE. Many students had achieved more than ten passes. One girl, Eleanor Chamings, had somehow managed to get Grade A's in 14 subjects, of which 13 were passed with distinction. The author, who had achieved no grade A's himself, gave a speech attempting to inspire them to future success, citing examples of other old boys and girls who had excelled.

Not all success in later life stems from academic excellence and many who fail to shine while at school may later surprise the teachers who despaired of them. Preston Isaac, founder of the 'Cobatton Combat Collection', was one such old Bardian. Brian Ford, founder of the Ford & Lock retail chain, was another. Teachers usually don't find out about their pupils' success and it doesn't help when girls change their names, as Ann Richardson did, for example, becoming a successful writer as Ann Cleeves. Former pupils have gone on to excel in most walks of life and previous chapters have documented some of the better known high flyers from the Grammar School era – people like David Shepherd, David Vine, Jimmy Isaac, Joyce Hill, and Vivienne Cox. Those who have been awarded Honours by the Queen include Keith Harding and John Gammon, who both earned MBEs during distinguished military careers, and Sir Kenneth Wood, who was knighted for business success. Others have been content to be team players and have largely gone un-noticed,

*Leavers' Board, 2009.*

like Margret Tamlyn who worked on the Human Genome Project and helped to complete the sequence for the first chromosome.

One of the large glass cabinets on display at Park contains cuttings from the local press of former students who have recently graduated, each with a photo and a brief description. This helps to stimulate a sense of institutional pride among current pupils, who no longer have sixth formers around to look up to. With no *Bardian* magazine and no Old Bardians Association there is more chance now than previously of someone leaving school and going off the radar. But nobody should think that career success ended with the Grammar School. Countless former pupils from the comprehensive era are flying the Park School flag as accountants, builders, civil servants, doctors, engineers, firemen, gardeners, hairdressers, I.T. consultants… and so on to the end of the alphabet…

In sport, Keith Gammon became World Surf Life-Saving Champion. Owen Pickard became a league footballer and then Manager of Barnstaple Town Football Club. Kevin Squire became Director of Rugby at Barnstaple RFC. In music, Philip Evans became Conductor and Leader of the Royal Marine Band, while Dominic Greensmith and Jason Knight became drummer and keyboard player respectively with chart band Reef, which produced six albums in ten years. In business, Paul Jury owns plant hire and haulage companies in North Devon and Tim Bailey is a property investment entrepreneur in London. Catherine Courtney became a journalist and so did Ian King, who is now deputy business editor at *The Times*, having been voted Financial Journalist of the Year. In TV and Film, Peter Lawrence is now an established Executive Producer at the BBC and Matthew Loudon, who achieved a BA in Film Production in 2009, has already been nominated for a BAFTA for his short film 'My Darling Wife'. James Grigg became a solicitor and took a high profile case involving frozen embryos all the way to the European Court of Human Rights. Stephen Masters runs a thriving Chiropractic Clinic. Sophie Isaac is back working at Park School as a Cover Supervisor, the first of another new breed, covering lessons when teachers are absent…

As it was in the very beginning some students have sadly died young. Neil Tucker, a bright scholar and athlete, became a mountaineer and was lost on Mount Pissis in Argentina in 2003. Christopher King joined the Coldstream Guards and was killed in July 2009 by an explosive device in Helmand Province, Afghanistan. His commanding officer said, *"He was a man of action who died doing the job he loved."*

Many of today's students will become the Mums and Dads of the next generation whatever else they do and some of their children and grandchildren may one day grace the corridors and classrooms their parents knew. Perhaps one of their great grandchildren may read this book in a hundred years time and be moved to write a sequel.

*Park School Campus at the centenary -viewed from Trinity Church tower.*

*No visible trace of the Grammar School from the 2010 main entrance.*

**The Park Community School**
Centenary Year Photograph
STAFF and GOVERNORS 2009-2010